PHILOSOPHY FOR A NEW CIVILISATION

PHILOSOPHY FOR A NEW CIVILISATION

Henryk Skolimowski

GYAN

GYAN PUBLISHING HOUSE

NEW DELHI - 110002

Philosophy for a New Civilisation

Rs. 690

ISBN : 81-212-0853-X

Published in 2005 in India by
Gyan Publishing House,
5, Ansari Road, Daryaganj,
New Delhi-110002
Phone: 23261060, 23282060
Fax: 91-011-23285914
Email: gyanbook@vsnl.com
Web-site: http//www.gyanbooks.com

Lasertype Setting by: Tact Computer Graphics, Delhi
Printed at: Salasar Imaging System , Delhi

Contents

PART II: LOOKING FORWARD TO A DESIRABLE FUTURE

Introduction

This book represents a journey of one human mind, one Western mind, which was brought to the world at the time when Western civilisation was at the peak of its achievement. This mind was thus inculcated with the idea that Western civilisation was the greatest, most rational and most powerful of all. These assumptions were further rubbed in, although in a subtle way, by great universities that finally molded this mind: Warsaw Technical University, Warsaw University (with its famous School of Logic) and finally Oxford University, which bestowed on this mind one of its most precious trophies — D.Phil. in Philosophy.

Well, in this book I want to describe my liberation from this precious yet poisonous cargo, which was thrust upon me. Yes, I received M.Sc. from Warsaw Technical University; yes, I received M.A. in Logic from Warsaw University; yes, I received Ph.D. (D.Phil.) from Oxford University. And very soon after I was offered an academic position at one of the universities in California. So all was well. Except that not all was well. Some inner forces were working within me, slowly but relentlessly, making me increasingly aware that this whole technological miracle of the world, which was surrounding me (as I continued to teach in California) was a sham and a fake.

How can it be, I was asking myself, while it was supposed such a splendid and superior world? Then another voice was saying inside: if it is so splendid and superior, why is it so flimsy, insubstantial and flaky? Then the first voice was responding: if those who live here say that it is splendid and superior, then it must be so... Who are you to question that? Then the second voice came back and said: perhaps they don't want to see how frail and flaky their world is. Perhaps they are deluding themselves about their superiority? The first voice came back:

And who are you to be suggesting such a thing? The second voice said: I am a philosopher. And my business and passion is to search. At the very least, I must attempt to find what is underneath, which makes this world so equivocal and flimsy and what makes me feel disturbed and questioning inside. Such were my dialogues.

Soon enough, after closer scrutiny, I discovered that the foundations of Western civilization, the so-called scientific worldview, are full of cracks and hidden myths and assumptions, which are accepted as evident truths. While searching for the causes of Western civilisation backfiring upon itself, I scrutinized the last four centuries of Western culture and especially Western philosophy. I came to the conclusion that the fault was in the very blueprint, right there, in the 17th century mechanistic philosophies which laid the foundations for the whole civilisation. It was then that we assumed that the universe is a machine, that knowledge is power, and that nature is ours for exploitation and plunder. We simply conceived of a wrong idiom for the interaction with nature.

Now, this I have found for myself. The problem is, however, that you cannot discuss the underlying assumptions of a culture easily. They are part of the prevailing daily ethos, and indeed woven into personal identities of the people. By questioning them, ordinary people feel that they are attacked; that their identity is threatened. And they are ready to jump to their own defense; and to the defense of the underlying myths. Deeper down in their minds they think: How can you be so stupid to question the obvious?

The difficulty with the learned is of a different sort. As soon as they detect that *you are undermining the assumptions of their thinking* (which often means the foundations of their livelihood) they sarcastically ask you whether you would like to return to the middle ages, or perhaps to the cave. In a more serious vein, they ask you whether you are tired of your rationality and would like to settle for a soapy sentimentality. In the corridors of the university you are teaching, your academic colleagues are asking themselves whether your Ph.D. is really trustworthy. Then they discover that it was published as a book; and is based on rigorous, exacting and impeccable arguments. So they are asking themselves: why is he so unreasonable as to question what is accepted and cherished as the foundation? For them, what is reasonable is the accepted rationality; this they consider untouchable.

Thus, when one endeavors a deeper journey (into the foundations of thinking and existence) one has to be simultaneously gentle and tough. One has to be gentle because only a great compassion can lead you to new insights and new understanding. One has to be tough in being able to defend one's new insights. One has to use appropriate language and arguments — the language which the establishment can understand, but at the same time such a language, which does not subsume you under the existing assumptions of the status quo. The point is that the scientific-rationalist mind-set is very aggressive and always ready to cut you to pieces or dispose of you as an unscientific quack.

Well, in my journey, I had to be patient and persevere...and persevere. The array of responses to a challenger of the present paradigm is almost endless. So often the defenders of the status quo simply blurt out: "but you can't be against progress!" Until recently progress has been a holy cow. And often used as a banner to discourage you from further questioning. Yet when you persevere and say: "Yes, I can be against material progress; after all, it has not delivered what it meant to deliver." Then you are being told: "Wait. It is a question of time. Give us more time. And all will be well." But we have waited a long time. And the goods (of prosperity and happiness for all) have not been delivered.

Actually, with the coming of the 21st century, the whole story has been changed. And the language and arguments have been changed. We are no longer told that science and technology will produce new miracles to make everybody happy. Rather, we are told, by the leading rationalists and representatives of the status quo, that the world is a mean and cruel place and that you should accept it. Those of us, who are still expecting the world to become a better place to live, are now called naïve and unrealistic.

Where is the logic, reason and rationality of this sudden vault? Why are the early promises denied and forgotten? Where was the logic, reason and rationality at that time when science and progress were making grand promises that everything would be well?

May be the process of mythologizing science and technology (as the almighty forces, which can do it all) is responsible for our present plight. If so, then the ardent prophets of science and progress are guilty of irresponsibility, recklessness, and deceitfulness. Now, which of the present champions of science and of progress is going to respond to our charges... the charges of deceiving the whole civilization? Or will the priests of science continue to pretend that all is well? Will the process of arrogance and deceitfulness continue?

Now, these were the kind of reflections and arguments, which prompted and compelled me to look deeper into the assumptions and myths of the scientific worldview and of the whole fabrique of our allegedly splendid civilization. As I kept finding that the whole structure was insecure, wobbling and full of rot inside, I was at first a bit uncomfortable and uneasy. Could it be that the whole thing was of a mythological nature and was going to collapse sooner or later because its myths were too shallow, too naïve, and not sustaining enough to carry on human kind at this point of its history? This is what I was asking myself.

There weren't many with whom I could discuss such things, or even to whom I could confide such fundamental doubts. So I kept searching deeper and wider. If the disease lay in the foundations then it had to affect all branches of knowledge stemming from the rotten roots. In this book, there is quite a number of chapters on Technology — not because I am such an expert in the field, but because technology embodies and exemplifies the promises and the diseases of civilization more clearly than other branches of present knowledge.

The poisonous chalice of technology. Modern technology, with its stupendous prowess and with its 'miraculous' achievements, has turned out to be a very mixed blessing. At one end of the spectrum, the phenomenon of technology is the proverbial horn of plenty. At the other end of the spectrum, technology has turned out to be a poisonous chalice; poisoning environments and creating weapons of mass destruction.

Among the negative aspects of technology, there is one, which we do not clearly appreciate or understand, namely, that it has become ruinous to economies of many nations. The arms race is but one aspect of the technology race. The most sophisticated weapons are technology-based. And they are very expensive. In trying to keep up with the continuous arms race, nations have become impoverished and are slipping into bankruptcy — including the United States.

Thus, the negative aspects of technology — its poisonous propensity, which is ruinous to natural environments; and its imperative to develop ever new arms, which is ruinous to nations — have undermined and nullified the dream of the early twentieth century that the world would become prosperous and people happy everywhere. As the technological race continues, it only promises more disparity and destruction.

After three centuries of the relentless pursuit of material progress which was supposed the solve all our problems; after having elevated Technology to the position of the supreme savior, the time has come to sober up, to remove the scales from our eyes, to wake up from a dream which has turned out to be a nightmare. The time has come to realize that only Imagination can save us, and not Technology; that only spiritual amelioration can bring us satisfaction and ultimately happiness.

We have tried to humanize technology. We have tried to create technology with the human face. To no avail. Technology, and its inner imperatives are not interested in any process of humanization, but only in the process of control, manipulation and the enlargement of its power.

Technology is not benign. Technology is not democratic. Technology is not a tool of equity. Technology is a tool for the barbarization of the world.

Jacques Ellul has proposed some similar ideas, already in 1965, in his book *The Technological Society*. He argued that technology couldn't be controlled because it wants to control. Its imperatives — of control, manipulation and expansion — are so strong that it subdues and subverts ideologies, economies and even sovereign states under its power.

We have been slow to perceive the imperious, aggressive and controlling aspects of technology because we have been mesmerized by its glamour and browbeaten to submission by the idea of technology as a Savior. While in fact technology has been a poisonous chalice.

The double-edged sword of science. Even if technology possesses certain "blemishes", science surely is beyond the pale, we are told. Not so. Science is part and parcel of the aggressive ideology, which we have developed to conquer nature; and then to conquer other cultures and people. It is in the very nature of science that it "attacks" its problems. It does so by dismembering larger wholes in order to investigate minute parts of them. In the process of this "objective" enquiry the meaning of the larger wholes is lost or obliterated.

We are told that science is based on objectivity. On closer inspection, we find that objectivity can neither be defined nor defended — as residing in the cosmos or in nature. There is no such thing in nature, which we can call objectivity. Objectivity is a postulate of the scientific mind. It does not have an objective justification in the world outside the confines of science. It is therefore a subjective creation of the scientific mind.

We agree that the clinical objectivity of science means detachment, separation and ultimately alienation from the subject we study. This mind-set has not enabled us to truly understand the meaning of the universe and of life. However, the attitude of detachment and subsequently of alienation has created a lonely universe outside of us and a sense of loneliness while we live in the human universe.

The other holy cow of science is called rationality. Nobody has properly defined what it is. It is that set of procedures, we are told, through which science obtains its impeccable and lasting results. In order to know the meaning of rationality, we need to know what science is. But we cannot know what science is until we know what rationality is. For science is this exemplary mode of knowledge, which proceeds on the basis of rationality.

Now, the real point is that the whole edifice of classical (mechanistic) science has collapsed. We don't know any more what science is and what is the scientific method; and thus what is the rationality of science.

Science and its rationality has been a double-edged sword. For too often by the application of science, and the rationality underlying it, we have created monsters and crimes. The rationality of science is blind. We need enlightened reason, which is seeing and which is friendly to humans and to the human quest for a good and beautiful life. Scientific rationality has not been such a vehicle. Therefore, we have to transcend it in favor of a more enlightened and compassionate reason. No, we are not throwing rationality over board. *We are seeking an all-encompassing reason as a vehicle of understanding the cosmos and ourselves.*

The blind leading the blind. By some kind of divine providence, I have been interacting with and teaching at many difference schools of learning, in addition to philosophy. During a visit to the University of British Columbia, at Vancouver, in the early 1970's, I gave lectures to four different departments in two days: Physics, Architecture, Philosophy, and Political Science. This is not to boast. But to explain my epistemological necessity.

My reason for being at so many schools at the same time was as follows. If we witness fundamental cracks in our metaphysical and epistemological foundations (I thought), then this should demonstrate itself in different departments of learning. Let us look into these different departments and see whether this is so. And thus I did. And thus I found that whole foundations were wobbly and collapsing... and everybody pretended that all is well.

Let me emphasize that I was not interested in just meandering from one discipline to another. But rather I was interested in some basic questions:

1. Why architecture — in spite of the fact that it possesses an enormous array of new materials and techniques (in addition to the old ones); and while being aided by so much knowledge — has been has been producing such drab, uninspiring and often anti-human environments?
2. Why biology — in spite of its dazzling successes in the molecular sub-fields — is not bringing us closer to the understanding life as a living process, and why is it not helping us to understand our own lives?

3. Why social science — in spite of the plethora of quantitative techniques it employs — is not helping society to become a more coherent and harmonious organism?
4. Why present physics — in spite of its spectacular new discoveries— is creating an ever more confusing picture of the universe instead of making it clear and comprehensible to us?
5. Why is knowledge unfriendly to humans?

Well, I have found that a very large cause responsible for all of this has been unthinking, dogmatic, and servile application of what is deemed as "the best principles of science" to particular disciplines. So often these disciplines, and their practitioners, have not yet realized that classical science (on which the Western civilization is based) has crumbled and that which has been considered as the foundation of science is in a mess — all coherence gone.

In order to be sure that what I was seeing was indeed a correct picture, I had to enter the lion's den and interact with the practitioners of various disciplines, on their turf and using their language. Thus, I gave quite a number of lectures to various Schools of Architecture in the U.K., USA and Finland, including a keynote address to the annual conference of the Royal Institute of British Architects, in 1976 at Hull.

With biology the occasion was perhaps even more auspicious. During an international conference at Bellagio, Italy, the foundations of biology were discussed among intellectual stars, of which there were four Nobel laureates. In this illustrious company of 20, I was the least of the stars. Yet, I had to say what I had to say. I challenged Jacques Monod and claimed that the principle of objectivity, which was supposed to justify the molecular ethos of biology, was a myth and a fiction. Actually all of our contributions were sent to each participant of the conference well in advance. Monod, as the super star, had decided to come to the conference three days after it started. Because I was the most critical of his views, as a gesture of courtesy, I chose to meet him at the railway station at Como, some 60 kilommeters from Bellagio (on the lake of Como). There were three of us in the car driving to the palatial surroundings of the conference: the driver, Monad and myself. I introduced myself: "I am Henryk Skolimowski." Monod looked at me penetratingly and with a disarming smile said: "So you are Mr. Skolimowski. You think that we disagree. But it is not so." I was stunned for a while. After a long pensive moment I said: "And yet we disagree." Now Monod became pensive and serious. After a while responded: "Yes, mistakes have been made. In the meantime the book has become a classic. And now nothing can be done." I could not believe my ears: mistakes were made but nothing can be done...because mistakes have become part of the canon.

We remained silent for the rest of the beautiful mountainous road to the palace. I was brooding to myself: is it the way that science operates — mistakes are made, then they become part of the canon, and then nobody dares to challenge them? Is it per chance the story of the apocryphal legacy of all science: mistakes were made at the outset, at the foundation level, then they were canonized, and then nobody dared to challenge them?

The rationality of human life. While looking at the spectacle of the decaying civilization and at the same time seeking viable alternatives to it, I visited many alternative communities. I was at first surprised that the main stream society has frowned upon alternative communities, considered them freakish, crazy, loony and even evil. In actual fact, these communities were made of gentle young people, who meant no harm, but were only searching for a better and saner way to live. I know what I am saying for I visited many such communities, and lived for a spell of time in some. I visited Auroville (in India), Finhorn (in Scotland), Arcosanti (in Arizona, USA) and wrote about each. I visited various kibbutzim in Israel and smaller, less known communities.

What has struck me was quite a diversity of ways of organizing life, of thinking, of envisaging the ultimate goals. Also a variety of rationalities. There isn't one rationality for all alternative communities. Well, one underlying reason of most of them was a desire to escape from the mechanistic Moloch of technological society. Otherwise, a variety of forms of life prevailed even when this life was frugal and modest; and especially then — when there are not enough material resources, then imagination and ingenuity must step in.

Yes, people in these alternative communities have been non-conformists. Even in well established communities like Kibbutzim. Actually I have found the Kibbutz experiment quite daring and important. On some Kibbutzim, I saw three generations living together: the founders, their children, and their grandchildren, living in harmony. Judged by standard criteria of materialist affluence, social cohesion, and ethical integrity, the Kibbutz has done well. At one point 6 per cent of Kibbutzniks provide 35 per cent of the food for the whole of Israel. However, as capitalism started to assert itself more and more aggressively, the kibbutz started to be deemed less and less important; not because its real value diminished, but because the capitalist ideology did not like its achievements. In the turmoil of recent violence, the Kibbutz has almost become forgotten.

Now, in addition to visiting alternative communities, I also visited many cultures markedly different from Western technological culture. India has been a revelation in so many ways. It has also been a continuous spiritual sustenance for me over the last 25 years. China, in spite of the Maoist revolution, has been a reminder of what a colossal culture flourished there. Against the breath and depth of India and China, Western Civilization, especially technological civilization is a midget; well an upstart.

Intoxicated by their mechanistic dogmas, facile gadgets, and technological powers, Western people tried to forget that there is a world outside their techno-sphere. I had to remind them through my dialogues with Marcus Aurelius (chapt. 10) and with Nandi —the Bull of Lord Shiva — (chapt. 11).

There is a pain in me when I see how the West has squandered its potential to build a peaceful and harmonious world; a pain to see the endless resources turned into machines of war and destruction, a pain to see the consciousness of Leonardo and Plato turned into the consciousness of slothful consumers; a pain to see small children and youngsters indoctrinated by stupid and violent films, which invite them to think that killing is an ordinary and banal affair; a pain to see millions upon millions of good people agonizing about how to help the world; who are, however, speechless and incapacitated by the conviction that nothing can be done to stop this civilization from ruin.

But we shall prevail. We, the people of good hearts of positive visions. We shall build a new civilisation for such is an imperative of evolution. And the desire of our deeper heart.

The waves of evolutionary becoming and of our consciousness arising will wash out the accretions of dirt, stain, and calamities, which have accumulated. We are not alone. The stars are with us, and evolution, and the genius of past cultures; and some luminous voices of individuals who cared.

Here I quote one such voice, that of Friedrich Nietzsche:

And how could I endure to be a man, if man
Were not also a poet and reader of riddles
And a way to new dawns?

This book argues that we, as a human race, especially Western Civilisation, have been deficient in ideas and visions. We are an intelligent race. But we have used our intelligence for inventing ever-new gadgets, which somehow make our lives more comfortable, but ultimately increasingly empty. We have used our intelligence for inventing ever new weapons, which we were supposed to make our lives safe but instead our lives are ever more fragile. The whole world has become a dangerous place to live.

We know that we are living in a dangerous reality; which actually is not dangerous by itself but has been made so by human beings. This reality, which we now find menacing, (let us be quite clear about this) has come about on the wheels of early utopias of the 16th and 17th centuries. These utopias have been carried out to their fruition through the vehicles of material progress, science, and technology. It is very strange indeed that the optimistic technological dreams have turned out to be calamitous.

In the first part of the book, I have tried to trace some of the important developments, which have led to our perilous slide from dreams into nightmares. I have tried to emphasize, especially, how tenuous and shallow were the assumptions on which modern science and modern technology have been based. While examining the developments leading to the emergence of modern civilization, we find over and again, that the visions on which modern science and the modern world view were established are lamentably inadequate, superficial, and completely skewed in favor of the pragmatic and the materialistic. The vision of the human life became so diminished that ultimately this diminished vision has diminished our horizons, visions and the understanding of life itself.

In the second part of this book we are proposing alternatives to the present dilapidated thinking, which has systematically misfired on so many fronts. Now, genuine alternatives to the present dysfunctional systems, including Democracy, will have to amount to nothing less than *a metanoia* — turning things inside out — with the aid of New Imagination, new visions, and a new will to inherit the earth as a garden of Eden.

This book is a primer for people who seek an alternative to the kind of thinking, which produces monsters, destruction, poisonous environments, and oppression of people. This book is a primer for the people of the 3rd world nations and societies, who are tired of the alleged superiority of industrial nations, which pretend that they know best, while themselves are groping in darkness and confusion. This book provides a way of overcoming the toxic thinking of technological mentality. This mentality has become a religion for Western people. The main civilizational conflict is not a religious one — Islam vs. Christianity, or Islam vs. Hinduism. It is the conflict between technological mentality against all religions. The destructive edge of technological mentality, guided by the imperatives of selfishness, domination, and exploitation, is directed against all religions of love and mercy — Buddhism, Christianity, Hinduism or Islam. Let us be quite clear that the rapacious, destructive and exploitive technological mentality has nothing to do with Christian values and the underlying tenor of Christ's teaching.

The two main conclusions of our examination of the legacy of modern civilization are as follows.

Technology is not the solution. And it will never be. **Imagination is the solution.** And it will always be. Imagination is boundless, infinite and generous. While technology is limited, confining and exclusive.

Imagination is a spiritual force. It is a superior expression of human intelligence. Making weapons of mass destruction is an inferior expression of human intelligence. Hence our choice: to follow our inferior intelligence and bring more weapons and more destruction to our environments and our inner lives; or to follow our superior intelligence and create the world in which our spiritual destinies will be fulfilled, and natural environments will be healed.

We need to remember with Socrates: "unexamined life is not worth living." I am inviting the reader for a tour of a deeper examination of our present assumptions and beliefs. They purportedly serve us. In actual fact, we serve them... and some strange merciless gods, which are hidden behind the scene.

The human condition is glorious. Yes, it has been sullied, diminished and dwarfed. So much dead accretion has been accumulated that civilization is petrified and human life is stifled. We need to break through this stultifying straitjacket with a blaze of new awareness so that we are not reduced to consumptive puppets.

Human thought is a vehicle of light. Human thought is a conveyor of joy and a source of illumination, through which human life is uplifted and the universe is understood in depth. At its best, human thought brings illumination, solace and inspiration. Such was human thought, which was guided by lucid Logos in ancient Greece. Such was the nature of thought, which inspired the *Upanishads,* the sublime discourses of ancient India, which have shone with brilliance and luminescence for millennia.

The Universe was created amidst the joyous celebration of the original potency of the Cosmos. And so it is presented by the *Upanishads,* where Joy was born before gods, who came to existence only later. We can return to Joy through the acts of thinking and of being, which are infused with light and guided by light. From Joy we have come, to joy we want to return.

Part : I
Looking Back at the Past

1

Does Science Control People or Do People Control Science?

1. Science as Eternal Truths

On 17 October 1780, the ship *Lincoln Galley* anchored in William's Cove on the east side of Isleboro, now in the state of Maine. On this ship there was a group of scientists and students from Harvard College led by the Reverend Professor Williams. Their purpose was to make observations of the total eclipse of the sun which was to take place in this part of the world on 28 October.

There is nothing remarkable about scientists making observations of the eclipse of the sun. What was remarkable about this expedition was the fact that it was in time of war and the part of the coast they were going to was held by the British. Earlier in October Professor Williams, representing the new American Academy of Arts and Sciences, wrote a letter to the British commander, Colonel Campbell, requesting permission for the expedition to enter British territory immediately. 'Our business,' he wrote, 'is solely to promote the interest of Science which is the common interest of mankind.' Whereupon permission was granted. The gentlemen from Harvard directed their telescopes on the sun on the specified day and made their observations. These observations are now a part of our scientific library.

Science, as conceived by Professor Williams and his assistants, is the embodiment of human dignity and eternal truths. This kind of science, or rather science conceived in this manner, transcends the idea of who controls whom for, as we have said, science here is equivalent to the pursuit of eternal truths. Let us therefore note the first conception of *science as the embodiment of human dignity and eternal truths.*

The idea of the untouchability of science, of its entirely beneficial nature was so strongly embedded in the minds of the people at that time (the end of the eighteenth century) that the gentlemen from Harvard could not only devise the idea of crossing the enemy's lines in order to make some scientific observations, but could actually carry it out—war or no war.

Let us contrast this kind of untouchability of science with the disgraceful misuses of science in the twentieth century. It suffices to mention IG Farben in Hitler's Germany—the infamous chemical concern which provided chemicals for the gas chambers in concentration camps; lunatic asylums and special camps in the Soviet Union as described, for example, in Solzhenitsyn's *The First Circle*; or research on biological warfare conducted on—American campuses, to see at once that in the twentieth century science can no longer be regarded as the embodiment of human dignity. Indeed it is often nowadays a disgrace to human dignity.

2. Science as Entertainment

Before we engage in a more detailed analysis of contemporary science, let us review some other conceptions of science in the past. From the seventeenth century on we can distinguish another concept of science, *science as a glorious entertainment*. Moliere beautifully satirizes this notion of science in his play, *The Learned Ladies*, where he shows science invading not only the fashionable boudoirs, but also the chambers of servant girls. Chrisalus complains to Belisa about his household.

No science is too profound for 'em; and in my house, more than in any other place in the world, the most lofty secrets are conceived, and they understand everything but what they ought to understand. They know the motions of the moon, the Polar Star, Venus, Saturn, and Mars, which I have no business with; and with all this vain knowledge, which they go so far to look for, they don't know how my pot goes on, which I have occasion for.

In the French salons of the eighteenth century, particularly those attended by the French Encyclopaedists, science as a glorious entertainment positively flourished. Voltaire's mistress, Madame du Châtelet, wrote a very learned and lucid account of Leibniz's philosophy (under the title *Institutions de physique*) of which La Mettrie said, 'Everybody understands monads since the Leibnizians made the brilliant acquisition of Madame du Châtelet.' In Madame du Châtelet's salon the charming Venetian fellow, Algarotti, presented and discussed his book, *Newtonisme pour les dames*. The learned duet, Voltaire and Madame du Châtelet, were slightly shocked by the frivolous tone of the narrative and by too many jokes in the text. However, *Newtonisme pour les dames* in a curious way epitomizes the conception of science as a glorious entertainment.

3. Science as Ideology

It might appear from these two conceptions of science that historically, that is before the twentieth century, science was an altogether benevolent entity, capable of causing no harm, ideologically indifferent, and exerting no significant influence on the destinies of societies and civilizations. Such a conclusion would be premature. For already, at the beginning of the seventeenth century, science can be seen in an altogether different role. The burning of Giordano Bruno in 1600 and the trial of Galileo in 1633 mark the appearance of science as an ideology, the ideology capable of swinging people's minds from the path of faith to the realm of doubt, from the truth as rendered by the Church to the inquiry of truth as rendered by human reason. The Holy Inquisition seems to have been perfectly aware of the potential of science. Hence Galileo's trial.

When Galileo was on trial, science was on trial. But let us carefully observe the circumstances under which science was on trial. Science was at that time undercutting the foundations of a decaying civilization. The medieval civilization was coming to an end, unable to sustain itself through its own means. Science was helping man to evolve a new civilization. Science was at that time the torch of light, the agent of progress and liberation. It was put on trial by the agents of the dying epoch. These circumstances must be very clearly borne in mind. For the main point is that science was on trial at the beginning of the seventeenth century for attempting to extend man and his universe beyond the limits in which they were bound.

But one may imagine that science could be put on trial for quite a different reason and in quite different circumstances. Might it not be the case that in the course of time, science itself became a bondage, restraining and suffocating us as people, as society, as a civilization? I shall return to the 'second trial' of Galileo at the end of this essay.

Nowadays we no longer believe that science is the embodiment of human dignity. And we do not believe that science is concerned with eternal truths either for we know that every theory established by science is tentative, subject to revision and replacement. Eternal truths are not replaceable. Replaceable truths are not eternal. Since every theory is replaceable, there are no eternal truths in science. However, the old idea of science as something beyond the sordid and immediate concerns of human beings still prevails in many quarters. Science is then equated with pure knowledge. Science handles ideas, as the argument goes. As such it is not responsible for the disastrous effects of the intrusions of technology into the fabric of society and into the sanctuaries of our private lives.

Science as pure knowledge is equated with the body of descriptions of nature, the sum total of ideas which illuminate for us the behaviour of nature. In this context Russell's contention that 'equations do not explode' seems to be valid and relevant. Certain ideas may or may not be illuminating for the problem under consideration, but they do belong to the realm of intellectual contemplation and not to the realm which can control the destiny of society or people. Thus science, seen as pure knowledge, *does* not and cannot control people. It is simply a category mistake to ask in this context whether science does control people. For 'control,' if it is to mean anything, must mean an influence on, and a determination of some courses of action of many individuals and ultimately the determination of the course of the whole society. When we equate science with pure knowledge, the centre of gravity remains within science. When we see science as *controlling* people, or people controlling science, we shift the centre of gravity from science to society. It is only by broadening the concept of science to include its *social* implications that we can talk either about science controlling people or vice versa.

To say it once more, the conception of science as pure knowledge precludes the problem of science versus people because the theatre of pure ideas is so hermetic that it does not include the social consequences of scientific ideas. The Pythagorean theorem, taken in its primary sense as expressing certain geometrical relationships, is a cognitive concept, not a social phenomenon.

Pope Urban VIII in Brecht's play *Galileo*, torn by indecision about what to do with Galileo, no doubt thought about science as pure knowledge when he said, "I want no condemnation of physical facts, no battle-cries like "Here the Church, there Reason!"" But then, under the persuasive influence of the Inquisitor, he is made to *see* that science is much more than physical facts and pure ideas, that its reach extends to the sacred shrines of the Orthodoxy. And the Pope, concluding that 'That is certainly an impertinence,' decides that the spirit that emanates from Galileo's mathematical tables must be destroyed. Galileo must be tried.

4. Science as a Civilisation

Now, science as an integral part of Western civilization is certainly much more than a collection of physical facts and a body of pure ideas. It is above all a social phenomenon. It is only with regard to science so conceived, as a social phenomenon, as a part of the fabric of society, that we can meaningfully ask: 'Does science control people, or do people control science?'

We have arrived at another conception of science: *science as a civilization*. The institution of science is the history of the development of science which includes its impact on and its interaction with society. The point is that our social institutions have been shaped by science, not only in their structure and organization, but in their goals and aspirations. Science has inspired us to set up such institutions that further foster the development of science. The most spectacular example illustrating this point is the United States space programme which fired the imagination of the whole society but which drained a great deal of the resources from this society. If there is an insidious intent in science to self-perpetuate itself in a variety of disguises, the elephantine space programme is a clear manifestation of this intent. Science is, as it were, a blind force which tends to multiply itself. Militarism, as an extension of contemporary science, is perhaps not so much an expression of the corruption of scientists' minds, but rather an expression of an inherent tendency of science to multiply itself in whatever form. Now, if it is true that science has pervaded the fabric of Western society, and if it is true that every established institution in society has a tendency to perpetuate itself, and if it is true that the American society is most saturated with science and technology, then it is quite natural that science will flourish here in a variety of forms of which militarism is one.

An even more striking example of institutions inspired by science to further foster science are the institutions of learning. The course of a civilization is determined by the quality, quantity and character of learning pursued in the institutions of learning in that civilization. Since science has continually shaped the character of learning pursued in our schools and universities, its influence should be expected to be profound. And so it is. For we inherit from our schools not only knowledge about the world. We inherit also a particular conception of the world.

Now, our *Weltanschauung*, our world view, is acquired with and through our knowledge. It is the scientific *Weltanschauung* that we acquire in our schools and in our academia. The nature of knowledge determines the nature of the world around us. We perceive and understand what we are made to perceive and understand through the knowledge we acquire. The dominant position of science in our system of learning assures a further perpetuation of what is called the scientific outlook and what is tantamount to a vision of the world through the spectacles of science.

Seen in this context, science does control people; it does control people subtly and indirectly because it furnishes them with the categories of understanding; it acts as a series of filters through which we view reality.

To put the matter in more general terms: our thinking is to a large degree determined by our language. The conceptual framework is a matrix which enables us to express certain relationships and does not enable us to express other relationships. Every civilization is under the influence of these subtle yet all-encompassing conceptual determinants. The conceptual framework of Western man in modern times has been profoundly influenced by science; and so was his language and his thinking. Here again we see an indirect but an important influence of science on the thinking of man, thus on the thinking of society. According to proverbial wisdom our habits control our lives. Is it not also the case that the conceptual habits of a society control the destiny of the society?

We have thus analysed science in yet another context: *science as a conceptual framework* (determining our thinking). This conception of science may be regarded as a part of science as a civilization. Yet this context is distinctive enough to deserve separate treatment. There is one aspect of science so conceived (as a conceptual framework) which requires special attention. This aspect is related to the notion of rationality as developed by modern science. It is this notion which often determines whether our behaviour, decision or action is deemed rational, thus acceptable or not. But it so happens that scientific rationality favours frameworks and situations which comply with the structure and scope of the universe as established by science. Our judgments (which are a subset of our conceptual habits) are without question under the influence of scientific rationality. There would be no room for conflict here if the universe of science encompassed everything there is, encompassed, in other words, all aspects of the human universe. However, since the universe of science does leave out certain aspects of the human universe, a conflict may arise between our human judgments and our scientific judgments. If the force of scientific rationality is such that we must obey it (for fear of being called unscientific quacks) even though we feel that some aspects of the human universe are violated, then the issue of science controlling us as people again arises.

5. Science as Technology

We are now ready to examine the last important conception of science: *science as technology*. A sharp distinction is often made, particularly by the priests of pure science, between science and technology; the rationale given is that science is innocent and that technology is responsible for the present crisis of society. This separation is, of course, artificial. Technology is a part of the rational *Weltanschauung* shaped by science. Technology is a part of the fabric of Western society which, for centuries, has been guided by the spirit of science. Technology, seen in the broad perspective of *science as a civilization*, is only an extension of science; and it is only within this broad perspective that we can meaningfully discuss the social consequences of either science or technology. One commits a category mistake, as we have argued, if one attempts to discuss the *social* function of science, when science is confined to the body of pure ideas.

Science is an integral part of the bloodstream of Western civilization. The new civilization was erected not only on the piles of Galileo's physics. Bacon's program, 'knowledge is power,' was equally important in secularizing society, in seeking fulfilment for man here on earth rather than later on in heaven, and in realizing the idea of progress conceived in human rather than in theological terms. From the beginning of the new epoch science was designed to be a servant of human progress; thus science was designed to serve a social function. Technology is only a more ruthless embodiment of the tendency toward material progress as exemplified by Bacon's motto, 'knowledge is power.'

To repeat the main point: within the over-all structure of the rational *Weltanschauung* there is not much room for the distinction between science and technology; both serve the same function—that of perpetuating material progress. This is clearly realized by technocrats and militarists who insist, and they are quite correct in this, that they only extend the scope of the rational universe; and this is also clearly realized by many young people who want to escape this rational universe altogether by flights into lyricism and mysticism.

We are now ready to pose the question again: does science control people or do people control science? The most obvious but mutually exclusive answers are:

(1) Yes, people control science because individual people make contributions to science following their chosen line of inquiry;

(2) No, people do not control science because even scientists and the whole institution of science are manipulated by the power structures of society.

Neither of these answers is adequate. Science is an exceedingly complex affair and our loaded question can only be answered by reconstructing the various contexts of science.

Science as the pursuit of eternal truths, science as a glorious entertainment, science as pure knowledge does not control people. But it could hardly be said that people control science in these contexts. The idea of controls is somewhat irrelevant here. Science as a civilization, and especially science as a conceptual framework, as a form of the rational *Weltanschauung*, does control people; although its control is indirect, its consequences are far-reaching. Our mental habits, our thinking and perceiving have been predetermined by the network of knowledge within which we grew up. And this network has been profoundly influenced by science.

We are even more obviously controlled by *science as technology*. There can be no question that our most grievous concerns are about technological change ruthlessly asserting itself over and above human controls. But technology is only an extension of our rational ideology.

Thus, when we question technology, we question our rational ideology, we question the whole enterprise of science. Our question at this point should be reformulated. What we are really asking is: do we control the course of our civilization ? And the answer is: we do not. The crisis of scientific civilization is the crisis of scientific reason, is the crisis of science itself.

When an experiment does not come out right, we blame either the instruments or the scientist, but not science. Only on rare occasions do we blame science. On such occasions we know that our anomaly is not really an anomaly, but a manifestation of a crisis. We do not try to improve our instruments or our performance, but look for a different set of theories. We switch the whole idiom of science, we switch to another paradigm, we change science, so to speak.

Perhaps our predicament nowadays is similar with regard to science as a civilization. Perhaps we should not ask who controls whom—for obviously we as people, as scientists, as scholars, as citizens do not control science in the most profound sense as a scientific civilization—but ask ourselves, what kind of new science should we or must we develop to disentangle ourselves from the present crisis?

Perhaps what we witness nowadays is another trial of science and thereby another trial of Galileo. But science is being tried nowadays in new circumstances. It is not tried as a force which attempts to upset the *status quo*; but as a force which represents the *status quo*. It is not tried as an emerging civilization, but it is tried as a part of a dying civilization.

2
Farewell to the Second Millennium

1.The Glory of Science...Or was it?

The Second Millennium was dominated by the white race. One of the proudest chapters of Western Civilization is science—its development and application. In science Sir Isaac Newton has been a towering figure. His book, *Principia Mathematica Philosophia Naturalis*, is considered to be the greatest scientific book ever written; and because science is regarded as the most important human endeavor, this book stands as a sort of pinnacle of human achievement.

Yet it is a curiously marred book. Newton was very anxious to present a very neat set of results. So he fudged some data which we discovered only recently. He wanted to formulate the ultimate *Laws of Nature*, which would stand in the treasury of human knowledge forever. Sir Isaac was so sure of the iron clad nature of his pronouncements that he emphatically insisted: *Hypotheses non fingo* (I don't feign hypotheses). Poor Newton, in the course of time his theories were found to be merely approximations, a bunch of tentative hypotheses, applicable only in some realms of our space-time; not applicable in the realm of subatomic particles, or in temperatures close to absolute zero. Twentieth century Physics has demonstrated that Newtonian mechanics was not the ultimate knowledge of the universe, and therefore not unshakable and unalterable. It was merely a frail fragment of physical knowledge.

In short with Newton's demise the whole presumption of Western culture that it found indubitable knowledge, based on firm scientific rationality, simply collapsed. We (in the West) know it. But we are so attached to the alleged glory and superiority of scientific knowledge that we don't want to admit it. Nor do we want to draw appropriate conclusions (from the collapse of scientific rationality) for the whole culture.

There is another peculiar aspect of the Newtonian legacy. There is a definite theological flavour in Newton's cosmology. The whole structure, with its insistence on absoluteness, unshakability, immutabity—to which we must succumb—is very much in the image of Jehovah. The ramblings of the Old Testament can be heard through the pages of Newton's *Principia*. Newtonian dogmatism and arrogance became hall marks for the whole Western culture, which has been subduing other cultures, assuming that it had the mandate from heaven and Mr. Newton.

The West celebrated the 300th anniversary of Newton's Principia in 1986—with some fanfare; and yet with some misgivings. I don't think this book will be so celebrated in another 300 years. In the long run, Cervantes' *Don Quixote* will be considered a more important book.

So what about the glory of science? At present the whole Western scientific knowledge is in shambles. Nobody knows what it is supposed to describe, what is its relationship with reality, and what is the meaning of reality within present science.

The protagonist of the Western scientific world may still argue as follows: even if science did not deliver what it had promised, look at our technology. Surely it is a success story of Western civilization. We may pause and ask: But is it really? What parts of it are so undoubtedly successful? The most spectacular examples of human prowess and power are nuclear weapons. Should we consider these weapons to be the greatest glory of technology? We scratch our heads and say, "no, not this. We don't wish to identify ourselves with these murderous toys." What then? Landing on the moon? Yes, this is a good example, we want to say. But is it? At the time of the event, we were all excited. Our imagination of reaching beyond Earth made us gasp with wonder. But what is the legacy of this moon landing now? How did it help the human race? What have we learnt about ourselves? Yes, there were some gadgets developed for the space travelers which spill over to society, such as teflon frying pans. Thus we have obtained some interesting gadgets. Sure enough, we consume some exotic items which would not have been available if it were not for space travel. Is that all?

While dazzled by technological gadgets, we forget to ask: who controls technology? Whom does it serve? Who reaps the major profits? But also such questions as: why have we devastated ecology through our seemingly benign technologies? Why have we cheapened human lives? Why have we eliminated the sacred from our existence?

One answer is because we have not been thinking but only obeying the scientific-technological imperative: what can be done (in the scientific material sphere) must be done. When the Chinese invented gun powder, they decided not to use it for destructive purposes. We did not have this kind of wisdom while developing our technologies.

We are now told that new electronic technologies will deliver us to the paradise of virtual reality. Is this not another delusion of arrogant unthinking people?

So many people have chosen Albert Einstein as the man of the 20th century. And even of the whole Millennium. But he is an ambiguous genius, as Newton was. He signed the letter which led to the production and explosion of the Bomb; this fact he considered the greatest mistake of his life. But he was a scientific genius wasn't he? Yes, he was. But would the 20th century have been better off if $E=mc^2$ were never discovered? I dare say—yes. Furthermore: if A-bombs and then H-bombs were never invented? All this stupendous technology has been a march of destruction. And who have benefited from it? Obviously not us, ordinary people, but big multinational corporations.

2. White Man's Burden

Our problems did not start with the abortive 17th century. This century had high dreams. They were laudable but not deep enough, as 17th century wanted to make people happy but only in material terms. Because the vision was too shallow the salvation proved to be abortive.

Deep problems emerged at the very beginning of the millennium. Many Christians expected that the year 1000 would signify "the end of the world, "that is to say, the end of the material existence on Earth. In great concentration, they waited. And waited. When "the end" did not come, the accumulated energy of waiting for Godot did not find any outlet. Here lies the beginning of a big problem. The people did not know what to do with this accumulated energy, born of the expectation of an early departure to heaven.

A similar situation occurred in ancient Greece; but with astoundingly different results. After the Greeks repulsed the Persians in the wars of 495-491 BCE, they still could not believe that they were so lucky and alive. They waited for another big Persian army to come and to crush them. They were concentrated. They were prepared to die. They waited. And waited. And the Persians were not coming. Then they started to use this accumulated energy in a most creative manner. They built the Parthenon, the Erachteion, the temple of Nike—all on the Athenian Acropolis. They exploded with creative exuberance in every realm of human endeavor and left the masterpieces which became the yardstick of what was highest and best in Western culture.

Medieval Europe after the year 1000 went another way. Instead of going from flowering to flowering, the path has become from conquest to conquest. First, the Crusades were organized to "liberate" the Holy land. The Crusades were a failure. But the accumulated aggressive energy was set in motion. Some crusader units attacked and sacked Christian communities. Then another Crusade was organized to stamp out what was deemed the Cathars' heresy. In the 13th century with the blessings of the Pope Innocent III, dozens of thousands of Cathars were killed with strange cruelty.

After the Cathars tragedy, the Institution of the Inquisition was established, in 1231. Its purpose was to "eliminate" infidels and heretics from among the Christians. The wheel of the Inquisition once turned on was revolving mercilessly for the next four centuries. Millions of alleged heretics died an unnatural death, being smoldered on the stakes. Among these heretics an overwhelming number were women, who were condemned as witches. Some six million of them were ruthlessly exterminated with the flimsiest of evidence, or no evidence at all, for their alleged involvement in non-Christian powers or practices. What a stain it must have created on the Western moral conscience. This stain is still not fully recognized, acknowledged and dealt with.

In the meantime, there were wars for domination between the emperor (German Emperor) and the Pope. And also religious wars between the Christians and the Moslems. Then later on we witness the religious wars of the 17th century between Christians and Christians. These were the wars of continuous religious slaughter.

These aggressive energies are also running high as Europe is preparing for the conquest of the world in the colonial wars. Far away countries are invaded. Populations are subdued. Natural treasuries and especially gold robbed. Resisting tribes slaughtered, sometimes whole populations; at times even those natives who cooperated with the conquistadors were killed.

One raises one's eyebrows while examining this history. For we are talking about a *Christian* civilization. Yet the modes of its behaviour were distinctly not the ones which Christ would condone. Are we truly Christian? Or only clever hypocrites? The turning of the Millennia would seem an appropriate time to reflect and meditate on deeper subjects such as: what is it in the Western psyche that makes it so restless and aggressive.

3. The Causes of the Demise

What were the main causes of the anaemia of Western culture in the second Millennium? What were the causes which led to the shattering of the whole culture, in spite of so much intellectual brilliance and undoubted technical achievement?

The first cause was the religious straight jacket. The intolerance of Christianity and its rigid and at times brutal control— at least during the first five centuries of the 2nd millennium— were constantly undermining whatever ascent to light and to truly compassionate society were undertaken.

This can be seen in the exploitation of peasants in the early medieval society. While the peasants were starving, the Church and the monks were having a ball, which Boccachio describes so vividly and eloquently in his *Decameron*.

This intolerance and brutal control can be seen in the institution of the Inquisition and its "works." This institution is one of the shames of the "enlightened" Western Civilization. (And also of the Christian Church, based allegedly on love).

This intolerance can be seen in religious wars which produced so much venom, tragedy and lasting bad *karma* which has stained Western conscience, and of which Western people are hardly aware.

One of the strange consequences of Christianity going haywire has been the treacherous and grasping legacy of modern capitalism. The foundation of Christianity is the teaching of Jesus Christ. The essential pillars of this teaching is the quest for justice and equality, is the care for the poor, is the disapproval of the rich. "It is easier for a camel to go through the eye of a needle than for a rich man to enter the Kingdom of God." This teaching has been altered by Calvinism and Protestantism, and then by the ideology of capitalism to such a degree that the poor are now seen as responsible for their own plight, while triumphant capitalism thrives on greed, exploitation, ruthlessness and utter social irresponsibility.

We may say, in brief, that the second millennium was not a good one for Christianity. By the same token, it was not a good one for Western Civilization; in spite of our claims to the contrary.

The second cause was the shallowness and timidity of Western thinking which turned potential brilliance and even genius into the civilization of trivial pursuits.

We did not have enough spiritual substance to safeguard the brilliance of our minds. We have become a cocky arrogant people who have become a menace to other people and the whole creation. Our alleged superiority over other races led us to blindness and cruelty. Only recently were we able to see this aspect of our nature. But instead of making amends and apologizing to the exploited and mistreated (by our arrogance and drunken power), we have developed globalism— a new tool for exploitation and colonialism.

The legacy of exploitation and conquest of many lands and peoples over centuries has been deeply unsettling for our psyche. These conquests were often justified as the white man's burden to bring civilisation to "savages". In actual fact, this whole story is one of colossal savagery. These savageries are not fully recognized in the collective memory of Western people. There exists a strange amnesia with regard to the wrongs we have done. Yes, the past millennium was the white man's millennium. But at what price? With what consequence and damages?

On the positive side, we have developed the Charter of Human Rights. We have tried to share with others our democracy which has been better than vicious dictatorships. However, this industrial democracy has so often proved to be a loaded dice. Instead of helping other people, we have reaped the major economic benefits. Hence the gap between the rich and the poor is widening.

The bad *karma* has been nagging our moral conscious all the time, the *karma* of war, aggression, conquest, poisoning the mind and consciousness of Western people. What is to be done to redeem this bad *karma*? Who is going to purify our sullied souls. Are we waiting for a new Messiah?

This is the real cross of the past millennium. Don't tell me about our technical achievements. Let us talk about our sullied psyche and how we can purify it to become human again.

4. The Redeeming Nature of Art

Against the spurious euphoria of technocrats, who have been destroying the earth, our capacity to think independently and deeply, and our communion with nature, I shall declare: "Long live art and the artists for they are the true redeemers of the world.."

The Italian Renaissance was a fresh breath of robust air. It showed what the human being can be when inspired by a great idea and released from the chains of dogmas. It is breathtaking to think that so many great individuals appeared on the scene at the same time.

Art was a great catalyzing agent, a miracle-maker. It released from humans their powerful energies. It unlocked the secrets of creativity. It taught people to be creative. The Renaissance alone would be sufficient to redeem the shortcomings of other epochs (but not to redeem our moral sins committed through conquests and barbarian behaviour).

Let us not forget that the West was blessed with sublime artists throughout the millennium, not only during the Renaissance period. Through their Protean visions and transcendental yearning, they kept us from our smallness and often from our misdeeds. To them we owe the fact that Western Civilization did not degenerate further and deeper.

For what we would have been if we did not have Giotto, Leonardo, Michael Angelo, Rembrandt; Dante, Shakespeare, Cervantes, Molier, Tolstoy, Dostoyevsky? What we would have been without Monteverdi, Vivaldi, Bach, Mozart, Beethoven? These are the proud names of Western culture. The celestial sounds of Monteverdi and Mozart have kept alive our souls in the last two centuries of darkness. The language of Shakespeare, of Cervantes, of Blake have been our nourishment counteracting the sterile jargon and flat philosophy of the positivists who have been destroying our minds and our language.

In every epoch there were the people who kept alive the flaming torch of light. They were usually artists. The creative light, burning bright within some individuals, is what brings us closest to Divinity. This is what makes us human. Everything else is a pale shadow. Long live the artists for they are the true saviours of humanity.

Summary

The Third Millennium will not belong to the white race if only because there will not be the white race at the end of the millennium. Our ranks have been diminishing. There were about 50 per cent of white faces at he beginning of the 20th century. Now there are about 20 per cent. Then we will become 10 per cent. Then 5 per cent. And then we shall be absorbed in the pool of more interesting colours. In this way we shall survive as a larger pool of humanity. A less interesting scenario would be if the dominant people of colour would decide to isolate the remaining 2-3 per cent of pure white faces and lock us in some kind of reservation—perhaps in the Scandinavian peninsula. That would be a bit cruel. I will not mention how paradoxical it would be.

Looking at Western People over the last millennium, one is struck with these impressions. Lots of energy bursting in so many places. Unfortunately, most of it has been an ill-directed energy. Thus the first part of our trauma: boundless but ill-directed energy.

So much activity. People always in a rush. Never having time for reflection. All action, action, action... but to what ends? "Never mind that. We are people of action. We don't have time for spurious reflection." This alone was bound to create problems in the long run.

So we see the spectacle of people always in action. But also suffering so much. Mainly because they elected as their guide the suffering Christianity. Throughout the millennium one is struck by the crucified Christianity. Painful and inflicting pain. Never able to get out of the cross to become a life-inspiring and life-sustaining religion... according to the words of Jesus Christ: "I bring you life abundant."

People were intoxicated with power, with the Faustian myth: "you only live once. Therefore you have a ball on earth, at whatever or whosoever's expense." Unsure of their identity, while losing their spiritual depth, people opted out for the aphrodisiac of power. And those lesser characters, settled for consumption.

This was the millennium of the brilliant flowering of a handful of great scientific minds, whose creative genius, alas, was used later to trivialise the whole civilisation and to negate the spiritual depth of the people.

Taking a more Olympian perspective, we can say that this was the millennium of lost opportunities. This was the millennium of some luminous lights burning on our horizons—such as early medieval mystics (including, of course, St. Francis of Assisi) and above all such lights as Leonardo and Michael Angelo. Only to be followed by much darkness, confusion and evil.This was the millennium of auspicious beginnings, such as the French and the American Revolutions, whose lofty ideals later led to vicious and degenerative ideologies of communism and capitalism, each equally devastating to human freedom and human happiness.

This was the millennium which has left behind wounded humanity, shattered dreams, skeletons of human beings—frantically searching for fulfillment and so often settling for addictive drugs, or in the least harmful of scenarios, for stupid consumption. The best thing we can say for the 20th century is that we did not blow ourselves to bits in one spectacular nuclear fireball. We were saved by the last vestiges of sanity and this indomitable human force called the courage to live. These elemental forces of sanity and courage are our best advisors as we travel through the Third Millennium.

3

Technology : The Myth Behind Reality

In this chapter we trace the historical development of technology, and in particular argue that there is an intimate relationship between our outlook on the cosmos and our view of technology. Before technology could expand and develop in the way it is today, we had to acquire a rather special attitude towards nature. Modern technology is an instrument designed to control nature. It could not have evolved, at any rate in the form it did, before we have conceived the idea of the conquest of nature. There is therefore a subtle and continuing dialectics between our larger ideas of the world and our views of what kind of instruments we should seek and implement.

1. Greek Ideals and Technology

The first and fundamental question is: Why did technology not develop in the ancient world? It is intriguing that the Greeks did not use technology in our sense as labour saving devices, as instruments for the mastery of the outside world. The Greeks were after all incredibly inventive. And not only the Greeks in the Hellenistic age, which is known for its mechanical inventions mainly owing to the genius of Archimedes and Hero of Alexandria, but also in the classical period.

We know a great deal about the intellectual and cultural climate of the golden period of Ancient Athens. But we are much less aware that all kinds of extraordinary gadgets were employed at that time; some very clever and sophisticated, as for example machines designed to mimic human behaviour. But it was all for the purpose of Entertainment. Hardly any attempt was made to employ these gadgets in the process of, as we would call it to-day, industrial production.

No doubt this can be attributed to the Greek ideal about what kind of life is worthy of a man. Witness in this context Plutarch's opinions about Archimedes and how disparagingly Plutarch talks about Archimedes' inventions:

> Archimedes possessed so high a spirit, so profound a soul, and such treasures of scientific knowledge, that though these inventions had now obtained him the renown of more than human sagacity, he yet would not deign to leave behind him any commentary or writing on such subjects; but repudiating as sordid and ignoble the whole trade of engineering and every sort of art that lends itself to mere use and profit, he placed his whole affection and ambition in those purer speculations where there can be no reference to the vulgar needs of life.

Archimedes is said to have constantly apologised for his inventions and justified them as mere amusements, as diversions, as useless toys. Thus, a human being or a citizen, as contrasted with a slave or an animal, was a man who did not sully his hands with manual work, whose art did not lend itself to mere use and profit. In such an intellectual climate, technology had little chance to develop, not because slaves were sufficient or slave-owners did not want labour-saving devices, but because it was morally and intellectually repulsive. And these moral and intellectual constraints had a great power over the Greek mind.

There is one element which I find constantly missing in various accounts of ancient technology. This element is the attitude towards nature. Around 600 BC the Greeks chased the gods from their universe and attempted to give natural explanations to phenomena which had previously been explained by reference to the intervention of the gods. Perhaps the efforts to comprehend the workings of nature in non-religious terms was great enough and the Greeks were unable to have gone a step further towards controlling nature. Yet, I believe that this was not because they lacked the capacity or mental resources that they did not attempt to control nature, but rather because of their basically symbiotic relationship with nature. It seems that the Greeks did not separate nature from the rest of their universe. Thus they did not consider nature as object outside, fixed and ready for exploration, independent for its existence from us. Nature, as it were, was too close to them to be objectified.

Perhaps the clearest evidence that the Greeks did not objectify nature sufficiently is the fact that they did not develop the experimental method. They did develop imaginative conjectures and hypotheses about nature. But they were satisfied with the rational power of their conjectures and explanations. They did not test these conjectures and explanations against empirical reality. The concept of nature, as something constant, immutable and firmly established out there, against which we test our hypotheses, was not a part of ancient science. The rationalist tradition in ancient Greece meant the capacity of the human mind to invent hypotheses and conjectures based on reason, which explain the behaviour of nature, but which do not have to be tested against nature. Because of their conception of nature the Greeks could not have developed the idea of empiricism as practised in modern science since Galileo. And this also explains why they could not have conceived the idea of controlling and conquering nature.

2. Medieval Theology and Technology

Another hypothesis which we must examine claims that the roots of modern technology are in the canons of the Judeo-Christian religion. The Judeo-Christian scriptures, it is argued, present man as ruthlessly lording over nature, and nature as the object of his will and rule. The basic premise of this argument appears to be that the destruction of the environment was written in the blueprint given to us in the Bible.

The view that modern technology is rooted in Judeo-Christian teleology is advocated vigorously even by such eminent historians as Lynn White. He argues that a new system of agriculture in the Middle Ages was an expression of a new attitude towards the soil and thus towards nature. "Man's relation to the soil was profoundly changed. Formerly man had been part of nature; now he was the exploiter of nature. Nowhere else in the world did farmers develop any analogous agricultural implement. "Is it coincidence," White asks, "that modern technology, with its ruthlessness towards nature, has so largely been produced by descendents of these peasants of northern Europe?" White continues his argument by suggesting that the new Frankish calendars set the style for the Middle Ages showing "men coercing the world around them—ploughing, harvesting, chopping trees, butchering pigs. Man and nature are two things, and man is master."

These are very interesting arguments. But are they substantial enough? Is ploughing really coercing the world? If this is so, then the coercion of nature started to occur at the time when man, the hunter, became man, the farmer. And then Lynn White's argument collapses. Moreover, is it not the case that the Middle Ages invented rotation farming thereby emphasizing their care for the soil? Furthermore it seems that Lynn White reads too much in the pictures of the medieval calendars. How much can we really deduce from calendars about people's world-views?

Thus, we need much firmer evidence for the view that the aggressive tendencies of modern technology have their roots in the Judeo-Christian tradition. Can this evidence be found in the book of Genesis as some wish to suggest? We read there that man was created in the image of God who gave him "dominion over the fish of the sea, and over the fowl of the air, and over the cattle, and over all the earth, and over every creeping thing that creepeth upon the earth." The crucial term here is of course "dominion." If this term is to be understood in the sense in which it was used with reference to political empires and dominions, such as the Roman Empire and the British Empire, then dominion is indeed the territory for exploitation and plunder. But there is no reason to suppose that this was the intended meaning of the Scripture. On the contrary, there is every reason to suppose that it was not. Man, systematically destroying his dominion, would be a very poor image of God. Alternatively, it could mean that God had wished to project a very poor image of himself, which is nonsense again; or that God is a malicious monster, who created the world for the pleasure of its destruction, which is again an absurd conclusion. Thus the suggestion that the aggressive tendencies of modern technology have their source in the Judeo-Christian tradition leads to nonsense. This suggestion is nonsensical for another reason. It is universally known that the idea of the medieval man was not the conquest of nature but of himself, not the mastery over nature but the mortification of his flesh. For the sake of eternal salvation, the external world had to be disregarded, treated as a transient stage full of temptations on the path to eternal glory. And indeed this world was disregarded, pushed to the periphery of human existence, treated a sinful bondage.

To the medieval man, inspired by the doctrine of the church, nature served no purpose in the overall scheme of salvation; indeed it was a hindrance. In this context, it would make no sense whatsoever to talk about man's expansive drive towards the domination of nature. Nature was a dormant aspect of man's existence, a bondage rather than an element of satisfaction and gratification.

3. The Discovery of Nature

When we compare the paintings of the Middle Ages with the paintings of the Renaissance we become immediately aware of the vast difference between the Medieval and the Renaissance outlook on nature. For the medieval painter nature hardly existed; the content of the painting was the inward world. This is also true of the great masters who lived in the period of transition from the Middle Ages to the Renaissance, such as Giotto. The Renaissance as we know, discovered perspective. The discovery, or perhaps we should say the invention of perspective, was necessary for the discovery of nature in a true sense. For the medieval painter perspective was not essential at all. For the Renaissance painter, on the other hand, so deeply steeped in the external world, perspective was of vital importance.

Turning from the inward to the outward world had innumerable consequences. One of them was the discovery of nature most strikingly manifested by the Renaissance painter. It is inconceivable that technology would have developed as an instrument for controlling nature without the prior discovery of nature. Nature became objectified: first an object of aesthetic contemplation, then an object of exploration, and finally the object of exploitation. We had to discover nature first in order to be able to rape her later. Seventeenth century science worked with the axiom that no authority whatsoever should be obeyed, that only the actual unbiased investigation of nature can provide genuine knowledge.

No one exemplified the spirit of the new science better than Francis Bacon (1561-1626). He was the most articulate spokesman for the new science, although alas not its most successful practitioner. Bacon was one of the prophets of the experimental method in science. We must purge our minds, he urged, of all prejudices, refine and purify it; and then in the state of intellectual *nirvana* we shall be ready for the communion with facts. Uncontaminated facts, shining out there in nature, will reveal their truth to the uncontaminated mind and this will be the basis of genuine knowledge. The concept of the unbiased investigation of nature was of course right. The concept of the mind entirely purified of all prejudices and preconceived notions was of course wrong. What is important in Bacon is not detail but the general concept of the experimental method. But still more important was Bacon's overall idea of knowledge. *Knowledge is power*, he announced at the end of the 16th century. The Baconian programme became a dominant characteristic of the Western intellectual tradition for next centuries to come.

Bacon's succinct motto is enormously important for another reason. In it there are the roots of modern technology. We need to change only one word in order to obtain a perfect description and justification of modern technology. Instead of saying "knowledge is power," Bacon should have said "technology is power." Then the overall Baconian programme fits perfectly the development of Western society during the last three centuries and the last century especially. Modern technology, I have argued, consists not only of tools, but also the ideology regarding the purposes these tools are to be used for, and also regarding the concept of man in the universe. The ideology for the expansive drive of modern technology was provided by Bacon. He wrote: "Man, if we look for final causes, may be regarded as the centre of the world, insomuch that if man were taken away from the world, the rest would seem to be led astray, without aim or purpose...For the whole world works together in the service of man; and there is nothing from which he does not derive use and fruit...insomuch that all things seem to be going about man's business and not their own." This is a bold and assertive programme, and terribly anthropo-centric as well.

Thus, one of the most important of Bacon's endeavours was the shift of our vision from knowledge conceived exclusively as the source of enlightenment, the Greek ideal, to knowledge conceived as the source of our domination over nature, the ideal of the modern occidental mind. We should not overlook the fact, however, that Bacon was not a crude pragmatist; he did cherish knowledge for the sake of enlightenment in the truly Greek fashion. But in addition to this ideal, he conceived of knowledge as the instrument of power. Obstacles to knowledge were to be removed and new strategies for the acquisition of knowledge were to be designed in order to make this knowledge useful, instrumental, powerful. In this scheme the value and utility of the knowledge of the ancients, Bacon beautifully argues, is of no avail: "The wisdom which we have derived principally from the Greeks is but like the boyhood of knowledge and has the characteristic property of boys; it can talk but it cannot generate for it is fruitful of controversies but barren of works." As with all ideologies, Bacon's programme served many purposes, one of them being the liberation of man from the hermetic castles of medieval theology.

What makes Bacon so important as the prophet of modern technology is his vision of knowledge as power, a concept alien to the Greek mind. However, the implementation of Bacon's programme was not possible without further explorations of nature and in particular without its quantification.

4. The Quantification of Nature

It was Galileo Galilei (1564-1642) who conceived the programme for the quantification of nature. In a famous passage on the language in which the book of nature is written he said, "Philosophy (which at that time meant science too) is written in this grand book, the universe, which stands continually open to our gaze. But the book cannot be understood unless one first learns to comprehend the language and read the letters in which it is composed. It is written in the language of mathematics...

without which it is humanly impossible to understand a single word of it; without these one wanders about in a dark labyrinth."

This programme was followed for the next three centuries of the scientific development. Galileo's mathematical vision of the world, it might be argued, contains nothing new. After all, it was the Pythagorean concept of the mathematical harmony, of the number, that holds sway over the flux. The similarity is striking but should not be over-stressed, for while Pythagoras was a mystic, Galileo was an empiricist. It was the empirical world discovered by the Renaissance which Galileo was exploring mathematically. But mathematics was only an instrument for the formulation of results. Mathematics alone could not be a method for the acquisition of new knowledge. The actual method of acquiring knowledge was experimental: empirical testing of the consequences of hypotheses by means of which we try to grasp the world around us. The basic difference between Bacon's experimental method and Galileo's is that whereas Bacon urges us to start with facts and experiments and to induce theories from them, Galileo insists that we must start with imaginative hypotheses and only at the end subject them to empirical tests. Imagination can and must violate common sense. "I cannot find bounds for my admiration," Galileo wrote, "how the reason of Artistarchus and Copernicus has committed such a rape upon their senses as despite them to make herself mistress of their belief." Similar eulogies about the value of imagination can be heard three centuries later from Einstein. "Imagination is more important than knowledge. Knowledge is limited, imagination embraces the world, stimulating progress, giving birth to evolution." Now, we must be perfectly aware that it was the Galilean conception of science that has finally triumphed, not Baconian. But we must be also aware that the clouds of the Baconian conception are still shrouding the minds of many people.

The supreme architect who executed the design for the quantification of nature was Isaac Newton (1647-1727). Newton followed Galileo's programme to the letter. But it took quite a few decades before the first alphabet for reading the book of nature was provided in Newton's *Philosophiae Naturalis Principia Mathematica* (1687). It took yet another century after Newton's *Principia* appeared before the mechanistic model of the universe, as based on Newtonian mechanics, finally appeared. The universe came to be viewed as a huge, but perfectly working clock whose laws are not only discoverable but discovered. All explanations to be considered genuine had to be mechanistic explanations or reducible to mechanistic ones. Now the quantification of nature was accomplished. Whatever was not quantifiable was considered either non-existent or unimportant. It was at that time that science completed its task for technology, and technology was ready to start its conquest and subjugation of nature.

We have reconstructed this story in order to show the intricacy and complexity of the process which led to the development of modern technology. This process contained a number of preconditions which had to be fulfilled before technology could acquire its full potential. In realising these conditions, we have acquired a certain frame of mind which is known as the rational modern European mind. Technology is thus not so much a collection of tools and machines *as a state of Western mind*. Heidegger's declaration that technology is the last stage of metaphysics becomes meaningful in this context. Our inability to come to terms with technology is no doubt related to our infantile naivete about its nature. It is still assumed that technology is "indifferent", that it contains no metaphysics, and that its relation to traditional metaphysics is none. All these assumptions are an expression of an infantile mind.

Technology, as we know it today, is a historical phenomenon born of a certain idea of nature, of a certain idea of progress, of a certain preconception about the deterministic structure of the world, and also related to specific social ideals and specific visions of the ends of human life. As such, it is laden with the elements of traditional metaphysics.

5. The Utopian Heritage

So far we have discussed mainly the intellectual and scientific components which were prerequisites for the emergence of modern technology. In addition to these cognitive factors, we must consider the social ideals whose influence has been profound but much less tangible. These ideals were embodied in some great Utopias of the Renaissance and post-

Renaissance period. When the religious structures which justified man's craving for the transcendent were punctured, secular structures offering man new transcendental goals had to be invented. It is at this point that the idea of progress was born. The concept of progress as a secular category thus replaced the old concept of progress which was a religious and spiritual category. We have secularised our goals but they were still the goals beyond our immediate reach; in this sense they were transcendental goals. Thus, we can easily see that the powerful sway of Utopian thinking pervades the development of modern science and modern technology. We simply delude ourselves if we think that this development was rational through and through, free from mythology and free from Utopian thinking. This idea will be further developed in chapter four.

Jean-Jacques Rousseau (1712-78) represents the first revolt against the ideology of modern science and technology. This revolt was carried on under the banner "down with civilisation." Civilisation for Rousseau was tantamount to the evil force which deprives us of freedom and thus of humanity. When we examine the notion of civilization as conceived by Rousseau, we realise at once that Rousseau fought against the programme of liberation as formulated by Bacon and the Encyclopaedists and as based on the idea of progress. But Rousseau's was also a programme of liberation. Man is born free and yet wherever we look as see him in chains, Rousseau emphatically announces. Thus, we witness here the clash of two programmes of the liberation of man from the tyranny of extrinsic forces. The extraordinary thing is that Rousseau wanted to liberate us from what has been previously conceived as a form of liberation from some other constraints and tyrannies.

Rousseau effectively argued that civilization has imposed on us artificial needs. The pursuit of these needs has alienated man from his essence, deprived him of his humanity. The tyranny of artificial needs is the greatest malady of mankind because it has fundamentally impoverished the individual life of man. This diagnosis is of course alarmingly contemporary. Rousseau was absolutely prophetic in analysing the predicament of the 20th century technological society.

How can we regain our lost humanity? asks Rousseau; a question even more relevant today than it was in Rousseau's time. Rousseau's solution was the doctrine of individual salvation. Civilisation and the artificial needs it imposes upon us must be defied by opting out from society and civilization. Man must return to nature, thus to himself, thus to his essence through the individual act of defiance—not a rebellion against the social system but rather a liberation from the web of artificial needs and phoney relationships of the technological civilization. The hippies had a great and outspoken predecessor in Jean-Jacques Rousseau.Essential to Rousseau's new philosophy was his new concept of nature. Nature was treated by Rousseau not as an object for exploration in order to satisfy man's material needs, but rather as a part of his spirituality, as a primordial state of harmony which we must reach in order to regain humanity. Nature is thus for Rousseau an imaginary matrix, the ideal where the symbiosis of the individual with the outside and with his inner essence takes place; is not an object but rather a subject.

6. Marx—a Revolt Against Progress in the Name of Progress

A century later another powerful voice protested against the suppression of the individual and the deprivation of human dignity by the all-enveloping system of expanding technology. This was the voice of Karl Marx (1818-83). I am referring here specifically to the philosophical views of the young Marx, particularly as expressed in the *Economic and Philosophical Manuscripts* of 1844. There is no question that Marx's primary concern was the liberation of the individual, of the human being, from the tyranny of objectified relationships which he inadvertently imposes on himself. Thus Marx's is Rousseau-like programme of the liberation of man from the constraints and tyrannies of the external world. But Marx saw these constraints and tyrannies through the spectacles of a moralist who witnessed the effects of the industrial revolution. The process of alienation, another name for which is dehumanisation or the estrangement of man from his essence, is the process of objectification, the process during which man, the human being, becomes an object. In Rousseau's times this estrangement occured through the submission to artificial needs (as Rousseau calls them). In Marx's time the main form of his objectification was alienation through the buying and selling of human labour. This was the negative aspect of the otherwise rational, secular and scientific world in which Marx believed so passionately. He set himself to rectify this aspect in his own way.

Marx's attitude towards technology is rather complex. But there is no question that he saw in expanding technology a necessary condition of the liberation of man. Man must first liberate himself from the constraints of the natural elements and then liberate himself from technology. The most important task for his own time Marx saw as the liberation of man from the tyranny of the machine, which was the result of the unfortunate social system. The reformation of society was the necessary condition for the return of man to himself, to his essence, to his lost humanity. The evils of technology are due to the structure of society. We must change this structure in order to enable technology to bring about the liberation of man.

Although Marx was intellectually independent in many ways, he was profoundly indebted to Rousseau in his conception of man not only implicitly, but in the very terminology, he used to defend the dignity of man. But there is one fundamental difference between Rousseau and Marx. Whereas Rousseau's programme of reform was individual and consisted of opting out from civilisation and society, Marx's programme was social and consisted in calling for a collective effort to change the structure of society. Thus we witness here two basic types of possible remedy against the suppression of the individual human being by objects and relationships he has inadvertently developed: Rousseauian-individual, and Marxian-social. Both have been tried. Both have failed.

The problem of alienation haunts us now more than ever before. We are at the mercy of the increasing quantity of objects which saturate and atomise our human environment, which constantly require our attention, and which condition us to ever new and often artificial needs. According to the original conception, spelled out in many Utopias, technologies were to be invented to gratify our genuine needs. Now we have reversed the formula and indeed perverted it: needs are artificially created to satisfy the demands of technology. (For further discussion of artificial and genuine needs see Chapter 6). This is by no means a trivial problem. We craved to be saved *by* technology; now we crave to be saved *from* technology.

Where shall we turn for a possible solution? As we have said, there is the individual solution, as exemplified by Rousseau and the hippies. And there is the social solution, as exemplified by Marx and the revolutionary students. Neither sheer escapism, as in the case of the hippies, nor anarchistic revolution, as in the case of militant students, will carry the day. The dearth of constructive programmes among various revolutionaries render their negations an act of despair, not a genuine revolution.

Can there be another solution? At first sight it does not seem so. Yet, when we analyse the situation with some care, the third solution can be discerned. We can distinguish two different approaches to technology and two different concepts of nature. The first approach to technology insists that the individual is first and everything revolves around him, including technology; the second approach insists that society comes first and that the primary purpose of technology is social. The first concept of nature treats her as an object 'out there'; the second as a part of ourselves, as subject. Now we have four possibilities (see diagram).

		Nature	
		as object	as subject
Technology Oriented to	Indi-vidual	Free Enterprise (Present System)	The Rousseauian Solution
	Socitety	The Marxist Solution	The Eco-Philosophy Solution

The first possibility is that of Free Enterprise System. We have tried it for a long time. It no longer works; the second is the Rousseauian solution; the third the Marxist Solution (in which nature is still treated as an object 'out there' to be exploited); the fourth—not yet tried in the occidental world, which I am here advocating—is the Eco-Philosophy Solution. (For further discussion of Eco-Philosophy see my book under the same title published by Marion Boyars Publishers, London, 1981). The few remarks I can here offer on the fourth possibility do not constitute a programme; only a bare outline of a direction. But basically I wish to suggest that we must work towards a new social utopia. I am using the term utopia advisedly and deliberately. And I defy all of those who deride utopia as something almost childish; their thinking must be insipient, their imagination must be barren, and their vision must be blurred. As long as man exists utopia—as a vehicle for expression of future hopes and aspirations—is an indispensable element of the human existence, and indeed a part of the human condition. Those who cannot see that this is so must have scales on their eyes and should keep quiet on the subject. Progress has never been promoted by and never depended on sceptics and cynics.

In the programme or utopia I am suggesting we must treat nature as subject, as a part of ourselves, as a part of our outer skin which cannot be damaged without causing damage to ourselves. This may require the development of a religious reverence of nature, characteristic of some Renaissance painters and of some oriental societies. And this will also require a change in our social institutions and social relationships which for the time being are set in the opposite direction—towards further growth of technology for the sake of personal profit, and at the expense of whoever and whatever is in the way. If this reverence for nature becomes a new imperative, then technology will become harmless. Whether this programme (the fourth alternative) can be implemented in a cold, rational way, nobody can say; more likely it will require a sort of religious inspiration and fervour, characteristic of new departures in human thought.

Summary

Technology is a part of our intellectual heritage; it is a component of our view of man and of society. We cannot redirect its course, by assuming, as is too often done, that technology is a huge chariot which will move whichever way we guide it.

Technology is not a chariot and what we need is not a more skilful charioteer. Indeed, technologists are the least suitable people for redirecting the course of technology because their thinking has been more corrupted by the concept of technology as power than the thinking of other people.

What we must do is to shift our vision in a fundamental manner, away from the ideology of modern science, away from the further quantification of nature, and from modes of life directed towards further multiplication of material goods (which will further atomise and mutilate the texture of our human and social life), and towards a model for a symbiosis between man and nature.

As it was difficult for the Greeks to think about their technical inventions in term of their utility, so it is difficult for us, and will be for a long time, not to think about technology as power, not to think about nature as an object of exploitation. We have to evolve new social models based on qualitative, not quantitative, criteria. The return of man to nature will be the return of man to himself; the restitution of the basic qualities of life will be at the same time the restitution of our symbolic relationship with nature. Once this new vision becomes a reality, becomes the defining characteristic of man's new horizons, we shall have to draw, relentlessly and unhesitatingly, the consequences which follow from it regarding changes in our economic and social structures. It should be crystal clear that this new vision cannot be maintained unless specific and appropriate changes are made in the social and economic structures of our society; and in the structure of our consciousness.

4

Technology as a Slayer of Democracy

1. The Ambiguous Legacy of the French Revolution

"Man is born free and everywhere he is in chains."

With these words, Rousseau starts his *Social Contract*. Rousseau's ideas reverberate with freedom. In due time, they become the dynamite for the Revolution.

The great French Revolution was fought in the name of liberty and freedom. This revolution was announcing the dawn of a new era. However, the dream of the revolution came only partly true. The revolution turned into a nightmare in a double sense. In the political sense, just after it happened in France. And in a larger—social and human sense, two centuries later.

I will argue in this chapter that during the last two centuries we have witnessed, on the global scale, the repeat of the tragedy, which happened in France a few years after the Revolution. Thus I will argue that the promise of liberty and freedom, which the Revolution had proclaimed, has been vitiated and fundamentally unfulfilled. The dialectics of freedom is never easy. It has been particularly ambiguous and double-edged when Democracy became a close ally of technology and together they embarked on a new era of freedom.

As we all know, the great French Revolution signified not only the bloodbath of the reigning aristocracy. Very soon, it became a bloodbath for the revolutionaries themselves. The great terror gradually killed all the leaders. The revolution was devouring its own children. The machine of the Revolution, the guillotine, once released, was relentlessly killing, as if it were.by its own will; and acording to its own imperative. The premise of the great freedom became the reality of a great terror.

By and large, we do not see (and we do not want to see) any parallels between the terror of the Great Revolution and the gradually increasing terror of technology during the last two centuries, and particularly during the last fifty years. Yet the parallels are quite striking. Like the Revolution, technology was meant to be a great liberator, and like the Revolution, it is now capable of killing us all. It hasn't killed us yet. But the fact that it has this potential, is quite chilling. Once the machine of the Revolution (the guillotine) was set up, there was no way to stop it. Is it not similar with technology, which, although in a more subtle and attenuated form, is a relentless slayer of our liberty, of social cohesion, and of our individual inner lives? It is this aspect that I wish to explore in some depth.

We are celebrating the achievements of the French Revolution. We are celebrating the achievements of Democracy. We are celebrating the achievements of technology. In these celebrations we must not ignore the darker side of the picture. We must ask ourselves whether the technological revolution, in the midst of which we are presently living, is not creating a similar legacy the French Revolution left behind—the legacy of the guillotine relentlessly chopping the heads which are on its way? Perhaps chopping the heads is too strong a term—extinguishing the soul and emptying the heart of men would be more appropriate.

Now the French philosophers of the Enlightenment were ideologues. They were more interested in influencing public opinion than in deep search for truth. They were brilliant conversationalists rather than profound thinkers. With the exception of Jean-Jacques Rousseau, who was Swiss after all.

Among French philosophers of the Enlightenment, there was nobody of the stature of Emmanuel Kant—who, although inspired by their ideal, was a thinker digging deep and confronting the great problems, which the scientific world view has brought about. Among these problems were: If science provides indubitable and ultimate truths; and if empiricism, which is the epistemological vanguard of science, is right, namely that all knowledge is acquired through the senses, then how is scientific knowledge possible? What is the nature of this knowledge? Let us be absolutely clear about the problem. If empiricism holds good (and if it is the case that knowledge acquired through the senses is unreliable, as the senses are unreliable), then it is obvious that knowledge acquired via the empiricist vehicle cannot be final, absolute, indubitable. If, on the other hand, the knowledge of physics is final and irrevocable, then it could not have been the product of the senses. This was the dilemma which Kant confronted magnificently, and to which he found a magnificent solution.

This was one problem. The other problem was: what is the status of the human person in the world defined by science, which is deterministic, prearranged, and clad in the iron cast of physical laws? What is the role of morality in the deterministic scheme of the universe? Again Kant confronted the dilemma with clarity and incisiveness as he declared: "the starry heaven above you; and the moral law within you." The moral law lies in the sovereignty of the individual. The human being is a sovereign. The human universe, with its moral and spiritual dimensions, is not reducible to the deterministic stuff of science.

The French philosophers were not concerned with fundamental problems. They assumed that all was well, and Science and Reason were the solution to all problems. They were propagators and popularizers of science and the scientific world view. They didn't see any problems with science and reason. They wore rosy spectacles of the scientific-technological optimism.

The whole culture was intoxicated with science and its achievements. Moliere beautifully satirizes the fascination with science in his play, *The Learned Ladies*, in which he shows science invading not only fashionable boudoirs but also the chambers of servant girls. In the French salons of the 18th century, particularly those attended by Encyclopaedists, science is one of the main subjects of conversation. Voltaire's mistress, madame du Chatelet, wrote a very lucid and learned account of Leibnitz' philosophy under the title: *Institutions de Physique*, of which La Mettrie said, "Everybody understands monads since the Leibnitzians made the brilliant acquisition of Madame du Chatelet." In Madame du Chatelet's salon the charming Venetian fellow, Algarotti, presented and discussed his book, *Newtonianism For the Ladies*. The learned duet, Voltaire and Madame du Chatelet, were slightly shocked by the frivolous tone of the narrative and by too many jokes in the text. However, *Newtonianism* in a curious way epitomizes the obsession with the triumphant march of science.

Now, Voltaire's philosophy itself was not really profound. Voltaire was a brilliant conversationalist, but far from a deep, let alone an original thinker. This became the legacy of the Encyclopaedists: brilliant talk but not much substance.

Voltaire was very vocal about liberty, including liberties of others. He was supporting all kinds of good causes, and sometimes financed them as well. But his moral conscience seems to be in doubt. For he was an arms dealer, making huge amounts of money on trading in weapons. There is at least some moral ambiguity here: to propound the philosophy of liberation, to raise one's voice in the name of liberty for others—while procuring the arms trade...the result of which must be the killing of others. Voltaire's conscience does not seem to have bothered him. Voltaire was not a particularly moral person. He didn't think that morality had much to do with liberation. This moral ambiguity is something we have inherited from the French Enlightenment. It is also inherent in Marxism, which was profoundly influenced by the Enlightenment.

What I am suggesting is that we have inherited from the Enlightenment not only some specific ideas concerning the great importance of Reason and the beneficial role of science and technology in human affairs. We also inherited a considerable ambiguity about the role of morality in the human world. Somehow we have been persuaded by the dictum of the Enlightenment: morality is for the church. For the enlightened man—it is material progress. This has become our credo.

I said that the Encyclopaedists were brilliant talkers without much substance behind it. Yet it would be unfair to say that they were just talkers. They had a project. And an important one, for that matter. This was the *Encyclopaedia*. The *Encyclopaedia* was the stupendous undertaking to envisage and to complete.

The thirty-five volume *Encyclopaedia of Useful Knowledge* was a triumph of human industry and of perseverance. The project was based on a philosophy. It was the Baconian philosophy. Bacon insisted that the ancient knowledge was but a boyhood of knowledge. It could speak but it could not generate. It was full of words but barren of works. He wanted knowledge that is potent of works, knowledge that is useful. And that is precisely what the Encyclopaedists meant to provide. They considered the *Encyclopaedia* to be the ultimate compilation of all useful knowledge that the human race could amass. A laughable claim from our perspective; but a noble one at the time.

The Encyclopaedists were so busy collecting useful knowledge that they did not have time and energy to think about deeper questions. This has become the hallmark of the entire technological/scientific civilization. We have been so busy gathering useful knowledge and improving our material condition that we have forgotten what the ultimate purpose of it all is, particularly as related to the life of beauty, dignity and meaning. It is in this sense that I consider the legacy of the French Enlightenment and the French Revolution to be a double edged sword. The ideals were noble, particularly as seen against the oppressive background of the church and the ruling aristocracy. However, in pursuing these ideals, we have cheapened our lives. We have been continuously acting. But our actions do not add up—to a life of meaning and coherence. The words of Macbeth are painfully relevant. Our actions are "full of sound and fury, signifying nothing."

2. The Insidious Role of Secularism

Let us look at the whole picture from a larger perspective. What we have to contend with, in our times, is not only a particular drama that has occurred as the result of the interplay between Democracy and technology. Both Democracy and technology have to be seen in a larger framework. This is the framework of the post-Renaissance secularism, which has generated the Enlightenment. Together secularism and Enlightenment have shaped our ideas of Democracy and freedom.

Actually, we need to go a bit further back—to the very cradle of Democracy. There was no question in the Greek mind of the connection between freedom and Democracy. Indeed, it may be said that the Greeks invented Democracy to safeguard freedom. The intelligent and enlightened man chooses to live in a Polis. And the best way of arranging the Polis—for the sake of the fullness of life and of safeguarding freedom—is Democracy.

Let us be mindful that under the auspices of secularism we have tried to de-sacralize the physical universe; and then the meaning of Democracy and freedom. We have somehow persuaded ourselves that the three concepts: secularism-Democracy-technology are inherently connected and co-define each other. That is not how the meaning of Democracy was envisaged by the ancient Greeks. they did not tie Democracy either to secularism or to science/technology. It is important for us to bear this in mind.

Let me spell out one of my main theses: *in imposing the harness of secularism on Democracy we have distorted its meaning; and in the process we have impoverished the ideal of freedom.* Secularism has been a disaster for Western culture in so many ways; and it has been a misfortune for Democracy as well, as Democracy has become subsumed under the imperatives of technology.

Confusing Democracy with the domination of technology has been one of the unfortunate aspects of our secular age. This confusion has pervaded our political thinking to such a degree that we simply expect technology to be a liberator and never a slayer of Democracy. When confronted with facts, we are continually surprised, if not confounded. We so often assume that the expansion of technology is synonymous with the expansion of freedom and of Democracy. But it isn't synonymous. It wasn't conceived by the Greeks as synonymous. Only in our post-Enlightenment thinking we tried to make it synonymous. It is time to dismantle this whole composition which inherently ties Democracy with secularism and technology.

The 19th century discovered that "God is dead;" that man is unable to live with the traditional images of God. The 20th century has discovered that man cannot live without God, without some spiritual sustenance and larger transcendental horizons. We are now aware that secularism breeds emptiness, out of which arises nihlism, relativism, and an atrophy of values. When we ponder over the meaning of Democracy in our times, let us be aware that the cherished post-Enlightened schema: Technology→ progress→Democracy→Freedom, simply does not work.

In a famous passage (in the Social Contract) Rousseau maintains that if there were a nation of gods, Democracy would be a suitable form of government for them; human beings are too imperfect to govern themselves democratically. This passage of Rousseau is usually taken on its face value. Democracy is too perfect a form of government for humans; and indeed to unattainable. Yet, there is another, more fruitful and deeper interpretation of this passage. In aspiring to Democracy, we are elevating ourselves over and beyond the cruel and unjust forms of government characteristic of tyrannies. In aspiring to Democracy we are divinizing the human society; we are in a sense putting ourselves on an equal footing with gods. Such an interpretation would not only be endorsed by Socrates and Plato. They would insist that this is a true interpretation of Democracy—as an instrument enabling freedom, and indirectly helping man in his quest of self-perfectibility leading to Godhead.

Let us draw some conclusions. Democracy and spiritual aspirations were not antithetical to each other for the ancient Greeks, but indeed aspects of each other. Democracy was the social structure helping the individual man to attain freedom and spiritual enlightenment—leading to liberation.

We have completely forgotten about this aspect of Democracy in our times. Instead, we have tied Democracy to the quest of technology. But the imperatives of Democracy and technology are different. Technology aims at efficiency and control, and often domination; which in our times increasingly means control over nature, and over all living systems, including human beings. The quintessential imperative of Democracy is the enhancement of human freedom, including spiritual freedom. When the technological imperative is given a free reign, it becomes antithetical to the imperative of Democracy. At such a time, technology becomes a slayer of Democracy.

3. A New Agenda for Democracy

Nowadays Democracy seems to be an irrelevance. Everybody pays a lip service to it but hardly anybody thinks that it works any more. We treat Democracy as a venerable shell which we admire as we admire ancient monuments.

Yet, the power contained in the idea of Democracy is still enormous. Why? Partly because it is a spiritual ideal, or perhaps we could even call it—a religious ideal. Similarly as with so many other religious and ethical ideals lies exactly in their transcendent reach. We consider them immensely worthy. We aspire to them, although most of the time we fail to embody them in our lives. Let's put it simply: the enduring power of the idea of Democracy lies in its spiritual content. Democracy does not only spell out equality as such. This very equality has deeper attributes: it is an essential ingredient of our freedom; and, on a higher level, of our sense of dignity, of our nobility and indeed of our divinity.

With the twilight and demise of technological Democracy, strangled by the tentacles of secularism, it is time to restore Democracy's ancient spiritual meaning. We need to return not only to the concept of Democracy as "power for the people." For both the meaning of 'power' and of 'people' need to be re-examined.

The idea of 'power' has been distorted and perverted by the Faustian concept of power—you only live once, therefore you live dangerously, and at whosever expense; usually by attempting to have power over things and over people. Power then becomes a spectacle of domination for the sake of the aggrandizement of one's ego. That was not the meaning of *cratia* and *demos* in the original conception of demo-cratia.

We need to re-sacralize the universe, and in the process re-sacralize the concept of power, including one which is a component of Demo-cracy. We cannot treat the universe as a heap of inexhaustible natural resources to be exploited to our benefit. We cannot treat other people contemptuously, which happens when we treat them as objects and pawns of our power games. To stop those fundamental processes of degradation of both the universe and of ourselves, we need much more than a re-distribution of power, or a re-distribution of justice—while the old paradigm of power, dominated by technology-triumphant is controlling our destiny.

Re-thinking secularism does not mean a better secularism. It means a fundamental realization that secularism has become a blind alley, that we are spiritually strangled by it. In the wake of this process we suffer the fallout of a shrunken concept of man and of the universe; and a cheapened conception of Democracy.

Re-thinking secularism means a re-enchantment of the world, a re-sacralization of nature and Cosmos, a re-introduction of spirituality to the content of our lives. We do not need to re-invent the wheel. In the great spiritual traditions of the past we have ready blueprints.

Let us realize that it is not a negation of reason to insist that we should treat all nature and the entire cosmos reverentially—because it is a sacred universe in which we are dwelling. From the sacredness of the ground of all being follows a revential treatment of nature (no longer to be ruthlessly exploited as the result of our power trip), of other people (no longer to be treated as objects of our faustian quests) of Democracy (no longer to be subdued to the imperatives of manipulative technology). It is time to change our spectacles and realize that the cosmos is not a quarry but a cradle and a nursery of our lives and our dreams, including one of a fair life.

The broadening of the concept of Democracy, to include its cosmic underpinning and enriching it by returning to its ancient spiritual roots, may be necessary for resurrecting the now dying ideal. It may also be a part of the process of our self-renewal. We become in the image of concepts we have created. If concepts become progressively empty and their symbolic content dies of atrophy, we slowly die with the symbolic products of our minds.

The renewal of Democracy, or a form of government which would serve its original intent—of enlarging man's freedom and of helping him/her on the path of spiritual enlightenment is a more vital task for our times than the invention of a new technology or an introduction of another utilitarian scheme of distributive justice, for such schemes and such technologies are but servants of the crippling secularist formation.

Summary

Democracy is a noble concept that has undergone various transformations during the last 25 centuries. Democracy is one of the modalities of human social experience. It can be renewed if and when human beings, collectively and deliberately, embark on a new form of social praxis. I have suggested that a renewal of Democracy lies in its spiritual regeneration, for, to begin with, Democracy was a concept serving spiritual ends.

Technology and Democracy are not aspects of each other. Nor do they co-define each other. In technological Democracy of our times, technology triumphs while Democracy suffers. In brief, technology is a slayer of Democracy. Technological Democracy is a progeny of larger forces and ideologies. It is a child whose parents are secularism and the French Enlightenment. Secularism, although it was once a liberating force, is now a crippling conceptual disease. Secularism is a culprit responsible for the demise of Democracy, which originally was conceived to spiritual ends. Democracy was a part of the process of divinizing the human society, whereby by inventing an 'ideal' political system, we tried to govern ourselves in a manner "suitable for gods" as Rousseau would put it.

Modern technology, especially in the 20th century, has been profoundly undemocratic. It has served the elites. It was invented by the elites. And the main financial rewards were reaped by the elites. The spread of Technology did not signify the spread of democratic values but rather profit and domination. In controlling the markets through the spread and dissemination of technologies—by the powerful financial elites—the democratic aspirations of unprivileged countries were not helped. For modern technology to be truly democratic and serving democratic values, we need to abolish patents and patent laws. Otherwise, market forces will be continually upsetting Democracy and the democratic process.

A fundamental renewal of Democracy is possible. But it will have to go hand in hand with a fundamental renewal of our thinking and our basic assumptions. We have to overcome secularism by re-introducing to Democracy its (presently missing) spiritual dimension. Secondly, we need to place Democracy in a larger context. This context, I claim, should be cosmocracy. A further discussion of Cosmocracy, as superseding Democracy, is carried out in chapter 19.

5

Human Values and Capitalism

1. Our Basic Problem—A Wrong Articulation of Human Nature

The present hosanna of Capitalism is distorting our picture of reality—making greed as the chief motif of everything there is, and it is obscuring and falsifying our future, that is the future of all humanity, as contrasted with the future of Western financial elites. What is cherished as a great victory of human industry is a concealed form of human aggression exercised on an unprecedented scale. In a society which is so successful and so affluent, there should be no aggression and violence. Alas, violence is nowadays structural, is part of the daily life. It is not limited to poor countries (according to the precept, poverty breeds violence) but is hugely evident in rich countries. The time has arrived to see with more clarity the whole picture and especially to see that the way by which we bring about our prosperity is steeped in violence and is a carrier of violennce. To put it bluntly, Western modes of economic development are not benign scientific models but hidden vehicles of violence.

We in the West do not want to acknowledge this hidden violence of our economic models; or else we justify them by claiming that human nature is aggressive and selfish. It is time we examine this pernicious assumption as well.

Let us look at some facts. While the prosperity of the rich is growing, the poverty of the poor is growing. This is a strange and disturbing spectacle. In the fault line which separates the prosperous and the miserably poor there lurks a great deal of violence, both overt and covert.

Neither poverty is springing by itself nor are riches growing by themselves. Responsible for both, especially in our tightly connected world are economic institutions and specific technologies—invariably developed in the West. Deeper down responsible for our exploitive technologies is our Western rapacious thinking which we have skillfully developed under the camouflage of Western democracy, more recently re-christened as Market Democracy.

Yet deeper still, there is something else which is responsible for our rapacious thinking and our exploitive technologies. I will come straight to the point: it is a wrong articulation of human nature. Out of many possible ways of developing and articulating human nature, we have chosen one which is aggressive to nature, destructive to other cultures and antithetical to human happiness; and to peace among people. Two main characteristics of the model of human nature which we have inadvertently (and more recently deliberately) developed are aggression and selfishness. Aggression is built into the modes of our economic thinking which means into the dominant modes of our Western thinking. And this aggression spills over to all spheres of our activity. In the final reckoning, we justify this aggression (which deep down we are ashamed of) by insisting that *human nature is aggressive.*

Now about selfishness. The pursuit of selfishness brings about unprecedented prosperity to some, while creating a sea of misery for others. And while creating huge injustices in the world—for which deep down we are also ashamed. (Again we justify this existential angst to ourselves by saying: 'well, human nature is selfish.') Another consequence of the pursuit of selfishness is a warped social reality: nobody is truly happy, everybody envies everybody else, people are trampling on other people or are being trampled upon. This is surely a cockeyed ideal of happiness. And this miserable ideal of happiness cannot be justified by our muttering that human nature is selfish.

Now, let us not be simple minded. There is no denying that there are selfish elements in human nature. There is no denying that we are capable of aggression and recognize it as a part of our nature. But this is only a part of the story. And not the most significant one, for that matter. Let us remember that the periods of unprecedented selfishness and aggression are not known as glorious periods of human history but as periods of barbarity.

Let us look at the picture of human cultures historically. Through millennia of human unfolding, we were able to transcend the principles of "might is right", "man with the biggest club rules" because traditional human cultures and great religions have emphasized the cooperative, the selfless, the altruistic. Great leaps forward in human welfare were made exactly when we were able to transcend and sublimate our aggression and instead built in peace and cooperation. Such an articulation of human nature is possible. Moreover, it is a cornerstone of what we call our humanity, our dignity.

The consequence of the recent intoxication with selfishness and aggression, which I consider to be a result of the wrong articulation of human nature, are disastrous. They bode ill for the whole of humanity in the future. Let me emphasize that we are not only concerned with the plight of so many individuals who have been trapped and crushed by the wheels and mechanisms of present economic models. We are concerned above all with the course of the whole of humanity which is on the wrong track. We all know, at least all perceptive people do, that we are out of kilt, that things do not connect, that the whole picture does not make sense, that our individual lives do not make sense—even among the most prosperous societies, and particularly those. Yet we have allowed ourselves to be duped by the unseeing and the unscrupulous, who have usurped for themselves the mantle of rulers and over-seers of this planet.

It is time that the thinking and seeing people all over the world put an end to this nonsense, put an end to this shameful spectacle which, by distorting the meaning of human nature, distorts our lives and cheapens our destinies.

2. Our Destinies Cannot be Guided by Lesser Beings

Americans are resourceful and enterprising people. But they seem to have too much of one kind of energy—for pushing and imposing their will on others; and too little of other qualities—for understanding, compassion and respecting tradition. Americans simply are not mature as a culture to be the leader of nations. Not having developed their own culture (there never was a Ministry of Culture in America and recently the Endowment for the Arts was eliminated), they cannot appreciate other cultures in depth. They can only appreciate civilization which they have frantically pushed and pushed forward. Frantic rush was probably in response to the feeling of inferiority which the Americans have felt toward traditional cultures.

Let us be quite clear about it. Our business is not to criticize America and especially Americans, many of whom are admirable people. I have many American friends whom I admire for their deep human qualities. What is at stake is the mentality of the whole civilization, which is run by the ideology of profit and greed, with disregard for truth, human dignity, future generations and the well being of nature. It is this mentality which is a menace. As one American writer has put it: "Americans worship their own points of view, and they aim to get them across in the plainest, fastest and most forceful way." All true. Except that this worship of their points of view is a bit too much for others and these plainest and most forceful ways do seem as ignoble arrogance at best and as bullying, coercion and exploitation at worst.

It is known that an American ambassador in Poland called the Polish Prime Minister to his office, shouted at him and stamped his feet in displeasure when the Poles were slow in purchasing American helicopters. This did not go very well with the Poles who remember only too vividly the Soviet ambassadors in Communist days doing similar things. The examples of bullying and coercion by the USA officials occupying high power offices, including the President, could be cited a plenty while the rhetoric of freedom and democracy are being constantly evoked. Thus Democracy so often appears to be a fig-leaf hiding for the bulldozer of American economic expansion.

The intimidation and exploitation goes on not only outside the USA. The unseeing greed of American political/business elites has no mercy for their own people. As a result, the gap between the poor and the rich has widened dramatically during the last 20 years. For many years economists, politicians and columnists sheepishly admitted that, yes, the fortunes of the rich were growing by leaps and bounds, while the salaries of working people and middle class people were stagnant. "Stagnant" was the term that was used for 15 years, as if these salaries were holding on about the same level. Finally the recent statistics has revealed the real story. The salaries of lower classes and lower middle classes have been markedly decreasing. To keep up on the level of their previous existence, and not admitting their own plight, people have been working longer hours, and so often more people in the family had to work.

This impoverishment of the working and middle class people (which involved hundreds of thousands below the poverty level) produced a social malaise and existential anguish unknown in American society.

So the empire is devouring not only distant lands but their own children. America is still the richest country in the world. Yet its vision is so narrow, its goals are so limited that it with impunity impoverishes the core of its working population, reversing the historical process of slow amelioration of underprivileged people and, in the process causing social and psychic traumas of huge proportions. Can such a country be a leader of nations? Is this the right example for the world? Is this what the future well being of the word requires?

It is quite apparent that the American example of greedy rapaciousness of some, at the expense of so many others, has been followed by many other industrial nations. This is a sure recipe for future strife and violent upheaval—as societies and nations will spontaneously seek a re-adjustment of these glaring injustices, inequalities and exploitation.

In the triumphant hosanna of American business classes, it is unashamedly declared that, human nature is 'spontaneously capitalistic'; and it is sometimes whispered that it is 'American.' This is dangerous nonsense. It is dangerous because it allows Americans to push their gospel of greed with impunity as if it were a law of nature, if not a law of god.

We need to examine all the assumptions and myths of present thinking in order not to be duped and manipulated into situations and destinies which are clearly undesirable and often anti-human and which are forced upon us by people of a lesser human substance who want to persuade us that their path of greed and our existential misery are inevitable.

3. The Erosion of Truth and the Corruption of the Intellectuals

Since the great debate over the nature of science in the 1970's, between Karl Popper and Thomas Khun, and their respective followers, science has lost its status as an unshakable rock of truth and a reliable criterion for all human knowledge. In this debate, it was revealed that the foundations of science are far more shaky than we had believed. It was also revealed that we don't quite know what science is. The various attributes which we took for granted, as being part of the nature of science, were shown to be a mosaic of question begging notions and assumptions. Moreover, the very notion of truth, this cornerstone of science could no longer be defended as an objective category. Thus during the last quarter of the century, truth has become an entity in retreat. Scientists and philosophers are unwilling to use it as the criterion of knowledge. They prefer not to talk about it.

In these circumstances truth has lost a great deal of its authority. This fact, among others, led to the proliferation of all kinds of relativisms. Finally post-modernism emerged codifying the death of objective truth.

In the final analysis, it turns out that we are living in a society where the bottom line is the most important truth. When the bottom line is the only truth, the foundation of our understanding is undermined. And we are paralyzed with cognitive confusion. In this confusion, those who shout the loudest and who have media at their disposal prevail. Bewildered by this whole spectacle, ordinary people are pushed to the margin. Some try to rescue their sanity and dignity by escaping into their individual gardens of indulgence and subjectivity. This subjectivity and escapism have led many to addictive substances which is a sinister consequence of the confused society in turmoil, led by the blind and the greedy.

Religious leaders, philosophers and intellectuals are of little help, as they themselves are confused and paralyzed with inaction. In the late 1960 and early 1970's intellectuals and thinking people showed a great deal of courage in challenging the status quo and in proposing new alternatives. This came to an end in the late

1970's and the 1980's; especially in the 1990's. The process of curtailment started in the USA in the mid-1970's. I was there at the time and saw it happening. In a subtle and gradual way, nearly all powerful minds were bought. The process was so subtle that it was almost imperceptible. I was approached in a subtle way by a prominent right wing foundation. But I saw the game through and declined their 'interesting' offer. Others were simply sucked in. It was lucrative. In ten years the whole ethos of thinking changed in the USA. And then in Western Europe, and the world over.

The result has been the muzzling of the minds of thinking people in servitude of the status quo and the ideology of Big Business. It shows nowhere more clearly than among economists. The inability of the economists to distinguish facts and reality from economic fictions and pseudo-scientific theories, is so glaring. When we turn our attention to the universities at large, we realize that they have become corporations, ruled by corporate mentality and corporate interests. So without much exaggeration one can say that high paid intellectuals and a huge army of experts now form a new class of prostitutes. I do not wish to insult anybody. But let us look at the picture. Where is integrity? Where is the responsibility? Where is dignity and honesty characteristic of traditional intellectuals who had moral conscience? They are not there. Intellectuals are pieces of commodities to be bought in the market place. They sell their minds and knowledge with little regard for the moral consequences of their services.

It is extremely difficult to hear the voices of sanity and truth nowadays. For the media are monopolized by those who are prepared to serve the interests of financial elites, and actually protect these interests. Intellectuals have aligned themselves to the interests of the mainstream. Younger thinking scholars are intimidated by the status quo and the power of money.

Those with alternative views are marginalized. They don't have any access to media. Alternative voices are invariably viewed as suspect. No longer a commie suspect but as some kind of weirdo suspect: as a myopic position of a person who cannot see what it is all about. And it is about money, money, money. The whole thing is, in fact, so one-sided and bizarre that it offends human intelligence and prompts us to ask: are we living in some kind of insane asylum? In brief, a buy out of intellectuals has occurred and there is nobody to protect the common men, society and future generations.

4. The Great Betrayal of the Middle Class

Since the Middle Ages, the middle classes have been the foundation of rising prosperity of Western Society. And this has been particularly so in modern times. During the last century, a myth was created which the middle classes have wholeheartedly accepted, that if you work hard and contribute to the mainstream of society, your lot will steadily improve, your own future and the future of your children will be secure. A hazy utopia has been continually lingering on the skies of Western people, reassuring them that all was well on the Western front.

Suddenly, the rug was pulled out of the cozy existence of middle classes. The myth has collapsed and the middle class finds itself shattered and bewildered. There is no longer job security, an assurance of job continuity, assured protection in old age. The welfare state says, with embarrassment and frankness, that it cannot afford the services it had promised, and on which the very existence of middle class is based.

The middle class is frustrated and feels betrayed. It cannot understand what has happened. Its leaders have no explanation either; nor are they promising any brighter future. The very myth of a brighter and brighter future forever is shattered. The whole social fabrique of liberal society is in pieces. Nobody within the established classes has any satisfactory answer, while the ruthless knights of triumphant capitalism are robbing the estate of the Middle Class with impunity and jeer.

The ex-champions of liberal ideology which is the foundation of liberal society are now curiously mute and appear confused. What strikes one while reading the ex-luminaries of Western liberal philosophy, such as Lord Ralf Dahrendorf, of U.K. or Lester Carl Thurow, of the USA is a complete vacuity of their arguments and a complete impotency of their vision. The self-brainwashing of supposedly great minds is truly pathetic. These men behave as if they knew nothing about the spiritual and cultural history of human kind; as if the only thing worth knowing were material progress and capitalist ideology.

Let us go a bit deeper with our analysis. It would be just too simplistic to say that a rapacious lot inspired by the American ideology of greed and conquest is steam rolling through all lands, while impoverishing other people in the process. The dice was cast much earlier. The pursuit of the superficial American ideology, which has produced a one-dimensional mentality, is not the only culprit to blame. The post Renaissance European culture created the foundations for this whole process. It was exactly the myth of progress, elevated and perpetuated by the most eminent philosophers of the Enlightenment and post enlightenment eras, that prepared the ground for the belief that all will be well in the future, that through material amelioration we shall solve all problems, and as the last consequence we shall assure happiness for all; at least for the industrious West.

It takes a momentary reflection to realize that present academic wisdom is but a perpetuation of the legacy of the Enlightenment with its belief in the primacy of material progress, and its conviction that scientific knowledge is the highest form of knowledge and the surest way to salvation. The myths of enlightenment has stayed unexamined for far too long. Unexamined myths finally decay and their putrefied fall out poisons us all.

From our analysis it clearly follows that our problem is neither unemployment nor creating a social safety net nor still a seasaw strategy of vacillating between the two but something else and much deeper. The policy of reducing unemployment at all costs, like in the United States, produces a new class of serfs who tremble in their boots for fear of their jobs. So much of new employment in the USA are temporary, part-time jobs, without any security, therefore full of insecurities. The policy of creating a safety net at all costs finally leads to the bankruptcy of the welfare state. There is another twist to the story. Fed by the fables of material progress, workers always expect more and more. This is part of their belief system, perpetuated by Western secular ideology. The ideal of leisure as the highest form of existence has been a poisonous chalice. The advent of the leisure society announces the death of civil society.

For quite awhile it has been obvious at least to some that we have been following a wrong route. It has been obvious that as technology presses more and more, jobs will necessarily be eliminated. Instead of endlessly discussing employment and unemployment—while we have been continuously wetting the appetites and increasing the needs of the middle classes—we should have been discussing the foundations of the creative society.

What is most important is not jobs, not safety nets but providing meaningful work to all people, work with dignity, in the pursuit of a fulfilling life. This requires increasing the creative elan of the whole society so that we continually re-educate ourselves to create new forms of employment and we joyously anticipate change in which we participate creatively. This elan is just the opposite to the one cultivated presently. In the name of a spurious entity called leisure society we have been killing the brains of humans who endlessly watch senseless tv programs. The future society will require resilient and creative people, not couch potatoes.

Here we come to our original point again. A superfical articulation of human nature has led us to the creation of a superfical and unsustainable world, in which we are suffocated and, at the same time, slowly drawn into a sea of problems.

Let us notice paranthetically that the betrayal of Western middle class is also a betrayal of all people in the world who waited patiently and hoped quietly that their lot will also improve. Instead the poor are further pushed in the abyss of poverty, while savage knights of capitalism are ridding high.

5. Alternative Visions and Values

The Chinese culture has existed for some 5000 years. The Indian culture has existed for some 4000 years. The European culture has existed for some 3000 years. The American civilization is merely 200 years old. We are already travelling through the third millennium, which we have hoped and trusted will be more harmonious and peaceful and less bloody and violent than the passing one. Let us remind ourselves what a tremendous wealth of traditions and cultural values we have inherited from the past. What a store of supporting structures and symbols for a dignified and spiritually fulfilling life! Let us remind ourselves that past cultures have articulated human nature in quite a different and much deeper way than technological culture has done so. Let us also remember that these traditional articulations proved sustainable for centuries and millennia, while the recent articulation guided by the techno-paradigm does not promise to be sustainable in the long run. Indeed, for how long can you maintain that "homo homini lupus est" (man is wolf to man)? Until all the wolves cut each other's throats?

The Chinese culture has left behind such towering figures as Confucius and Läu Tzu. Their legacy has been lasting and sustaining. And it is being rediscovered again. We need to bow to greatness wherever we see it. For it is only through greatness of others, who have shown us the way, that we ourselves can become great.

The depth and strength of the Indian tradition has been undiminished in spite of the centuries of conquests. We don't need to invent an alternative to the shallowness of Western materialist civilization. India has always been that. Its philosophy has never relinquished its ambition to be a path of Moksha (liberation), in addition to being a set of explanations of the world. Nor should we forget about cultures, traditions and values of Africans, of Australian Aborigines, of Native Americans which are proving curiously resilient and sustaining to deeper quests of human life, while Western rational precepts lead us to blind alleys of confusion, anxiety, and existential anemia.

There is therefore a vibrant store of values and spiritual energies for our renewal as we go through the new millennium, and as we are determined to recover sanity, peace of mind, and peace with all creation. We are not simplistically maintaining that we can effortlessly return to old values and cultural patterns. We are arguing, however, that there is ample evidence in human history that human nature is deep and glorious. We don't need to accept the present emaciated skeleton of greed as our true nature. While we look with hope toward the future, let us be clear about who is leading whom ? For what good reasons? And with what consequence for future generations?

The problem of values is of great importance. Western thinkers and ideologists are becoming aware of it. They are actually becoming nervous when Asian values are evoked. This is for two reasons. They don't know what these value are. Yet deep down, they feel that there is much more to these values than can be off-handedly dismissed. Secondly, they are at least half aware that any acceptance of the validity of Asian values casts a shadow on the universality of Western economics and on its supposedly universal values; as well as it undermines the universality of the Western paradigm of material progress. So often the Westerner's response to Asian values is to suggest that Asian values are like Western ones or are increasingly becoming so. Which is a far cry from the truth.

Confucian values emphasize: respect for tradition and old age—as a repository of wisdom; respect for communal values and social ties—in contrast to rampart individualism; respect for the sense of solidarity among the people who are meant to help each other in the pursuit of larger common goals. The consequences of these values are quite clear and not welcome by the present Western economic paradigm.

Taoist values spell out (among other things): respect for truth which is always deeper and never merely linear; respect for complementarity and for the vision of things and their interconnectedness as based on complementary harmony. Traditional Indian values are pervaded by: respect for Ahimsa (non-violence) which has found recent embodiment in Mahatma Gandhi; respect for the human as an embodiment of God, which lifts the human life so extraordinarily and so beautifully. All these mentioned values (and they are just a sample) are antithetical to present crassness, materialism and the unseeing narrowness.

Our times will be known as one of the crassest in recorded human history. Our grandchildren will not be proud of their crass grandfathers. Those of us who can see and empathize with future generations and with higher requirements of human spirit must do whatever is possible to make younger generation aware that there is much more to life than the pursuit of selfishness. We have an evolutionary agenda on our shoulders—the agenda of self-realization which is a part of the destiny of the cosmos.

The time has arrived for non-Western people, especially for Asian people, to take the keel of human destiny into their hands and direct the ship of humanity to lands and shores which are peaceful, non-violent, equitable and based on justice and love. For such surely is our common human destiny in the long run. It is time to give tired Westerners a break, send them to some kind of fishing holiday, perhaps in North Alaska, so that they don't mess up the future of all humanity.

Each civilization has its span and usefulness. Beyond that, it is destructive. At this point new life must take over and build forms of life which are life-enhancing and which are conducive to higher goals of evolution and of human kind. The plastic civilization which is smothering spiritual values and the elan of life cannot be regarded as the apogee of human genius.

Summary

Communism has failed. And Capitalism has failed. The two are not the only alternatives we have had. Actually each one of them represents a distorted idea of human nature, therefore of human life. Life based on the ideal of material satisfaction is fatuous and ultimately unsatisfactory. It rings hollow and it is hollow. Thus we need to see new paths, beyond selfishness and aggression which destroy us in the process.

Selfish is stupid. The term 'idiot' comes from the Greek work 'idio'—the self. Harmonious is wise because it means weaving ourselves into right balances and patterns which are life enhancing. Inner peace is worth any money and it is beyond all money—as it is the source of true happiness. We were born to live in harmony and dignity. Without them we are crippled as human beings. We are spiritual beings and spiritual nourishment is as necessary for us as oxygen is for our lungs.

The next transformation is our new journey. We need to transcend all the messes we have created. Evolution is transcendence. And it wants us to transcend our present limitations. We need to liberate our human nature from the tethers of capitalist ideology. We need to create together—all humanity—patterns of cooperative behaviour, whereby spiritual nature of the human will flourish, unconstrained by religious divisions and dogmas, unhampered by greed and divisive nationalism, freed of hunger and destitution.

We can do it. And we shall do it. Because it is in our evolutionary destiny, because it is a desire of our burning heart, because it is a yearning of our soul, because this is essentially what we were created for.

6
Technology and the Sanctity of Life

1. The Structure of Thinking in Technology

I first studied civil engineering at the Warsaw Institute of Technology—for five and one half years. Then taught the subject for the next five years at the same Institute. While I was teaching I simultaneously pursued my studies in philosophy at Warsaw University, specializing in logic and semantics. Then I added to those years four further years of graduate studies at Oxford University from which I obtained a Doctorate of Philosophy in 1964. Now after those fourteen years of rigorous analytical objective schooling, I was a herald of Western rationality.

When I started to analyze phenomenon of technology, in the mid-1960s, while I assumed my first university post, quite predictably I tried to analyze the phenomenon of technology by concentrating on its cognitive structure. In a way, it was a typically positivist/rationalist exercise. Through trying to understand the structure of the phenomenon—its cognitive structure and its logical structure. My endeavor was very similar to what was going on in the philosophy of science. I tried to understand the phenomenon of technology by understanding its structure.

However, though positivist my approach was, I was not an innocent positivist, who simply believed that if we can reconstruct the structure of any phenomenon in some ultimate logical terms, all is well and good. By this time, I had been through Popper's exciting seminars in London in which a new perspective on the nature of science was revealed and hammered in. This was the perspective which emphasizes that in order to understand the nature of science, we have to understand the nature of its growth. This growth is fluid, dialectical, punctuated with discontinuities. Within the Popperian dialectical perspective to reconstruct the structure of science in logical terms was an interesting exercise, but a bit trivial—for it did not reveal the most important aspect of science; namely, how it grows.

While contemplating what would be the most fruitful way of looking at the phenomenon of technology in its growth and as distinguished from the phenomenon of science, I slowly developed the idea that the development of technology is governed by different forms of thinking from that of science. The result was my article, "The Structure of Thinking in Technology," published originally in 1966, and republished a couple of times since. In this early piece I argued that technological progress is the key to the understanding of technology. Without the comprehension of technological progress, there is no comprehension of technology and there is no sound philosophy of technology. Attempts that aim at reducing technology to the applied science fail to perceive the specific problem situation inherent in technology.

Although in many instances certain technological advancements can indeed be accounted for in terms of physics or chemistry, in other words, can be seen as based on pure science, it should not be overlooked that the problem was originally not cognitive but technical. With an eye to solving a technical problem, we undertake inquiries into what is called pure science. Our procedures are extremely selective. Out of infinitely many possible channels of research only very few are chosen. Problems thus are investigated not with an eye to increasing knowledge but with an eye to a solution of a technical problem. If it were not for the sake of solving some specific technological problem, many properties of physical bodies never would have been examined, and many theories incorporated afterward into the body of pure science never would have been formulated.

The growth of technology manifests itself precisely through its ability to produce more and more diversified objects with more and more interesting features, in a more and more efficient way.

It is a peculiarity of technological progress that it provides the means (in addition to producing new objects) for producing "better" objects of the same kind. By "better" many different characteristics may be intended, for example:

(a) More durable
(b) More reliable
(c) More sensitive
(d) Faster in performing its function
(e) A combination of the above

In addition to the just-mentioned five criteria, technological progress is achieved through shortening the time required for the production of a given object of through reducing the cost of production. Consequently, two further criteria are reduced expense or reduced time, or both, in producing an object of a given kind.

The criteria of technological progress cannot be replaced or even meaningfully translated into the criteria of scientific progress. And, conversely, the criteria of scientific progress cannot be expressed in terms of the criteria of technological progress. If an enormous technological improvement is made and at the same time no increase in pure science is accomplished, it will nevertheless mark a step in technological progress. On the other hand, it is of no consequence to pure science whether a given discovery is utilized or not; what is of significance is how much the discovery adds to our knowledge, how much it contributes to the comprehension of the world.

To summarize, scientific and technological progress are responsible for what science and technology, respectively, attempt to accomplish. Science aims at enlarging our knowledge through devising better and better theories; technology aims at creating new artifacts through devising means of increasing effectiveness. Thus the aims and the means are different in each case. The kernel of scientific progress can be expressed simply as being the pursuit of knowledge. The answer seems to be less straightforward with regard to technological progress. However, in spite of the diversity of criteria accounting for the advancement of technology, there seems to be a unifying theme common to them all, or at any rate into which they can be translated. This theme is the measure of effectiveness. Technological progress thus could be described as the pursuit of effectiveness in producing objects of a given kind.

Then I went on to claim (in my paper on "The Structure of Thinking in Technology") that specific branches of learning originate and condition specific modes of thinking, develop and adhere to categories through which they can best express their content and by means of which they can further progress. And I went on to distinguish various styles of thinking in various branches of technology. Such was my early struggle with the philosophy of technology.

I could have gone thus developing this structural-historical approach to technology and its forms of thinking; and after having spent ten years with this kind of endeavor would probably have convinced myself that this is the best way of studying the phenomenon of technology. Yet I felt and knew, in those early days in the mid-1960s, that it was a limiting approach and that the phenomenon itself was so complex, so all-pervading, so much determining the destiny of society and encroaching on the existential domains of individuals that a much broader approach was needed within a framework of understanding much transcending the tidy cognitive categories of the structural approach.

Incidentally, while my paper (on the structure of thinking in technology) was presented at the AAAS meeting in San Francisco in 1965 one of the persons in the audience was Paul Feyerabend (a renown philosopher of science). After the discussion he asked me point blank: "How does your philosophy of technology help us to live?" I was stunned by the question, but somehow recognized its validity—although not in the framework of discourse I outlined for myself at the time.

Quite independently Patrick Suppes (a renown logician) read the paper. When I asked him about his reactions, he said,

"Pretty good. But why won't you make it more rigorous?" What he meant was: why won't I formalize the whole discourse, and really express it in neat logical structures as it was customary among logical empiricists?

After the San Francisco meeting I knew that I would go more the road Paul Feyerabend suggested than that of Suppes. The limitations of logical positivism were too obvious at the time, while the phenomenon of technology was crying the social, existential and ethical analysis.

Around this time (in 1965) Jacques Elul's book *The Technological Society* appeared in English (the French original, entitled *Le Technique*, appeared in 1955!). This book was quite a challenge, at least to me personally. And I knew I could not remain in the neat boxes of the structural analysis of technology.

2. A Philosophy of Needs

I came to think at the time that to understand the true nature of the phenomenon of technology is not merely to understand the internal development of technology—from one invention to another—but to understand the peculiar dialogue which is taking place between technology and society; or more precisely between the potential of technology and the needs of society.

Technology becomes what society elicits out of its potential. In itself, technology is mute and dumb, like the universe which has not yet developed life. Out of its extraordinary, almost limitless potential, society elicits and articulates certain options. Once certain options are elicited, there is a tendency to keep developing and articulating similar options. Once a certain direction gains a momentum, other options are, as it were, suppressed, or at least neglected, as it happened with the nuclear option, which has been developed (some feel) at the expense of the solar option (solar technologies).

The nature of the dialogue between technology and society is subtle and all pervading, to the point that society may inhibit the development of some technologies, or of all technology; or may accelerate or boost their technological development.

There were societies which had much greater technological potential than they deemed it wise to use. Such was the case with ancient Greece in the Hellenistic period. Such was the case with China in the 14th and 15th centuries A.D. Throughout the history of human societies, technology is not simply used because it is there. It is used if and when society begins to consider it important in the overall social project. The will of society to use or not to use technology is all important, although it may be indirectly expressed.

That is not how things are seen in the context of the present technological society. Rather it is assumed, particularly by the protagonists of the technological society, that technology is there to help us to live. On a more sophisticated level it is argued that technology is here to satisfy human needs. And it is up to us to determine which needs are important to harness technology to this purpose. This argument requires some examination, particularly as the notion of needs which is quite a complex subject. Indeed a deep philosophical problem.

What is the right way of looking at needs as a part of a right perspective of how technology should develop and what kind of research should be undertaken? Let me then attempt to spell out a philosophy or a concept of needs which may be important not only for guiding research in technology and applied science but also for understanding the direction of technology in the 21st century.

To begin with, let us observe that the recognition of human needs may sometimes clash with the recognition of human rights. Human rights, once articulated, seem to be a universal category defining us as human beings. In this sense to deny human rights to a person is to deny his/her humanity.

I will start with some examples. Let us suppose a person, shall we say a busy executive, comes home from work and immediately pours himself a Martini. We say he is tired, perhaps even stressed and exhausted and he needs a Martini to relax. We recognize this need. Let us suppose that after finishing the first Martini he pours himself the second one. We are still inclined to say he needs it. It is his right to have it. But what do we say when he reaches the sixth Martini and says he needs it? Well, we are less certain to agree that since he says he needs it, it is his right to have it, and that it is his genuine need. When he reaches for his eleventh Martini of the evening, our immediate reaction is that it is not good for him, he better not drink any more—regardless of whether he says that he needs that eleventh Martini or not. We seem to know better—it is no good for him. When we learn that he reaches for the eleventh Martini every evening, we are assured that we know better: "The man has a problem." That is what we say when we want to use an euphemism. If we want to be straight about it, we say that the man is an alcoholic.

Let us analyze the situation in some depth. Who are we to say that the eleventh Martini is not good for him, if he insists that it is his need, and he insists on his right to have the twelfth Martini? On the surface we cannot deny him this right, particularly since he demands it explicitly. Yet in our heart, and in our better judgement, we do deny him this right. Why do we do it? Because—we reason—the man does not know what he is doing. He is destroying himself. And he has no business of doing that. Twelve Martinis in a row is not a genuine need of any normal person.

There are some deeper criteria which speak through us. Those criteria enable us to assert with clarity and certainty—in critical situations—what is good for a person as a human being. On another level, these criteria inform us what are (or can be accepted as) genuine needs, the significant ones, as contrasted with artificial needs which are trivial at best, destructive at worst.

The overall criterion that works through us is that of *the sanctity of life*. The principle of the sanctity of life which we share universally—actually in all cultures—speaks through us when we say to a person on the eleventh Martini that, "It is not good for you," even if the person insists that it is his right to have the twelfth Martini, or if he feels he needs it.

If the example with the Martini is not yet persuasive enough, and is not strong enough (because alcoholism is often a hidden disease), let us take a more drastic example. Let us consider a heroin addict who insists that he needs his heroin fix—regardless of the consequences. Do we recognize this need as valid? Do we recognize his human right to demand what he wants—in the circumstances in which he destroys himself? No, we do not recognize this human right and his alleged need in those circumstances. And we are quite unanimous in this non-recognition. There is nothing subjective about it. Again what motivates us and gives force to our conviction is the imperative of the sanctity of life.

The imperative of the sanctity of life generates its own sub-imperatives.

To treat human life with dignity

To treat human life with respect.

To treat human beings as authentic irreducible beings.

We have now obtained a backbone for a philosophy of needs. To begin with, needs are not subjective or relativistic. They are intersubjective, and rooted in the concept of human nature. Whatever our disagreements about the nature of human nature, the right treatment of human nature is one which respects the imperative of the sanctity of life which is the foundation of any conception of life worth living.

Secondly we now have the basis for the distinction fo genuine needs from artificial needs. Genuine needs are those whose satisfaction does not go against the principle of the sanctity of life. Thus destroying oneself through the use of heroin or through the abuse of alcohol cannot be deemed as satisfying genuine needs. Moreover, in our overall imperative of sanctity, we have the basis for a much sharper delineation of genuine needs from artificial needs.

Genuine needs are those whose satisfaction, in the long run, is life enhancing; or whose satisfaction contributes to the life of quality and meaning.

Artificial needs are those whose satisfaction, in the long run, is not life enhancing. The satisfaction of artificial needs at best, contributes to the trivialization of human life; at worst is life-destroying.

Now let us not quibble who is to determine which life is significant and which is trivial, for we know pretty well what a significant life is (as contrasted with the trivial one); just as we know at what point an alcoholic is ruining his life and a drug addict is destroying his. The principle of the sanctity of life is working pretty well and universally through nearly all of us.

And it is a beautiful principle indeed. Nor am I denying that the boundary between genuine needs and artificial ones is difficult to draw in some cases, as we have to weigh very carefully the respective merits of the satisfaction of different needs—often on different scales. What I am insisting on is that the distinction can be drawn and that it is a meaningful one. Only after this distinction is drawn can we look again at the phenomenon of techology and re-examine the dialogue between technology and society. Technology is indiscriminate. It produces everything: good, bad, indifferent, life enhancing, trivial, wretchedly unnecessary. But we, as humans, have to discriminate.

Our principle of discrimination, by which to evaluate a given technological process, or a given piece of research in technology is by means of asking: to what degree a given technology contributes to the satisfaction of genuine needs? We now have a rational criterion for technological research.

It simply would not dos any more, when we are in a reflective state of mind, to accept the argument that all technology is good because it satisfies some need—otherwise it would not be here. This argument is unsound and ultimately trivial. So many alleged needs technology satisfies are trivial needs, are superficial needs, are, to put it in our language, artificial needs—the satisfaction of which contributes nothing or precious little to the life-enhancing process. So many of our needs are induced and outrageously manipulated. The fact that we seem to go on satisfying them (at least many of us) does mean that they have inherent grounding in our nature, or that they contribute anything to our status as autonomous beings.

There are many products and processes, and a great deal of research that goes with them, whose purpose it is to destroy life—such as nerve gasses and weapons of mass destruction. From the standpoint of genuine human needs these technologies are evil: they are not life-enhancing, they cannot contribute to the quality of life. Their only justification is the paranoia of fear which itself is not a life-enhancing phenomenon, but a life-reducing one. The paranoia of fear does not create strengthened security. On the contrary, it weakens us as resources are being dissipated in the acts of continuous worry.

There is always a dialogue going on, as I mentioned before, between technology and society. In traditional cultures, society has an upper hand in this dialogue. It is different in our society which is, not without a reason, called the technological society. In our society, technology calls the tune, so much so that its imperatives become societies' norms. The dialogue has become lopsided. Deeper cultural and social restraints have been eroded in this climate of the technological domination.

Technology claims that it is the major force of social and existential amelioration. It claims that it satisfies genuine human needs. It claims furthermore that whatever it satisfies are genuine needs. It is this last claim that must to be challenged. Because it has been unquestioned, and as society we have become increasingly trivialized.

Now, whoever thinks that he contributes to the well-being of society, through his research or actual design of technological products, must ask himself at one point or another: What is the net result of my activities? To what aspect of the well-being of society or of individual human life do I contribute, and in what way?

There is one aspect of human needs that we should further reflect upon. It is claimed that although technology may not be able to satisfy more refined social, cultural and spiritual needs, it is, at least, an undoubted champion in satisfying basic human needs: food; shelter; material standards of living. Those are undoubtedly basic needs, but not the only fundamental basic needs.

When I was in India in 1981, I visited Calcutta, and while there I met Mother Teresa, who took me to "the Home For the Dying." That is what the place is called, and that is what it actually is. Mother Teresa, and her sisters, called the Missionaries of Charity, pick up from the streets of Calcutta people who are obviously dying—of hunger, and are going to die... and only those. The idea is to give them shelter for the hour of their dying. But more than that. Mother Teresa contends that to be unwanted and to be totally rejected by everybody is the most terrible thing that can happen to a human being, worse than starvation and death. Thus one of the fundamental needs, as basic as food or shelter, and even more so, is the need to be cared for. That's what the radiant sisters in the Home For the Dying attempt to give to the people in the last days and hours of their shattered existence: love and the sense of being cared for. This need—to be cared for as a human being—cannot be measured by any technological scale. Technology has very little to contribute to this need.

The reflection on this need, and the entire discussion of genuine human needs, makes us aware that technology cannot guide itself. It requires some deeper principles for its guidance and direction. Otherwise it gropes blindly. Or arrogantly asserts that what it does is right because what technology always benefits society.

The last conclusions also apply to research in technology and applied science. Left to itself, this research is a ship without a rudder.

3. Technology Cannot Guide Itself—It Needs a Comprehensive Philosophy to Guide It

It is surprising that although we have dealt with the phenomenon of technology for such a long time, and on such an immense scale, we still do not possess any comprehensive Technology Policy, let alone a comprehensive philosophy of technology. The result is that when things backfire, and they backfire rather often nowadays, we don't know how to respond rationally. The responsibility is often passed from engineers to planners; from planners to politicians and finally businessmen. It seems that in this large equation, nobody is specifically responsible for what technology does, and for its consequences in the long run. Technology, as it were, is guiding itself.

But the point is that technology cannot guide itself. It doesn't have enough wisdom, foresight and social acumen to do that. The free market, as a guide, is a poor guide indeed, as it is only interested in short-term gain. Besides, it is erratic and irrational itself—at times.

Let me put the proposition in more general terms. We can be rationally stupid. And we can be irrationally wise. The former case may occur when a researcher develops a new chemical product which dazzles the market—but for which the next generation of babies will pay through their infirmities. The latter case may occur when a group of protestors stages a sit-in, day after day, shall we say on the site of a rare bird sanctuary—which is condemned to become a new industrial site. The protestors may know that their protest is futile because a new industrial plant is going to be built there. But they may choose to take their stand not because of what is expedient, (and therefore seemingly rational) but what is right—and therefore wise in the long run. This distinction between what is expedient, and therefore considered rational; and what is right, and therefore wise in the long run, is by no means a superficial one or concocted for the occasion. It is a fundamental one.

It is futile to argue about the rationality of technology and its alleged efficiency if one does not take into account the adverse ecological consequences of technological advancements. It is futile to talk about the social benefits of technology if, at the same time, one does not take into account the adverse social consequences of these very technology. It is futile to praise technology as the savior of humanity if, at the same time, one does not take into account the individual alienation it brings about, and also one does not consider how much meaninglessness it creates.

In the very least we must take into account four large consequences on which technology constantly impinges. And these are: ecology, society, human life, ethical values. Whatever research and development we engage in, we must know what happens to the planet as the result. The planet earth is in our custody. If we loose the environment, we loose God, so maintains the philosopher-theologian Thomas Berry. I would add that if we lose the planet earth we have lost all our laboratories for research, including our neat rational models. What is at stake here is not spurious moralizing but a clear awareness that in so far as we effect the well being of the planet, through our research and development—and the consequences following from this research—we must take the responsibility for it all. For who else will do it? We know how thoroughly and often adversely our technologies can effect the environment. Yet we equivocate.

Ecology is only one of the four large-scale consequences. Another is society. Most of the arguments which we spelled out vis a vis ecology apply to society. What are the social costs of the development of certain technologies? Who will be footing the bill? Is it rational to claim that a given technology is cheap and easily available if the bill to be paid later will be enormous? Let us not fool ourselves that these are 'externalities.' These 'externalities' are an inherent aspect of technological progress.

The premise of all technology is that it brings social and human amelioration. We are proud to point out some of the lasting and beneficial consequences of technology. Technology takes credit for these beneficial consequences, and rightly so. The situation is a bit strange, the protagonists of technology are quite quick to take credit for large scale beneficial consequences of technology. As for the negative consequences of technology, they think it is not technology's fault. That kind of attitude is based on moral fudging or simply cynicism.

We talk so much about material amelioration. What about the quality of human life? What about the meaningfulness of human life? Is it rational to say that yes, technology contributes to the quality of human life by raising the material standard of living and stop at that? Is it not another exercise of moral ambiguity and poor reasoning?

We must not be naive or foolish to argue that it is all people's choice: people are not compelled to choose the values technology offers them, if they do not so desire. We must not argue so while we deliberately set up structures and choices which compel people to choose what technology offers. Social determinants created by technology are strong indeed. These determinants effect our choices. These choices effect our values. These values effect the very core of our life—its meaning, its significance, its worth. In actual facts we have always known that technology effects our values and the meaning of our life.

Now we have spelled out some of the consequences of technology. These consequences cannot be by-passed or brushed aside by anybody who claims to do his/her research in a truly rational and conscientious way.

The consequences of technological progress on ecology and society effect human life and ultimately values. We cannot assess these consequences piecemeal. We need one comprehensive framework in order to see how these things are related. (I am for the moment ignoring other consequences, such as political, in order not to complicate the picture any further.)

While thinking through those large scale consequences of technology, I came to the conclusion, already in 1970's, that what we need is a comprehensive philosophy which would guide and direct technology. Nothing short of it really will be adequate. My thinking about this comprehensive philosophy, which would effectively guide technology, resulted in a large philosophical project which I finally called ECO-PHILOSOPHY. Simply put, eco-philosophy is my philosophical response to the problem of technology; as well as to a variety of other societal and metaphysical problems which have been plaguing the technological society for quite a while. My Eco-Philosophy was partly created in response to the challenge of Jacques Ellul (whom I mentioned earlier) and of E.F. Schumacher who claimed, in Small is Beautiful, that what we need is not only an alternative economics and an alternative technology but also a metaphysical reconstruction, as our problems are much deeper and cannot be contained in economic-technological frameworks alone.

In due time I published the book on the subject: *Eco-philosophy, Designing New Tactics for Living*, 1981. The choice of the sub-title was quite deliberate. What we need is not another set of philosophical abstractions but a new philosophical framework as a foundation for the right tactics of living.

Technology is a moral enterprise, and we have every reason to judge it by moral criteria; but not the criteria of technological/instrumental values only. There is actually a deep moral ambiguity and double mindedness toward technology, particularly among the protagonists of technology and big foundations—both private and federal. These foundations are the beneficiaries of science and technology. On the one hand, they attempt to make us see the interactions of science and technology with society at large; on the other hand, there is an built-in constraint not to find that science and technology might possibly have large scale deleterious consequences for society and human beings. This attitude of moral ambiguity pervades the academia and quite a large segment of society. In such a climate technology is not guided. The tiger of technology is running strong.

We have created the world of good and evil through the unleashing of our technologies. We have to bear the consequences. Or amend the situation if we deem it undesirable. "Of all you have done in the past, you eat the fruit, either rotten or ripe," so says the poet T.S. Eliot. Technology will not do the work for us.

Summary

The original premise of all technological solutions is the amelioration of the human condition. This premise, however, has often been vitiated and, at times, totally ignored.

Now this original premise was part of a larger philosophy. The aim of this philosophy was a liberation of the human person, and in general the enhancement of life. Thus, the original context of all technology, and of all applied research, was a noble impulse to help the human condition. This original context is the historical mandate which (in public opinion) has never been altered, and therefore is one to which technologists are accountable.

What to do and what not to do in technology and applied science is a matter of a right vision of man, of a right philosophy which is comprehensive enough to assess any piece of a given research (and its consequences!) as to how it affects (in the long run!) the vicissitudes of individual human beings, the well-being of society, and the health of ecological habitats, including the well-being of all life-forms in it. Only such a philosophy constitutes a framework rational enough to guide our research in a true way.

The time of innocence is over. We have signed a Faustian bargain with the forces, which are beyond our control and sometimes beyond our understanding. To guide ourselves out of this awesome and intricate situation will require more than mere rationality, for so often it is this very rationality that is an inherent part of our problem. What will be required is foresight. And wisdom and vision—and the courage to act in a not trivial way.

7
Education for the Real World

1. The Triumph of Capitalism?

A Chinese proverb says: "I curse you to live in the times of change." Which is sometimes translated as:"I curse you to live in interesting times." In such interesting times we are living at present. Big changes and re-alignments have been taking place in front of our eyes. The specter of Communism seems to be no longer haunting the Capitalist world. On the contrary, in the battle between Communism and Capitalism, over its social superiority, Capitalism has handsomely won.

Yet, we need to pose a significant question:"Is capitalism working well enough?" Once we have asked this question, we confront a very serious problem indeed.

Our first response is an automatic one: yes, of course, it is working well enough—look at the material prosperity in the west and how capitalism outperforms communism. This is one kind of answer.

But actually a rather obvious answer, if not a trivial one. This answer relates to the bottom line economics. Our bottom line shows profit. So, all is well.

The economics of the bottom line has been so impressive to some that they began to mystify it. The result is economism, a philosophical doctrine which claims (implicitly or explicitly) that economics—the bottom line economics, that is—determines the structure and the ethos of society and should be unconditionally obeyed for it is our god. This last conclusion is not spelled out so clearly but it is nevertheless implied.

Now I will attempt to argue that this whole line of thinking and the entire philosophy underlying economism is basically wrong. Let us return to our question: is capitalism working well enough? My answer is that it isn't. The bottom line, economics is a misconceived idea. When we observe how life actually works, then we realize that the genuine bottom line is the quality of life. Unless an economic or a social system meets this ultimate criterion,that of the quality of life, it is an incomplete, inadequate, if not fraudulent one. In this sense economism, or the bottom line economics, may be considered fraudulent. Let me explain why.

The distinguished British writer Anthony Burgess writes: "turning humanity into something far less than it could be is what vulgarity is about."That is precisely what economism is attempting to do to us: it tries to reduce us to something less than what we could become. In this sense economism is pushing us on the road to vulgarity, and is itself an instrument of vulgarity. Advertising and the ideology of consumerism are its allies. When one looks perceptively at the cluster of those forces that spiritually diminish the human society, one realizes that consumerism and advertising are only tools of economism.

Thus on the first level of analysis economism must be questioned and opposed because it impoverishes us as individual existential beings, cheapens us with regard to what we can become, it robs us of our spiritual heritage.

On the second level of analysis, economism must be questioned and opposed on ecological grounds. Economism is based on false accounting. The much celebrated bottom line is really fictitious. What it shows is often illusory profit. Why illusory? Because some parameters and costs are hidden and omitted. Those costs are called 'externalities',which economic models hide. These externalities show up as enormous bills - going into billions of dollars - for cleaning polluted environments.

It must be emphasized that the ecological factor is not one of those externalities, the nuisance value which one can easily shrug off. The ecological parameters are now of such a crucial importance to our survival that an economic system which is sane and accountable in the long run must include these parameters as integral parts of all economic equations.

On the third level of analysis, economism is to be questioned because it is based on a wrong ethics. The ethics of selfishness, of competition, of ruthless disregard for all being - in the pursuit of material profit now, is unnatural from the standpoint of human history and human ethics, as well as from the standpoint of evolution. Evolution is a hymn to symbiosis. Human societies are monuments to cooperativeness and solidarity. The ethics of unbridled selfishness, which economism promotes, is not a great new invention to be welcomed - but an aberration, and an insult to our noble ethical heritage. Let us also notice that the ethics of competitiveness contains in itself potential violence. The ethics which encourages you to tread on the bodies of others cannot be right as a human ethics. The ethical imperative of economism, expressed in the simplest way, would read as follows: tread on the bodies of others or hang yourself if you are not successful.

On the fourth level of analysis, economism must be questioned because it is based on a myopic concept of reality. Any sensitive person, who has experienced the richness and the versatility of reality, including its magical aspects will perceive the reduction of all reality to its economic substratum as a farce, not a true rendition of the real world. What economism does is an extreme form of reductionism - reducing the world and human beings to economic categories and commodities. This represents a further vulgarization of the world, this time on the ontological level.

Now we have an answer why the economics of the bottom line is a fiction - not the ultimate criterion for accounting of all there is, and why economism is such a profoundly unsatisfactory philosophy, if not a fraudulent one. In so far as the economics of the bottom line is so crucial to present capitalism, we have an answer why capitalism does not work well enough - because it lives on the capital which belongs to future generations; because it undermines the foundations on which it rests: nature and natural cycles; because it reduces the human being, a noble animal to a vulgar consumer.

While examining the shortcomings of economism as a universal philosophy, I have argued that it is crippled on four grounds. Its conception of reality is myopic; its values are one-sided and distorted; its accounting is grotesquely inadequate and distorted; its concept of life is vulgar. By spelling out these shortcomings (of economism) we now have a clear direction concerning desirable and worthwhile education.

2. Education for the Real World

Thus we come to education. In one of the most memorable scenes in Hamlet, the king asks:"now, Hamlet, where's Plonius?" "At supper", Hamlet responds. The king:"At supper? Where?" Hamlet:"Not where he eats, but where he is eaten."

Mutatis mutandis this could be said about present students: they are devoured by the present system of education, not nourished by it. They are not educated in the true sense of the term (educare-I lead), but manipulated.

Plato says: "The direction in which education sets a man will determine his future life." This is as true now as it was in Plato's times. What kind of direction is our present education setting for our young people? How are they being guided and led? To what ends and to what purposes? Are they not per chance so socialized and programmed as to be good consumers and work for the glory of the consumerist ideology and the bottom line economics?

Education as a social and civilisational enterprise must ultimately serve the quality of life. If education ignores or neglects this vital criterion it is not an adequate education and may indeed be a misguided one.

Ultimately all systems of education, as well as systems of philosophy are about how to be human, not how to be a consumer. We must not misread our mandate: we are here to lead our young to be deservedly human and not to manipulate them for the sake of the status quo, which anyway is undermining its own existence.

It is quite clear that we are now opening a new chapter of history. This is an ecological chapter. Our responsibility entails and necessitates ecological responsibilities. We cannot be human, in a deeper sense, unless we make peace with nature (and with ourselves, for while waging the war against nature, we have been waging one against ourselves). Thus an ecological dimension must be a part of our education, our philosophies, and of our religions.

It can be said that the West has won the battle against communism. But winning this battle - is it a victory? Or perhaps a pyrrhic victory? Entranced and mesmerized by this battle, we have perhaps neglected to see that we have been losing another, a more important battle - the battle to save the earth and also to save the meaning of our lives.

The ecological reconstruction, the healing of the earth should be now among our most important imperatives. Education, if it is genuine and comprehensive, should help this process of healing and integration. We should steep the minds of our youth in the great, everlasting liturgy of nature and teach them reverence for life and for all creation. This is an imperative of our economic survival in the long run as well as an imperative of our psychological sanity.

Ecology is about a new shape of life. Ecology is about the dignity of life. Ecology is about the dignity of human work. Present economics is suicide economics, not a proper accounting of our household. We have been incurring an enormous debt to nature, and asking future generation to foot the bill. Future generations are refusing to do so. Future generations speak with the voice of eco-wisdom and eco-values. We were not brought to this world to lead an alienated, estranged, deracinate and uprooted existence. We were brought to this world to celebrate the glories of the cosmos and to live in solidarity with other beings. Genuine and significant education must be one which helps to live life fully, meaningfully, with inspiration and with a modicum of grace.

Summary

Education for the real world is one which respects the world in all its dimensions, in all its richness, including its hidden and mysterious aspects. Such an education respects evolution in its profound unfolding as it builds ever more subtle structures and beings, ultimately the ones which reach out to heaven.

Let us take the human condition seriously. Let us take predicaments seriously. Let us take education seriously. And let us design educational and social structures which are congruent with the evolutionary imperative, with the desiderata of life unfolding, bountiful and ultimately radiant. To win an ideological battle while losing the environment and the quality of life is no victory. Let us clearly see what our aims and goals are—in education and culture at large. These goals have to do with the liberation and fulfillment of the human being on the highest level of cultural and spiritual attainment. We need the courage, determination and vision to put one—dimensional theories of man—whether of capitalist or communist variety—to where they belong, on the shelf of history, and start evolving ideals, theories and practices in the image of man, a transcendental being.

8

Ecological Foundations of Politics

1. From the Technological Euphoria to the Existential Despair

The 20th century started with a cascade of optimistic euphoria, and it ended with the existential angst, amidst the poisonous rivers and the earth crying in the pain of continuous violence. The thinking people at the beginning of the 20th century were convinced that we were at the threshold of the era of fulfillment. The dream of self-realization, of prosperity, of the harmony among the nations seemed to be around the corner. The dream is now shattered. Instead we are confronted with a nightmare. This is so not because we were insufficiently intelligent, or resourceful, or creative. Perhaps we have been too clever; victims of our own demonic intelligence.

Who is responsible for the present condition of the humankind? Poisonous, pernicious ideologies? In part. Let us be aware that these pernicious ideologies were themselves the poisonous flowers spreading out of the cracks of the 20th century fractured psyche. Moreover Hitlerism and Stalinism are gone. But the hell on earth is continuing. Who is therefore responsible? Examining causes and effects, we could say that technicians are the most responsible ones; especially for the destruction of the environment. For the truth is that the more powerful the technology the more powerful means for the transformation of the earth; thus the more powerful means for the destruction of nature.

But such an analysis would be superficial. The technicians did what they were ordered to do. To put it more precisely, they were an instrument of execution of commands coming from above. They point their finger at the economists. The economists, in turn, point their finger at the politicians. The politicians say that they only put forward what the experts advised them to do. And the merry-go-round continues.

In the final analysis the responsibility for the withering of our civilization lies with the philosophers. They are the ones who created the foundations of the new world view and a new way of thinking. Our present civilizational illness is based on specific philosophies and styles of thinking. Thus philosophers are responsible for the triumphs and pitfalls of our present civilization. Without Marx, there would be no Marxism. But Marx himself was only a continuation of a certain line of thinking. This line of thinking favored the domination and exploitation of nature; and it conceived the human ends in materialist terms alone: utopia was to be reached by ignoring man's spiritual nature and man's spiritual potential.

The Marxist line was a specific articulation of positivism which has been the dominant ideology of the western mind in the post-enlightenment era. The western mind is very proud of its enlightenment, particularly as it became formulated by the French thinkers of the 18th century. Yet on a closer analysis this enlightenment is a misnomer. What kind of enlightenment is it which does not bring light, but, on the contrary, brings about the tyranny of a narrow scientific reason? We have been too hasty in congratulating ourselves on how enlightened our civilization has been.

Positivist philosophy (a rather rigid interpretation of the world through fact and number) crystallized on the ruins of the past religious world view. Whether this European mind had to go through the purgatory of positivist thinking in order to free itself from the tyranny of religious order, is an open question. However the consequence was as follows: while freeing ourselves from religious dogma, we have lost the sense of transcendence, and we have pawned ourselves to a rather savage god of instant gratification. The transcendent mind, for such was the earlier religious mind, became the empirical, pragmatic and technical mind; in the final reckoning it became a trivial mind. The world conceived as a huge clock-like mechanism has dominated our horizons and obscured the vision of the multifariousness of the universe. From this point on, we have been treading a narrow path of technitism with its characteristic instrumental thinking, which is atomistic, purely analytical, amoral in its very premise. Thus, it is indifferent to the great concerns of the human heart and the human soul.

It is precisely this narrow thinking, in a sense degenerate thinking, which is the root cause of our disasters: ecological, social, existential, religious and political. This form of thinking generated specific doctrines which have incapacitated our minds and poisoned our souls. We shall presently examine some of these doctrines so that we can see how unreal and fictitious are the foundations of that which we consider a palpable, practical and pragmatic reality.

2. Philosophical Fictions as the Foundations of our Civilization

Let us examine the major visions of the western mind which chiefly contributed to the making of the brave new positivist world. These visions, when articulated, assume the form of philosophical assumptions about the nature of the world and about the nature of human beings. These assumptions are philosophical fictions to begin with. At the time they were proposed there was not justification of their validity. As I said, they were of the nature of visions and fictions which we wanted to believe. Each of these visions was usually proposed by a singular philosopher who articulated what was in the air; or who had the power to sway people's mind in a new direction. All these assumptions (visions, fictions) have added to each other. They have formed a mutually supportive network.

In the final analysis I will present them in the form of an octagonal mandala. The elements which make the mandala can be seen as one connected structure. I will be very brief in presentation of the philosophical assumptions being the basis of our civilization—for in themselves they are well known. What is less perceived is a specific structure these elements (assumptions) form; and the consequences they lead to.

I. The world. The world is conceived, particularly as articulated by Newton, as a clock-like mechanism, a huge deterministic machine. From the time of LaPlace it is assumed that every thing there is must be subsumed under mechanistic and determinist laws. Note: there never was any proof given, especially a scientific proof, that the world is but a machine, for such a proof clearly lies outside the domain of science. And if it is outside the domain of science, it is not a proof, but a conjecture.

II. Nature and the language in which it is written. From Galileo it has been increasingly assumed that, to put it in the memorable words of Galileo himself, "The book of nature is forever open to our gaze but in order to read it we must understand the characters in which it is written. It is written in the language of mathematics." At the time when Galileo postulated the idea, it was just a postulate, a kind of fiction—with no proof of it given whatsoever. True enough, Pythagoras postulated a similar fiction which was even more enticing as it was connected with Harmonia Mundi. Now we wanted to believe in Galileo's scheme and went along with him towards a radical quantification of nature.

III. Knowledge as power. From the time of Francis Bacon the idea of knowledge as spiritual enlightenment (Plato's ideal) wanes, and the idea *scientia est potentia* gains in ascendance. But again, when Bacon proposed it, it was a mere postulate. Knowledge as power was in its infancy. It was but a dream. In the course of time, we have made of knowledge an immense power... a power which has become a nightmare. Strange: human fictions turn into realities of dimensions staggering the imagination.

IV. Man as homo homini lupus. As we go along the new path of the western mind, we redefine not only the world outside us but the nature of man himself. Thus Thomas Hobbes proposes that man is a wolf to man. *Homo homini lupus est* is another strange fiction. To consider man as vicious to his fellow humans was a bad turning point in the Western odyssey. We have become so transfixed by this fiction that (through our behaviour and thinking) we have almost rendered it into reality. Yet we must ask again: was there ever any proof given of the supposedly inherently aggressive nature of man? There wasn't. The human is aggressive. And the human is divine. And the important thing is what a given culture elicits from us.

V. Progress as material amelioration. We are so used to the idea of progress that we consider it quite natural to assume that progress is a part of the rational legacy of the western man. Yet we forget that it is a newcomer; a myth which we have elevated to the role of a deity. In the absence of transcendental schemes, material progress, until recently, has been our guiding light, ipso facto our deity. Even now, when we see that progress is a mixed blessing, we have difficulty in distancing ourselves from it. For it is a part of our eschatology.

VI. God as the hand of Free Market. When the transcendent was expelled, when the Newtonian machine began to represent the divine design, as its equivalent in the human affairs, Adam Smith conceived the idea of Free Market as the hand of destiny. What a strange fiction it has been from the beginning! And still is! There never was Free Market, particularly as the Will of God. Yet in the name of this fiction we manipulate people and sometimes crash whole societies. While religious ideals are derided as spurious fictions, this particular one, Free Market, is enjoying intellectual respectability. Is this how rational men behave?

VII. Evolution as Social Darwinism. In the 19th century, mainly through the articulation of Charles Darwin, we discovered evolution. But our understanding of it became very much tilted towards other assumptions of western man. So very soon (and up to our times) evolution came to signify Darwinism, and Darwinism has been often equivocated with social Darwinism. Thus evolution came to signify the process of the survival of the fittest. Within the framework of homo homini lupus, it came to signify the survival of the vicious. Thus another fiction was created, which then became perpetrated by the dominant social and economic institutions. Let us reflect: through these various assumptions and myths, we have been creating the disinherited world of ruthless competition. As a result, we have been gathering a bleak harvest.

VIII. Rationality as the optimization of profit. In this whole scheme of things, we have reduced rationality (a very noble human faculty) to the optimization of profit, to a manipulative instrumental faculty, which helps us in the conquest of nature and in other exploitative schemes of Western man. So often rationality is understood as practicality, pragmatism, a hard-headed approach. Yet the other side of the coin of this pragmatism is greed, aggressiveness, exploitation.

The sum total of the assumptions presented here has led many to the conclusion that we are living in the cold, competitive world, in which the cut throat competition is the order of nature. Surely, this was not part of the design of the noble schemes of the Enlightenment!

We have now completed our mandala

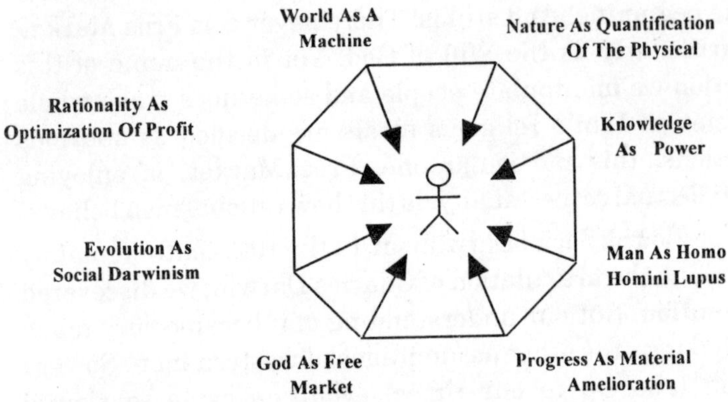

When we look at the main actors of our civilizational drama, we are rather astonished to notice how many of them were English (British), particularly among those who pushed the world towards ruthlessness, exploitation, selfishness. Bacon, Newton, Hobbes, Smith, Darwin—proud names on the pages of the British history. Perhaps not so proud in the history of humanity.

A perceptive mind will no doubt notice that those new thinkers (Hobbes, Smith and then Darwin) lived and acted at the time when Britain was expanding, conquering, enlarging its domain. Is it a coincidence that dominant thinkers of the British empire simply justified the power of domination, of ruthlessness, of exploitation? One does not have to be a Marxist to perceive how insidious this whole process was—of conquering and crashing, and then justifying the process through "new" philosophical doctrines.

The conclusion that appears is as follows. We have been kidnapped by the imperial interests of the British Empire, which have been deviously justified by British thinkers and inadvertently begun to be the basis of a destructive civilization. We know the end result of the whole process. The devastation of nature and the increasing bleakness of our future is enough to convince us that something radically wrong has gone with our secular dreams and materialist utopias. Yes, we know the effects. Yet we are still bewildered by what has happened. We apply our best rationality to understand the situation. We invent ever new technologies to mend the cracks in the boat of civilization. But to no avail. For this rationality is manipulative, and it still serves the old goals of maximization of gains and profits.

We need to notice that there is something radically wrong with our knowledge. Our knowledge has created so much harm. This is the result of some deep-seated ignorance—in spite of our conviction that this is the best knowledge available. We simply don't know, if through our knowledge we destroy. We have been much too busy in changing the world. The point is, to understand it better. We are thus reversing Marx's Eleventh Thesis on Feurbach.

One way of understanding in depth our predicament is to notice the contingent nature of all evolving reality. We know that in the real world, which is always impinged upon by all kinds of contingencies, no trend can go on ad infinitum. Regardless how strong is the trend, after a while it looses its impetus. Its force flattens out. Depicted graphically, the trend (almost any trend in the real world) could be represented by Bell's curve. After its rapid ascent, the curves flattens out, and then it goes down.

The same tendency can be seen in our story of material progress and of Western civilization at large. The meaning of Bell's curve expressed in a simple language says that the further pursuit of material progress is not worth it. Material progress was meant to bring us the continuous increase in the quality of life. We have realized of late that after a certain point this process brings about so many uninvited negative consequences that its very purpose is undermined and annihilated. This idea could be expressed by Bell's curve in the following way.

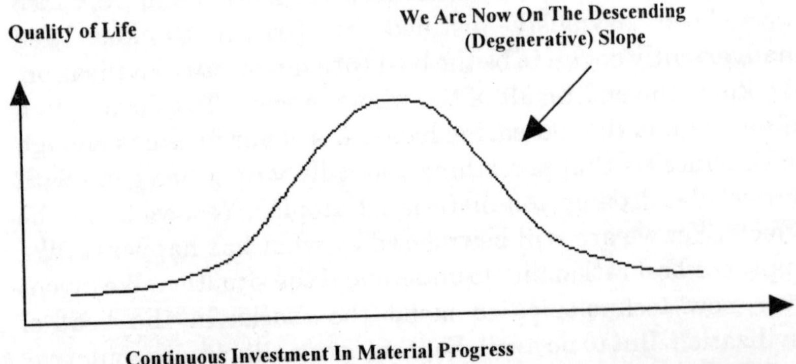

Perhaps a similar story has happened to our entire western civilization. Perhaps the cost of maintaining the present mode of Western civilization is higher than the benefits from it. Expressed by Bell's curve:

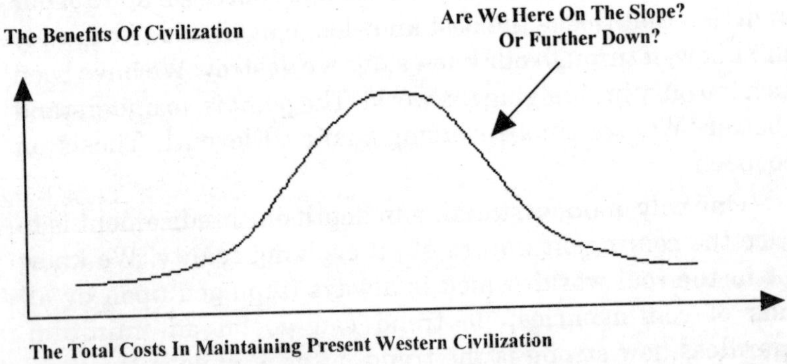

I am not the first to notice these strange propensities of our civilization (perhaps all civilizations; for each has a limited span). In a different context, Ivan Illich has persuasively demonstrated how the consumption of energy—beyond a certain point of use per capita—becomes counter-productive with regard to equity and good life. (See: Ivan Illich: *Energy and Equity* (1974). Equally persuasively, Illich showed a similar tendency in modern, high-technology based medicine, which now brings more harm than good (see *Limits to Medicine*, 1976)

We are the victims of philosophical fictions. Fictions cannot be overcome by philosophical analysis. Important philosophical fictions generate their own form of rationality, which supports and re-affirms them. Philosophical fictions have the character of a myth. Myth can be overcome or transcended by another myth—not by a cold, abstract analysis. What I am suggesting is that we must move out of the controlling circle of old assumptions, which are at the root of our problems. We must transcend the whole mandala—for it is bearing rotten fruit. In the words of the poet

> Of all you have done in the past
> You eat the fruit
> Either rotten or ripe. (T.S. Eliot)

3. The Peculiarity of Philosophy and Its Assumptions.

This discourse may lead some to a disturbing conclusion that the foundations of our thinking and being are very frail indeed. An even more disturbing conclusion is that: if philosophy rests on fictions, then how can we take it seriously? How can we take anything seriously? Well, these foundations are frail—in the sense that they are a work of human imagination, and in the sense that there is nothing inevitable or necessary about them. They could have been articulated and formulated differently; or something else could have taken their place. But once these basic philosophical assumptions become translated into the forms of human culture and become embedded in human practice, they show extraordinary strength and endurance. They seem to be clad in iron.

Philosophical fictions are thus a very special kind of fictions. When they express some enduring aspects of human nature, they are called sustaining myths. Now the myths which have outlived their potency and are no longer nourishing and inspiring us, become empty shells; really at a certain point they become spurious fictions. The distinction is subtle. But it can be drawn and must be drawn.

The ultimate tribunal of the validity of philosophical myths is the historical life of the human species. Myths and other symbols of human activity must be life enhancing in the broad and deep sense.

In the branches of philosophy, which is aspiring to be scientific, we do not talk about fictions and myths. These are supposed to be pejorative terms, unworthy of our respectable cognitive claims. We talk instead about assumptions! Although we can call them assumptions, these ultimate presuppositions are exactly of the nature of myths. Before they were proposed and articulated, they were not there. And after they were put forward, they were only tentative and tenuous entities. However, a rebuttal may immediately follow, namely that these assumptions are directly confronted with empirical reality and tested constantly in our social practice.

Our response is that this is exactly how other myths and large philosophical fictions are validated—by confronting them with reality and testing them in the context of social practice. But one thing must not be forgotten, namely that various assumptions (myths) envisage reality in different ways and test themselves exactly against that which they assume! No wonder they are being validated; even the weird ones such as: "homo homini lupus est" and "free market is a hand of destiny." Thus, various assumptions (myths, fictions) organize reality differently and elicit from us different aspects of our being. They cannot be judged by their internal coherence. They must be judged by the tribunal of life in the long run.

The peculiarity of philosophy is that it takes centuries before it shows its real worth or worthlessness. A pair of shoes shows its worth in a few weeks after they are worn. A bad meal manifests its nature the next day. Philosophical assumptions, being the roots of our social and individual life, take decades and sometimes centuries before their fruit is thoroughly tested—yes, by life in its multifarious aspects over a long span. Therefore don't expect philosophical ideas to work like nails. Two nails driven through two planks of woods hold these planks; their job done. If you treat philosophy in this instrumental crude way you can expect nothing but trouble; or a crude way of life with innumerable human problems following. Is this not what we have gathered as the result of the reign of our present pragmatic philosophies?

We need a broader perspective. We need to have an evolutionary perspective. Caught in narrow pragmatic strategems, we completely miss our place in history. During the last five centuries we, the Western people, have been on a trip of adventure and conquest. Consequently, we have developed a philosophy of adventurism and conquest. It is not a philosophy of mature minds. It is a philosophy of teenagers who have gone on a reckless trip of discovery, of probing their physical strength, of imposing their egos—whenever they can.

Now the philosophy preceding this Faustian trip—the ten centuries of Christianity prior to the Renaissance—was a similar trip of adolescence and immaturity, as Christianity attempted to impose its will through conquests and religious wars.

Whether we had to go through those adolescent epicycles, as a part of our evolutionary growth, we cannot be absolutely certain. What is certain now is that we have reached a new evolutionary level of development. This new evolutionary development requires an altogether new kind of philosophy. This must be a philosophy of maturity, of sustenance, of wisdom, and not of adolescent adventurism.

While we develop this new, mature, and evolutionarily sound philosophy, we must look beyond the next 5, 10, or 20 years. We must look into next five hundred years, nay, into the next fifteen hundred years. Do we have the courage and vision to do so? If not, then we shall remove ourselves from the driver's seat and give our place to those with courage and vision. The future generations will not judge us by our dexterity in driving nails or in operating smart computers, but by our courage, vision and wisdom in designing realities which represent evolutionary maturity.

4. Towards a New Social Order

We have been half-hearted in our search for new, more radical alternatives. We have somehow assumed, or wanted to believe, that the prowess of our technology and of our rationality will deliver us, will get us out of this unpleasant pitfall within which we have remained agonizingly long. Our past assumptions have conspired to make us indolent, for they want us to perpetuate the present status quo. Yet deep down many of us feel and know that there is no way of resolving our grave dilemmas without going to the foundations. This also means cosmological and theological foundations.

We have constructed a deficient code for reading nature. Hence our deficiency in interacting with nature. We have constructed a very limited conception of reason. And this reason leads us to a one-sided, and indeed myopic conception of reality. Perhaps the poet T.S. Eliot is right again, when he writes:

A wrong attitude towards God
And the consequence is
An inevitable doom.

The mechanistic reason and its excessive tendency to manipulation, to controlling often in a brutal insensitive way, grows out of mechanistic cosmology. Within this cosmology the world is viewed as a clock-like mechanism, as a huge machine. This metaphor, through which we have viewed the world, has done us a lot of harm. It has led to a myopic, one-sided, impoverished reading of the contents of the universe. On the human level, it has led to the impoverished conception of what it means to be human.

We need to find a new metaphor within which to view the world, and which would enable us to interact with the world differently. Within Eco-philosophy, which I have developed, the world is viewed as a sanctuary. The world as a sanctuary immediately opens for us new vistas on all there is. A new cosmological departure is our Copernican turning point. The old fashion Newtonian conception is already abandoned in the New Physics. We cling to it in lesser sciences, particularly in the social sciences. Why? Because we do not have enough imagination, because we are still brow-beaten by the shadows of Newtonian mechanics.

The world as a sanctuary immediately re-defines for us the multiplicity of our relationships with the cosmos. The conception of the world as a sanctuary is not only an idea; it is a guideline for action; a vehicle of values. In the world viewed as a sanctuary the most appropriate attitude is that of reverence. How much we need reverence in our brutalized world everybody knows! Thus we receive the first guideline—not a manipulation and exploitation of the world (so characteristic of the mechanistic cosmos) but reverence, compassion, a deep empathy for the world.

From reverence there immediately follows another major ecological value—responsibility: for our own life, for future generations, for the future of the planet, for the underprivileged on this planet. Responsibility is reverence in action. To understand the world as a sanctuary is to take responsibility for it. Furthermore, to act responsibly on behalf of the underprivileged. To be compelled to do so, we need something stronger than the sense of human solidarity. We need a conviction that the world has a sense, and that it is a beautiful place to live in. The idea of the world as a sanctuary provides this deeper foundation which supports and justifies our responsibilities at large.

A true comprehension of individual responsibility is enormously important in our present world in which we are continually diminished, reduced to insignificant pawns, deprived of dignity, of sovereignty, of essential human freedoms. Sovereignty, freedom, dignity and responsibility mutually supplement each other, and co-define each other. Responsibility is this splendid human attribute which enables dignity and freedom to exist and flourish. There is no true dignity and no true freedom without responsibility. So important is responsibility in our lives.

In this world of responsibility we must secure justice for all. Justice is a consequence of responsibility and indeed a form of reverence. Eco-justice, or justice for all, is the third important ecological value of our new world view. The sense of justice must be seen not only as a moral ideal, but a vehicle of action. One of my learned Indian friends asked at the end of an important scientific congress: "And what do we do about poverty?" There was deep silence... and a tinge of embarrassment. Whatever improvements we make in the world of the affluent, poverty remains. Poverty is now structural. But poverty does not make itself. People do not choose poverty, as president Reagan suggested in some of his infamous speeches. Poverty is the daughter of injustice. It is as simple as that. The dream of an equitable world is a dream of a just and fair world in which everybody is given a fair chance; not exactly an equal chance, but a fair chance. Only such a world is sustainable in the long run.

Thus sustainability, and especially a sustainable society, implies at its foundation justice and equality as conditions sine qua non of survival. In our equation of justice we must include other beings—in addition to human beings. They are all our brothers and sisters. Every form of life is unique, warranting respect regardless of its present worth to man. Fairness and equity for all beings of nature is a condition necessary for our survival.

Justice is a matter of belief in some ideal, is a matter of conviction that we are not selfish hogs. Therefore it is a matter of a certain conception of the world. In the cosmos supported by the eight pillars of selfishness (our philosophical fictions analyzed in Section 2), justice does not fare very well. In the world of the ruthless, justice is for the birds. This is another reason why we need to change our world view—its destructive selfishness is not sustainable.

Poverty and injustice are very palpable problems of everyday life. Any future world order, based on a sound and sane social contract (yes, we need a new social contract), will need to start with the idea of justice and of equity as its centrepieces. But the re-examination of justice cannot be confined to the old framework of class struggle and class interests. Universal justice, or simply sustainable justice, must now include the interests of future generations, and the interests of non-human-beings for their sake and our sake. Enlightened concerns for the interests of human beings now include the interest of other beings and all of nature. Thus our new social contract should not only have green tinges. It should be based on some kind of ecological philosophy. I have elaborated such a philosophy in various works.

I am saying above all that we need to change our lifestyles. When we look deeper into ecological values we realize that responsibility for our lifestyle has one specific consequence: the awareness how our lifestyle may impinge the lifestyle of others, may actually impoverish others. It is hard for us to swallow that our lifestyle may be a source of injustice to others.

So one part of the solution is: consume less and be more. We are touching on yet another, the fourth important ecological value—frugality. Frugality as a manifestation of responsibility and also as an instrument of justice in a larger framework. Frugality should not be thought of as a diminishment, impoverishment, abnegation. It is indeed a positive value. Frugality is doing more with less. Frugality is grace without waste. Frugality is empowering! Frugality is a precondition of inner beauty. Frugality is a majesty of simple means. Frugality is a rational strategy of survival for all. It may be difficult to change the mind-set of people who are used to waste as their way of life. Difficult but not impossible.

We have thus distinguished four basic ecological values which are articulating the idea of the world as a sanctuary. These values support each other and co-depend on each other.

The Wheel of Ecological Values

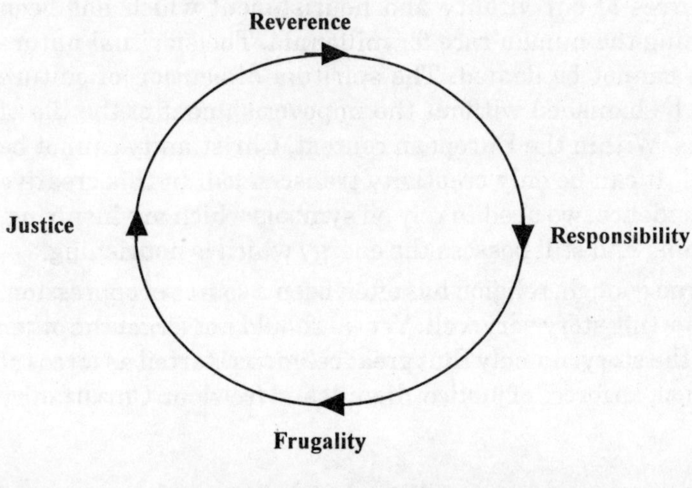

In the miasma of nothingness of our present nihilistic world, we need sustaining ideals. We need enduring convictions which are based on something firm and lasting. In short, we need spiritual ideals for inspiration, to hold us together and to propel us with extraordinary energies, will, and determination. We need not to be afraid of spiritual ideals. Nothing that is human is foreign to us.

Now the idea of the world as a sanctuary provides us with a deep spiritual basis—without committing us to any religion, any dogma, and especially any church. We are in the church called the cosmos! Is there a more magnificent temple than that? If we are not prepared to be worshippers in this temple, we must be at least intelligent enough to realize that without a transcendent dimension man shrinks.

When we look at the past with a discerning eye we can see that the major religions of humanity were champions of justice and protectors of the underprivileged. That they became twisted to serve the interests of privileged classes—this is another matter, and so was Marxism twisted as a matter of fact.

We can create a new world order, but not on the old foundations, which are cracking and going to pieces. New foundations means a new world view, new values and a rehabilitation of man's spiritual nature.

5. The Franciscan Legacy

In our quest for a new future we cannot cut ourselves from the sources of our vitality and nourishment which has been sustaining the human race for millennia. The spiritual nature of man cannot be denied. The spiritual dimension of culture cannot be banished without the impoverishment of the life of humans. Within the European context, Christianity cannot be ignored. It can be only creativity transcended. In this creative transcendence, we need to rely on symbols which are inspiring, sustaining and still possess the energy which is nourishing.

True enough, religion has often been a source of oppression. We know this story very well. Yet we should not forget the other part of the story, namely that great religions started as forces of liberation, as forces of justice, dignity and freedom. Christianity itself started as a form of liberation theology, as it attempted to help the poor, the wretched, the oppressed.

Let us make a major point. We cannot dream about a new social order, about justice in the world without confronting the problem of religion, of God, of spirituality. Those are not old fashion issues. Ultimately justice is a spiritual issue—even if we do not believe in a personal god or any institutional church. We can live without the church and personal god. The Buddhist tradition has shown how. However without spirituality, without the sense of transcendence which goes beyond mundane consumption, the human person withers. Thus, in our reconstruction of the world order to secure world's sustainability and a decent future for all, we must not forget about the spiritual reconstruction. But this spiritual reconstruction must be done aright. It cannot be a return to some dogmatic teaching of antiquated churches. As I mentioned, we need to rely on symbols which are inspiring and sustaining.

One of such symbols is the life and teaching of St. Francis of Assisi. He is a saint dear not only to many Christians but many non-Christians, who see in him a universal symbol of human justice, of human care, of compassion for all—including the non-human universe. Francis also possessed the courage of standing naked, both in the literary and figurative sense; of confronting human misery and injustice directly. He insisted that redistribution of wealth is our responsibility. The unjustified accumulation of wealth by some is the root cause of misery of others. Francis was convinced that we ultimately stand God's tribunal, which means the tribunal of our conscience. To this conscience we are ultimately responsible; especially as the existing laws so often protect the rich at the expense of the poor. We thus have the divine duty to help. This could be a foundation of our new spirituality. Needless to say, Francis was a great paragon of simplicity and frugality. We may not be able to emulate his extraordinary simplicity, but to see him as a sign post leading in a right direction would be an excellent idea indeed.

In brief, the teaching of St. Francis is still an inspiration, a yardstick of justice, and a challenge of how to be committed and courageous. It was a great tragedy for Christianity that it did not embrace St. Francis's teaching, and instead accepted Thomas Aquinas as the core of its orthodoxy. If St. Francis became the nourishing stream of Christian religion, we would have had a different Christianity, and in all probability a different world.

It was a tragedy for Marxism that it allied itself with vulgar materialists, such as Feurbach, whose creed was an aggressive atheism. Had Marx embraced the teaching of St. Francis, who was so close to Marx's ideals, we would have had a different Marxism. And a different world again. But perhaps historically it was not possible. But it is possible now.

I am thus proposing that Franciscan socialism might be a real possibility. We may have to find another label, for we have become allergic to the term "socialism". The basic point is to combine social justice for all with a spiritual ideal which resonates in us all.

Every religion has various threads woven into it. At certain points of history, some of the threads, hitherto neglected and ignored, begin to shine with a new beauty. In critical situations, when people need new perspectives and a new lease of life, new patterns are woven around these shining threads. The teaching of St. Francis is such a thread within Christianity—now shining with a new beauty.

Francis is an ecological saint and this makes him particularly suitable as our patron in our works of the ecological reconstruction. In a sense it does not matter whether he belonged to the Christian church or not. His message is universal, and so appropriate for our times.

6. From Democracy to Ecological Democracy

Democracy is in trouble. We all know it. Alas, there is no better system around. Put otherwise: other alternatives are less promising. So we have to cling to what we have. Now, what do we do with old garments which are in tatters? We improve, refurbish, and renew them. This is what we need to do with present democracy. We need to refurbish it at its seams, not only on the surface.

One of the most crucial problems of our times is that Western democracy is at odds with the environment, which is to say: our efforts to protect the integrity of the earth and to make it sustainable to future generations are not aided by present democracy. Let me explain. Western democracy over the last decades has come to signify the form of government which is elected every few years—which is not too bad. Yet we must look deeper, beyond the superficial trappings of democracy—free voting of allegedly free people. Politicians of leading democracies have become selfish individuals caring mainly for their own reelection. We don't see real statesmen among them, and they have no vision. Every four years or so, there is another scramble to get the votes of voters—in whatever manner you can. We all know the spectacle. The point is that policies established by politicians who only care about their next reelections are very short sighted, while the protection of the environment requires prudent planning over many years.

You cannot have any sane environmental policy for particular nations and for the whole globe when democracy signifies a merry-go-round from one election to the next. Present democracy is an enemy of the environment. If this conclusion seems too startling, I ask: How else would you describe this form of government, which is so geared to selfish interests of individual politicians that it is prepared to sacrifice nature, other species, and future generations for the sake of temporary glory of narrow-minded people?

If this system is still to be called democracy, we need to see how very inadequate it is and how unviable in the long run. Some may want to construe my arguments as an attempt to throw out democracy altogether. I am not advocating any such thing. As I mentioned earlier, like an old venerable garment, democracy must be refurbished to serve new realities and new imperatives of life.

Democracy cannot survive if it does not become a friend of and supporter of the environment. If we lose environment, we lose democracy and everything else. The democracy of the future will need to become more responsible and less self-serving. It will need to recognize in its universe of discourse not only humans but other beings which are a part of our world. It will need to recognize the interests of future generations of people.

In brief, I am proposing here Ecological Democracy.

Ecological democracy recognizes the rights of other beings (and of nature herself) in addition to the rights of human beings; for if we lose environment and the whole support of the biotic community, we lose democracy.

Ecological democracy recognizes equity and justice among nations. For if injustice prevails, the whole world will burst at its seams as the poorer nations will violently protest against a privileged clan of rich nations; alternatively, rich nations will have to cordon off poor nations and create some kind of world prison—which would be a far cry from democracy.

Ecological democracy recognizes the rights of future generations, and explicitly protests against the exploitation of natural resources at the expense of future generations. These future generations are already with us—we simply need a special ear to hear how these future generations are advising us to vote now. Their vote must count!

Ecological democracy is a stark necessity of our times, on the one hand, and common sense of the ecological era, on the other hand. Ecological democracy broadens the scope of traditional democracy by including rights and votes of:

(i) Nature and other beings of the Earth.

(ii) Underprivileged and exploited nations of the Earth.

(iii) Future generations of human beings.

Those three groups of voters, although invisible, are very much present, and we must include them in the genuine democracy of the future. Democracy has been changing historically, and it is bound to be changing further as the world changes, as our consciousness changes, as the imperatives of life change. Democracy was meant to serve people. Among people must be included these beings which are part of the web of life which supports us; and those unborn generations which are a part of the continuing history of humankind.

This is the meaning of ecological democracy: Power and justice to the people—not only a privileged few, but all others who form the interconnected network of life. Only such democracy will survive which respects life and its imperatives; which is based on wisdom and right prudence and not on ignorance and selfish interests of privileged groups. Such is ecological democracy.

Ecological democracy is much more akin to ancient Greek democracy than present anarchistic, rampant, unseeing democracy in its jittery run from one election to the next. For the ancient Greeks, to exercise democracy wisely was to choose freely what was right and best for the common good. This is the quintessence of democracy. This is the quintessence of ecological democracy, which is the democracy for our times. In chapter 18 we shall carry the discussion of ecological democracy futher to its ultimate fruition, which is Cosmocracy.

Summary

The new dawn of humanity is not yet on the horizon. But a mid summer dream is a part of our capacity to imagine the world as it ought to be. The gloomy prognostications of the prophets of the doom will not discourage us. For what they take to be a reality and a necessity is a nightmare and it will pass. Yet it will not pass by itself but through our stupendous effort—to bring about that which assures our survival and our flourishing, and which is potentially within us.

We are at a new evolutionary juncture and nothing short of a radical rethinking of our foundations will do. We shall emphasize that the old conceptual, economic and spiritual foundations are cracking. We cannot accomplish any lasting reconstruction of them. A new attitude toward nature, a new attitude toward God, a new attitude toward ourselves is necessary. For remember—a wrong attitude towards nature brings as a consequence an inevitable doom.

Karl Marx claimed that philosophers so far only tried to understand the world—the point is to change it. We are now in a new situation. We have changed the world. Only too much. the point nowadays is to understand it better. We do not understand the world if we destroy it. It is spurious knowledge of the world which claims to understand it and instead mutilates it.

Ecological philosophy provides a skeleton for a new understanding and a new social reconstruction. It does not shy to combine the spiritual with the ecological and with the economic. For the three is the right way to SEE (Spiritual, Ecological, Economic). If ecological philosophy does not suffice in the future, we shall invent new ones until we create the world that is worthy of the species which deems itself both rational and compassionate.

9

My Encounters with California

1. The USA—A Land of Unreality

In April, 1964, I received my doctorate in philosophy from Oxford University. In July, I found myself in New York, and in August in Los Angeles - as a professor of philosophy at the University of Southern California. What a change! My first encounter with New York was via a taxi driver who took me from the ship (those days, one still travelled by boat from Europe). He raved what a great place New York was, and how great and smart New Yorkers were... and he promptly added forty percent to the meter charges. I was too surprised to protest.

In Los Angeles I learned that New Yorkers are braggadocios and conceted hoaxers, and that the ultimate reality is here in Los Angeles. I was told that beyond California, there is no further West. For California is it. Such pronouncements of such blatant self-adulation were bound to raise an eyebrow of a European who just came from Oxford, where everything is understated. But then, one was prepared to be surprised by America, and especially California. Yet, this sycophantic bombast adulation of Californians was something that continually surprised me.

The scenes of material progress were at first intoxicating. The five-lane highways which were criss-crossing the whole city were dizzying to one's senses. Later on, however, I found this whole scene in which everything was moving, at least millions of cars were continually moving, to be rather boring, and a real menace to genuine city living. The wholesale optimism which described everything as "great" and "super" was uplifting and inspiring at first. But when one looked deeper into the phenomenon of the greatness of California living, one found a smiling facade empty of content (a kind of television screen).

I was told over and again during the first months of my stay in California that the whole world apes America; America follows California, and Los Angeles was the navel of California. The inference was clear: The future is forged out here. The laboratory of the entire world was here in Southern California. Which in a way was true—for better and worse. For better, because the Flower Children revolution and the Hippie revolution happened there, were ignited on the boulevards of Los Angeles—under my very eyes. And then spread to San Francisco and elsewhere.

The Western world has never been the same after the shake-ups of the 1960's, which brought about the new awareness and perspectives. Those late 1960's was a great and salutary period of human history. The late 1970's and the 1980's represented, in contrast, a period of conservative repression and counter-revolution, which attempted to turn back the clock of history. In the conservative era of the last twenty years, it has been difficult to appraise and clearly see earlier years. What a glorious period it really was—with a fundamental challenge posed to all the stale dogmas of Western civilization. As I said, being a witness in the late 1960's in L.A. was a great experience, for here was a laboratory of the future, which was forging out new forms.

Yet, one needs to remember that in the U.S., particularly in California, everything is so transient and ephemeral. You feel that something is beginning to emerge. And a day after tomorrow, it is gone. Something else has climbed on the stage of public life, clamoring for attention. Thus, a sense of perpetual change has been a most frustrating aspect of my American experience.

This phenomenon of perpetual change is fascinating to observe. It reflects America's historical rootlessness. We don't have history, Americans seem to be saying, all right, we shall bank on the future, we shall be a cutting edge on the future. Thus, an obsession with the future is an expression of the American ahistorical mentality.

Yet there is another important force which propels this incessant preoccupation with change and future. This force is mass media. The media are very powerful in the U.S.A. And they continually crave novelty. Media thrive on new things—whether real or invented. The whole American reality is partly an invention of the media. What media projects, that becomes a reality. Indeed, the influence of the media is so strong, particularly of the TV, that at one point it is difficult to distinguish what is real and what is imaginary. Facts and fiction, imagination and reality, are blended together—all in the pursuit of novelty, progress, future.

The relentless drive of the media is overwhelming. And you need to be a fastidious and critical philosopher in order to discern what is imposed and fabricated, on the one hand, and what is presented and elucidated, on the other hand. The boundary between these two realms is elusive and uncertain. And it is nowhere more elusive and uncertain than in California. You may say that Californians live in the imaginary world. The whole American experience sometimes strikes you as the journey through the land of unreality.

2. Grand Illusionism

If I were to reconstruct the ontology or the view of reality which emerges out of the mosaics of the American experience, I would call it grand illusionism. Americans, especially Californians, never think little of themselves. Indeed, they think of themselves as great, grand people, chosen by God to lead humanity into the future. If this strikes you as megalomania, it is a daily occurrence of life that is so common that one doesn't perceive it anymore. Thus, the illusion of grandeur pervades the lives of individuals, and the whole nation. At the same time, one sees a tremendous will to conjure up new worlds, new possibilities. There is no question, the Californians are creative people. "The sky is the limit," as the expression goes. So we are free to invent new options and new worlds. This kind of attitude is tremendously liberating to human imagination. The Europeans have little notion what a freedom it is to feel that all is open, can be reconceived and reconstructed. This openness of the mind is an invitation to imagination, as well as to fiction making. Thus, the relentless drive to unfold (or create) new future, plus a relentless drive to create novelty and mold people according to desirable fictions, plus a relentless drive of human imagination to feel free in inventing new reality, results in a great deal of inventiveness (which is usually free of critical constraints) and whose final result is a form of illusionism, a metaphysics in which reality blends with imagination so subtly that we cannot distinguish one from the other. Since this metaphysics is held by the people who have a grand opinion of themselves, I call is grand illusionism.

If I were to reconstruct the underlying epistemology of the California mentality, I would call it cognitive voluntarism or cognitive dadaism. In the mill of perpetual change, one soon realizes that anything goes. You can embark on anything, pursue any line of inquiry, craft or art, and it will be tolerated and applauded. But only for a while. For in the paradigm in which anything goes, nothing stays. For a European, it is a very frustrating feeling, for one realizes that there are no criteria of quality, either in theory of knowledge, or in aesthetics, or in ethics.

The epistemology of "anything goes" has created a total chaos of values in the United States, in aesthetics and ethics in particular. The attitude of "anything goes" has created a value vacuum, nihilism, cynicism, which are all daughters of spurious cognitive proliferation.

Let us quite clearly realize that "anything goes" is not just a half-baked methodology of half-mature hazy California thinkers. It has a seal of approval of representatives of highly acclaimed school of philosophy deriving from Karl Popper. Popper has relentlessly driven the point that any theory and idea should be open to criticism and questioning.

Paul Feyerabend was one of the brightest and colorful of Popper's disciples. He carried out Poppers program to its logical limits. If anything is open to criticism, then let us clearly realize that none of the established and celebrated scientific theories holds. They are all approximations, really useful fictions. We should not be bound by them. Instead, we should opt out for the principle of cognitive profligacy. We should generate ever new theories and conjectures. There are no scientific laws, and no pet methodologies, such as the scientific method. Anything goes—was Feyerabend's new epistemological cry of the 1970's.

Now, one should be aware that, while working out his methodology of cognitive proliferation, Feyerabend lived and worked at Berkeley in California. There is no question the California ethos has affected his thinking, and that his thinking—which seemingly applies to the methodology of science—was a legitimization of the ethos of California thinking. Feyerabend called for a total cognitive freedom within which one is not constrained by any scientific and rationalistic strictures, but by one's own aesthetic predilections. (See: Paul Feyerabend, "Consolations for the Specialist" in *Criticism and the Growth of Knowledge*, Imre Lakatos, ed., 1970.)

When one attempts to summarize Feyerabend's rationality and overall epistemology, the closest description is cognitive dadaism. And this, I claim, could serve as an overall description for the epistemology of what could be loosely called the California Weltanschauung. Anything goes in the carousel of perpetual change.

How can you build within the paradigm where anything goes but nothing stays? Not very well. Hence, no enduring achievements in humanities, social science, and philosophy that I could record in California and America at large. Yes, there are those enduring achievements in science and technology. But these are accomplished on the basis on the old-fashioned Newtonian worldview, not on the one expressing the ephemeral New Age philosophy.

3. Pop-culture and Con-men

How does it feel to live in the California reality? A bit unreal, as I said. I could never reconcile myself to this make-believe pantomime. Of course in life, one plays many roles. One is an actor, and occasionally one plays out an act or two. But there is a time for acting, and there is a time for returning to reality. In a sense, Americans and particularly Californians never leave this stage. Is it a liberation? Or is it a new form of prison? It may be conceived as a liberation as one is freed from the anchors of traditional dogmas and assumptions. It may be conceived as a form of prison as one is always flying and never has a chance to look at one's roots, and not much chance to ask what it is all about.

I have found life in America rather shallow, as compared with my European experience. To be sure, there are lots of groups, which practice meditation and spiritual discipline. These are the enclaves of sanity, connectedness, high-mindedness, and the search for the deepest in our soul. But these groups are ignored, derided, and deliberately marginalized by the mainstream society which is controlled and manipulated by the media. And this manipulation is frightening and thorough. Let no one have any illusion that it is otherwise.

Now, when we talk about California mentality, California worldview, or this special brand of mysticism, which we might call California mysticism, we do not talk about the people in the streets who are manipulated by the media. But we talk about a special kind of people who stand over and beyond the media. Seemingly it should be so. But in reality it is not. For the media approach, the media mentality is all pervading. This grand illusionism which I have described as the ruling ontology, this make-believe attitude in which you try to capture the stage and beam your message as all important, has pervaded the minds of major thinkers in America. One is so conscious of the importance of the media, one is so continuously trying to broadcast his/her message with an eye on the media, one is so constantly exaggerating and simplifying one's message to fit it to the requirements of the media, that after a while the critical mind gives in to the illusionist's mind. We can then legitimately say that the medium is the message. But this is so much deeper and more sinister sense than Mac Luhan's idea had been able to convey.

One has the feeling that Americans themselves are constantly promoting themselves. What is important is not the beauty and novelty of ideas, but how you promote them. In this commercial, "illusionist", "anything goes" climate, ideas are strange commodities. If this picture appears to be unflattering to the American mind, let it be said that it was drawn be an unreconstructed European who has resisted the lures of

American reality. To the American mind, my description would be thought of as a picture of essential fluidity, adjustability, American pragmatism, the possibility of embracing change and forging out new futures. Whatever the description, the fact is that this most effervescent mind-formation, which the California mentality has been exploding with the past few decades did not produce any lasting fruit. The beginning was made—yes—by the flower children and the hippies (which I must emphasize once more) were true and significant revolutionaries. But these were almost children—acting out their guts, not any well-articulated form of mind. In spite of the prodigious effort and continuous flowering of the California culture, which has been an inspiration for many, has not produced lasting achievements comparable with the lasting achievements of other cultures.

The California mentality is an ephemeral one. It spends its genius on creating various fascinating fireworks, which titillate the senses but do not ameliorate the human condition in any basic sense. Are we perchance dealing with a hedonistic culture, which delights in self-destruction and ephemeral epicycles? Such a description would perhaps be too harsh, but maybe not far from the truth. Future historians will resolve this matter.

Yet, a note should be added. Among various institutions of California, and there are many of them which are inspiring and really innovative, one is called New Dimensions Radio Program. This program has hosted over three thousand individuals, many of them from California, who are interviewed in-depth in a program each lasting for an hour. In these programs, which have been going for over thirty years, an alternative culture has been laid out and articulated. There is a coherent California Weltanschauung and something that can be called California culture, contained in these programs, which have been broadcast throughout the United States, and the world over, but which so far (as far as the dominant American culture is concerned) have been cries in the wilderness.

Yet another note should be added. I have described California ontology (grand illusionism) and California epistemology (cognitive dadaism). What of the concept of the person? What kind of human being emerges out of this new metaphysics, enacted in the ever changing reality? This being is surprisingly free and creative. As there are no limits, you are constantly challenged. Your creativity is taken for granted. The whole culture bubbles with new options. They may be immature and half-baked but no one is going to curtail your novelty and originality in the name of existing dogmas (oh yes, there is a subtle and pervading control of the minds by the establishment and mass media, but this control is hidden and never openly expressed.) So, at its best, the California mind emerges as Protean, Promethean, entirely free, almost god-like, in its capacity to remake reality and one's own future. To experience such a mind, even if it is not manifested by many people in its complete form, is a liberation. The other side of the coin is that there are too many con men in America.

How could I summarize my experience of California and the American mind? It has been an exciting experience, but also tinged with the awareness that these people are not quite serious—the con-man has been too often tripping the serious thinker within the unfolding spectacle of the American reality. From Socrates we inherited the idea of self-knowledge—know thyself. This ideal of self-knowledge has been changed into one of self-massage—feel good. It seems as if the name of the game is searching but not finding. The intoxication with newness is so profound that it creates an amnesia with regards to the past. If one compares various styles of thinking, then the obvious contrast is the German drill vs. California mist.

Yet my California experience has been a challenging and broadening one, and very liberating. You are always called to stretch further and further. The universe is forever open, and you have the sense of tremendous freedom. I do not think I could have advanced my ideas as far (particularly those of Ecophilosophy and Eco-mind) in any other reality. But at the same time, I have felt that America has been the land of lost opportunities. Here was a chance to create something new, significant, and redeeming for the whole race. This chance has been missed in the twentieth century.

We have to continue our quest in the 21st century. But this time, I think, outside America.

Part : II

Looking Forward to a Desirable Future

10
Dialogue with Marcus Aurelius

H.S. Marcus Aurelius, what do I call you? Your Imperial Majesty?

M.A. Marcus would do.

H.S. Are you surprised, and perhaps delighted that your little volume, which we now call *Meditations*, has enjoyed such an enormous popularity and has inspired people throughout the centuries, including present times?

M.A. I am surely astonished that they found my scribbles. And even more so that they published them in ancient times, and republished them in various languages ever since. I didn't think I was writing for posterity.

H.S. So were you writing for yourself?

M.A. Well, sort of. I had to concentrate my mind on something more sublime than the military affairs of my legions.

H.S. You wrote your thoughts in most uncomfortable of conditions, while being in camp with your legions, somewhere near present Budapest—being in the terrain of barbarians, which you attempted to contain. Why write in such conditions? Why write at all being an emperor? And furthermore, why write in Greek, while you were a noble Roman?

M.A. Well, it was perhaps the severity of the camp life that prompted me to reflect on deeper destinies of man. Fighting these brute barbarians in the endless forests of Europe was no joy. My soldiers were not doves either; coarse men indeed. So in order not to be depressed by the brutality of war and the barbarity of the human condition, I wrote...as a kind of solace.

H.S. Why did you write in Greek? After all it is a bit unusual for a noble Roman and an emperor as well, to write in a foreign language, the language of small people whom you conquered centuries ago?

M.A. To begin with, the Greeks were never small people. Even after they were conquered by us. Interestingly, through the empire we built and extended, we were ambassadors of Greek culture. It has been said, not without some justification, that the conquered Greeks culturally conquered the Romans.

I wrote in Greek partly to be safe. I didn't want anybody poking into my notes and spreading the word that the Emperor writes about miseries of life. But more importantly, the Greek language was for me deeper and subtler than our Roman language—which you call Latin. By submerging myself in the Greek language I felt a sense of freedom, I felt I grew in substance, my soul was so comfortable. While writing in Greek, I could be much more myself. When I used Latin, invariably it was in order to attend the affairs of the State. How should I put it? The convulsive tremors of the empire, the seedy undertones of political life, the smelly aspects of Rome, were always somewhere there—whenever I used Latin. I wanted to escape from that. In contrast the Greek language was more pure, more elevated, more divine. Language does not only convey meanings of a people. It brings with itself all the fluff and muck of ordinary life. One has to be careful in using language, for it can be a messenger of stars but also a conveyor of muck.

H.S. You were an emperor. Yet in your philosophy you were a stoic. Why this stoicism? Stoicism is considered to be a philosophy fit for the slaves, not a philosophy for emperors?

M.A. We are all slaves. Alas, most of us do not realise that. Stoicism signifies an aware life—of its pitfalls, hidden traps, agonies, great complexities. Human life is frail. The human condition is trembling. The beauty of reason is to reveal our true condition. Thus by reflecting on life's vicissitudes, its depths and its shames, its agonies and its glories, we can become free. This is the path of stoicism. This is the path of freedom. On this point stoicism is quite close to Buddhism. Both Stoicism and Buddhism declare that reason is not to be despised. But to be used as a ladder leading to heaven.

Stoicism teaches you distance towards life. Really, this is what philosophy is about—to teach you distance towards life so that you are not overwhelmed by trivia and vulgarities. Because Roman emperors and Roman nobles were not stoic enough, their empire fell apart.

This is also your problem in present times. You are overwhelmed with minutia, with a sea of disturbing trivia. Your daily life is full of stress and agony because you are overburdened with trifling petty concerns. You do not have enough distance towards life and yourself. You are not stoic enough. For this reason your lives are a bit of a sham; and often fall apart; also for this reason your society is anemic, disconnected and chaotic.

H.S. How does it feel to be the most illustrious of Roman emperors—on account of your philosophy?

M.A. I wouldn't call myself the most illustrious Roman emperor. Augustus was certainly the greatest. He excelled in every way possible. He laid the foundations of the greatness and glory of Rome. He supported artists and philosophers in an open and generous way. I had to scribble my philosophical thoughts as if clandestinely. I was not made of the material of which emperors are made. I was dragged into becoming an emperor. I didn't want to become one.

Another emperor who was great was Constantinus in the fourth century. He saw that Rome was declining—mainly because of her spiritual atrophy. He allowed Christianity to become the official religion. He built a new centre of the empire and of the new religion in Constantinople. The Basilica of Santa Sophia which he constructed was a great masterpiece then as it is now. Truly a great masterpiece.

H.S. Whether his whole achievement was a revival of Rome or a kiss of death is another matter. Rome never recovered after Constantinople was established as the capital of the Eastern Roman empire. Now, was Constantinus fleeing from Rome or establishing its new boundaries?

M.A. What you are saying has a ring of truth. Perhaps Western Roman Empire was already doomed. Those Northern barbarians were plenty tough. And they were coming and coming. And we didn't know what to do with them; they could neither be absorbed into our empire nor contained.

H.S. How would you compare the Roman Empire with the United States, which is often viewed as the Roman Empire of present times?

M.A. Well, I do not wish to say to whom this comparison is flattering and to whom it is unflattering. No doubt, we mighty Romans were overshadowed by the scintillating glory of Greek culture; just as America has been by the cultural achievement of Europe. However, and take heed of that, we had enough sense to spread the Greek achievement, Greek logos, Greek sense of harmony and beauty to all corners of our empire. Western Europe became what it is because Rome implemented the canons of understanding, civility and democracy invented by the Greeks.

We were builders. We built for permanence. We established and cultivated the law. Our laws have been endlessly copied in what was to become European countries. We built roads and aqueducts. And they were splendid edifices! They would have survived to our times (some actually did!) if you didn't start destroying them through the vehicles of your progress.

H.S. How does it compare to American civilisation?

M.A. The comparison is obvious. While we built for permanence, America is building for impermanence. It is a flimsy civilisation. Just think of that: built in obsolescence—what an absurdity. While we were spreading the best of Greek culture, American civilisation is spreading its rubbish culture, which so often propagates violence, egoism and impermanence. We attempted to spread good laws, civic virtues, responsibility for the common good. U.S. excels in lawlessness and violence.

You need to remember that the empire entails not only power but also responsibility, the responsibility for lasting and enhancing values, for nature which is our home. You are so destructive. In the name of what? In the name of your flimsy and so often trivial needs. Some restraint and a measure of stoic philosophy would be of great help to you.

H.S. But we have Christian values to guide us.

M.A. On paper, yes. But not in actuality. Of late you have been losing both Greco-Roman values and Christian values. You have unleashed within your civilisation some destructive forces which are neither an expression of Greek Logos nor of Christian love and compassion. There are some diabolical forces underneath this whole process. You better watch it. This is not the road to a flourishing and balanced civilisation. This is a road to extinction.

H.S. You seem to be a bit too holy about the virtues of Roman civilisation, while we know that the Roman empire was brutal and at times destructive.

M.A. Well, yes. This has to be admitted. Empires are never pretty things. They rule by force. This is their nature. Otherwise they would fall apart. But there are some fundamental differences between us and present America. We built for permanence. You do not. We built aqueducts. You are poisoning the environment. Virtual reality will not save you—if you kill nature or poison it too badly. This you must understand. Otherwise your understanding, whatever powerful computers you have at your fingertips is shallow and deficient.

H.S. You are not quite answering my question. I have been suggesting that the Roman Empire was quite a bully, at times brutal and destructive. Very similar to the way the USA has been behaving. Both empires, whether intentionally or not, acted like bulldozers flattening the lands and minds. Invariably they made things simple, uniform and somewhat trivial. All for the sake of running the empire efficiently.

M.A. Yes, I must admit it, this flattening out effect is characteristic of all empires, at least the Roman and American. They are very much alike in their insensitivity, intoxication with power, inability to understand subtlety, difference, the things which are of a deeper nature. Perhaps it is a matter of size. Giantism breeds indifference. Excessive power corrupts. Combined: excessive power and giantism spell out evil.

H.S. Is the matter as simple as that?

M.A. Perhaps it is. Logically and rationally it does not have to be like that. But giantism has got its own logic. When we look around, we see empires as bullies—particularly with respect to sensitive and different minorities. On the other hand, when we see thriving cultures, we see them thriving through and amidst tolerance, variety, difference, subtlety. Giantism always flattens smaller things. Uniformity nearly always attempts to eliminate exquisite diversity. Hence it is intolerant to significant differences.

H.S. One of the characteristic features of empires is that they think of themselves as ultimate things. They assume that they will last forever; not infrequently that they represent the final stage of history. I wonder whether you would agree with that.

M.A. Yes, I would. The Roman Empire was so sure of itself and assumed that it would last forever. It also assumed that nothing of importance existed before it and nothing of importance could exist after it.

H.S. This certainly must breed a sense of megalomania and a certain historical numbness, this notion that "we are the world"; that "history will end with us."

M.A. Yes, this is how power and giantism effect you. This was so in Roman times and this is so with regard to present America. At a certain juncture, the empire begets its own ideologues who become defenders of the status quo, the defenders, so to speak, of the "Sacred Status" of the empire. Take for example Francis Fukuyama with his idea of the end of history. What a silly idea indeed. But the empire needs such schemes and ideas to feel comfortable, important, self-assured.

H.S. Are you sure that it is such a silly idea, that of the end of history?

M.A. Of course I am. Already Hegel pronounced such an idea. History and the world were supposed to come to an end when everybody would accept his scheme of the ideal society. The same idea (of the end of history) was proposed by Karl Marx. Needless to say the ultimate order of things was envisaged differently by Hegel and by Marx. The realised communist utopia meant the end of history for Marx. For Fukuyama it is the realised capitalist utopia, or whatever you call it—the kind of society that enshrines the values of the American empire. Now, while Hegel and Marx were intellectual giants, Fukuyama is much less so. Poor man, he does not realise how the empire is using him. Or perhaps he does realise that... The result is the same: a triumphant peddling of a one dimensional idea of man by a simplistic mind.

H.S. So how will America dissolve, and where do we go from there?

M.A. That one... is a far more difficult question. Each empire is different and it dissolves differently.

H.S. Can you envisage what will come later when we are well in the third millennium?

M.A. The middle of the third millennium, eh? You will be already in the next civilisation.

H.S. Can you just outline briefly what it might look like?

M.A.........

H.S. I wonder why you are so reluctant to talk about the future.

M.A. Well what cannot be put in words, should be consigned to silence—as one of your philosophers says.

H.S. You mean, Wittgenstein?

M.A. Yes, Wittgenstein. He was obsessed with mathematical logic. He was a technician in many ways. Yet he was also a wise man, of a considerable depth. Pity that he did not choose to write on the moral dilemmas that tormented him..... I suppose a lack of courage. He was inhibited by his own strictures that you only talk about things which you can express with a precision and clarity. What a lamentably limited programme. It prevents you from talking about deep things, important things, immortal things.

H.S. What would you suggest that our epoch does to overcome the present paralysis and decay?

M.A. Hmm...

H.S. No word of advice whatsoever?

M.A. You should acquire some modesty. Modesty is good for attaining some inner depth. Most of the time you are immodest buffoons. This alone makes you forget your inner selves. Modesty is good for your balance, for your daily harmony—as it protects you from the invasion of your overblown egos, needs, desires and whims. Modesty is good for your sense of equity, as it makes you realise that other people have rights too. Modesty is good for your morality, as it makes you aware that human justice cannot prevail if and when some groups hoard exorbitant resources and monies, while others starve.

H.S. So, your sermon on modesty is your modest proposal to rectify the present imbalances of the world?

M.A. Yes, precisely. May you have enough depth and wisdom to perceive how important modesty is in understanding yourself and your place in the universe.

H.S. What words of caution or encouragement would you offer to present philosophers?

M.A. Don't sell out. At any rate don't sell too cheaply.

H.S. What do you mean by that?

M.A Preserve your dignity and your nobility. Maintain longer perspectives. Don't be narrow technicians, like W.V. Quine; or servants of the status quo, like Fukuyama. Philosophy is a noble and significant endeavor. It attempts to understand the depth and meaning of the phenomenon of man. It attempts to grasp the meaning of the cosmos, its grandeur and glory. It attempts to show that we are cosmic beings, and as such we need to behave responsibly. Philosophy is not the most important thing in the world. But without it, nothing is important.

11

The Silent Conques of Nandi

1. Being Puzzled by India

India is a fabulous country. And a continually surprising one. While all countries around it have been economically crashing, India refused to do so. What business did it have to stand aloof from the present turmoil? What an indolence indeed, while her neighbors, considered so much "better managed", have crashed one after another. Curiously enough, the learned gurus of the economic gospel of the West, have kept silent on India in recent years. Somehow they did not have anything to say on India, especially, why it survived so well.

I have always felt that there is more to India than meets the economic eye. I have been an eager scholar of past civilizations and—strange to say—of future civilizations. I believe that the next civilization will be much better than the present one. I am convinced that the turn for the better will not come from the treasury of Western wisdom. It will come from the East. India will play a major part in shaping the Third Millennium.

In the course of this essay I will explain some of the circumstances that have led me to this opinion. But first, let me share with the reader some of my background. I was born in Poland and spent the first thirty years there, living through the WW II and the Marxist debacle (until early 1960's). The next thirty years I spent in the West: five years in Britain (mainly at Oxford) and twenty seven years in the USA, mainly teaching at The University of Michigan at Ann Arbor. I am a Western man. Yet, being born and brought up in Poland, in rather difficult times, made my perceptions and thinking different from the standard Western man.

While in the USA, I observed and experienced the so called melting pot, the wonderful cauldron in which all nationalities were supposed to melt into standard honest to goodness Americans. In the early 1960's, the Asians were still at the bottom of this melting pot, treated with some disdain as a slightly inferior race. The situation started to change dramatically in the 1980's when it was discovered that the top 5 per cent of graduating students of the best American universities, such as Harvard, Yale, Berkeley, Stanford, were mainly Asian students. This caused a consternation, amidst inaudible murmurs "How can these coolies do so well?" The trend has continued. In around 2020 many of these outstanding students of the Asian background will be national leaders. Will they continue the same line of "business as usual"—favoring mainly big business at the expense of the people? Or will they per chance embark on new visions and perspectives, rooted in their Asian values and their profound cultures? I have got my answer to this question.

In 1994 I visited a friend in Southern California, whose wife is a piano teacher. Well, not just a piano teacher but an outstanding piano teacher. Year after year her students have been invariably winning important piano competitions—to the disbelief and envy of other teachers. I visited her studio in Pasadena. She had about 25 students in her classes at the time, the overwhelming percentage of which were Asian. It is precisely these Asian students who have been winning the competitions.

What is the secret, I asked. There is no secret, was the response. These are very talented people who work very hard. They revel in being at the top. They love submerging themselves in culture, especially high culture. What about American students from the main stream, I continued asking. Are they not talented? They are talented, she responded. Otherwise they would not have been here. But they have a different attitude to practice and art. They do not take culture so seriously. Somehow the dominant American culture makes them excel in other things rather than high culture.

I thought it was a bit odd. These Asian students coming from poor emigrant families could excel in Western music, which they did not have in their bones and in their cultural roots, while white Americans, coming from well to-do homes, in which they floated in Western culture (even it was a bit superficial) were unable to do so. The achievement of these Asians kids made me feel puzzled, particularly as they were not only musically gifted, but many of them so bright that they went to top U.S. universities on special scholarships for brilliant students.

What was it in the Asian values that enabled them to do so? What was it in the Asian spirit that motivated them to do so? Why are so many Indians (with degrees from Indian universities) in the Silicon Valley in California, excelling in the very Western game of computer programming? The obvious answers were quite unsatisfactory. I kept searching, hoping that there are deeper answers to these questions somewhere.

I also remember a moment of astonishment, while being in India in 1995. I learnt that the graduating students from Madras Institute of Technology were all hired (100 per cent of them) by foreign countries upon graduation and immediately employed abroad. It should be mentioned that Indian Institutes of Technologies (I.T.T.), of which Madras I.T. is one, are the best and most prestigious universities in India. They are modeled on the M.I.T. of the USA. They admit only the very best of Indian students. Education is free.

After I learnt that the graduates got their jobs abroad, mainly in the West, I thought to myself: "What a success!" But immediately another idea struck my mind: "What a phenomenal waste!" How can a country as poor as India afford to educate their best for free, and then let them go to foreign countries without any compensation? There was something not right in this whole process. The Indians cannot be so bright, on the one hand, on so dumb at the same time. I was puzzled by this dilemma.

2. The Unexpected Emergence of Nandi

In the late 1990's I was in India again. In the precincts of a Shiva Temple, I saw a big standing Shiva. In front of the statue there was a bull carved in the stone, in the sitting position, facing Lord Shiva. The bull in the front of Lord Shiva, in all temples, is called Nandi. He is a protector of Shiva, a servant, a messenger, a symbol of Shiva in so many ways. While his master bristles with restless energy, is full of creative tension, Nandi is passive, is forever watching, being present.

Upon leaving the temple, I looked again at Nandi. He smiled passively, as usual. Yet, when I cast my last glance, his eyes were as if animated, as if he wanted to tell me something. I was in motion, actually passing him. When I did pass him, I thought to myself: How extraordinary was his last glance. I decided to return. I stood in front of him again. The same passive smile, curved in stone. The stone is the stone, it cannot tell you anything. As I was leaving again, I looked from a corner of my eyes. Again there was something animated and revealing in his eyes. I am a tough rationalist. I do not hallucinate. I kept walking. But inside me there was this funny feeling, the realization that Nandi's glance was really revealing.

The days and weeks were passing by. Occasionally the mysterious smile of Nandi would come back. What does it mean, I asked myself. Then I changed the question: Does he want to tell me something? The idea struck me as rather preposterous. Yet from time to time Nandi would appear with a hint of urgency. But I was in no great hurry. Then I changed the question again: Does my sub-consciousness want to tell me something through the agency of Nandi? We all know that statues of either gods or animals do not talk. Yet we are also aware of the power of symbols and myths which work through our subconscious mind. We are aware that much more is going on in our subconscious mind than we can grasp and express. Thus my imagination and subconsciousness were watching. I was also cognizant of Karl's Popper methodology: it does not matter where the answers come from, as long as they are good. After you have got your answers, test them, see how explanatory they are, how much more they explain beyond what we have known already.

All the time, sometimes consciously, sometimes sub-consciously, I was looking for a solution to the dilemma of Western civilization: why has our great technological prowess led us to a consumptive quagmire and the smallness of thinking which subverts our very being? Nandi's appearances and disappearances were in the context of this larger search. Actually I got used to Nandi visiting me. He usually did so when I was in meditative spaces.

After a time—in my meditations or when my mind was not busy-busy with immediate concerns, I started imaginary conversations with Nandi. I found it surprising, to say the least, that he was so forthcoming with his answers. Although these answers came from imaginary dialogues, they should not be dispensed with too easily as futile imagining. These answers struck me as very penetrating and illuminating.

Thus in my meditative states, I called on Nandi to respond to my queries about India, about its curious paradoxes; also about the world at large. One of my questions was: why is India so stupid, well, at least so impractical as to educate its best minds at its best universities and then let them go to be employed by other nations which can well afford to train their own minds? Would it not be simpler and more reasonable to keep these bright and sparkling minds at home and improve the common lot of India?

It is not as simple as that, Nandi responded. We need to take a much broader perspective and employ a much deeper and far-reaching rationality. These young people from I.I.T.'s (let us take this as a classic example) go to America and get reasonable good jobs there. Soon enough they bring their families—whomever they can. As a matter of fact India is exporting a lot of people, with good minds and good genes. These exports are heavily subsidized by India. Imagine that! A poor country like India is subsidizing these exports to rich countries. These good minds and good genes are thrust in cultures which are denuded by materialism, bogged down by a very lowly conception of life. You see (Nandi would continue in a philosophical vein) Western cultures are slowly withering. They need to be renewed somehow. They cannot renew themselves.

I would intervene with my questions: are you telling me that these bright Indians who are going abroad to greener pastures are going there not only for jobs but for a larger mission? Are you proposing to save Western civilization by injecting fresh

Indian blood into its tired veins? Nandi would ignore the sarcasm of my questions and would reply simply. And why not? Except that the mission is not so much to save Western civilization but perhaps replace it with something else.

But you don't have enough people to do that, I would inject, even if your mission had any rhyme or reason.

Yes, he would respond, we have enough people! Our strength is in numbers. We can send 100 million people abroad without being pinched in the slightest in India, whereas 100 million Indians in Europe, or in America, would alter the whole sub-continent and the entire culture.

But why are you sending your best, I would insist. Because (he would reply) the world needs the best to renew itself. I would press: and you are just doing that? Sending people with good minds and good genes? What is this business about good genes?

Nandi was very patient in responding. You are still not grasping the larger perspective. For centuries, ruthless and barbarous armies were invading India and dismembering it. Also exploiting it to the hilt. India has survived it. Because it has had spiritual strength. The materialist and savage giants are still tramping all over the world. But it is their twilight. They are exhausted. The glimpse of a new dawn is on the horizon.

The world must renew itself—humanly, socially, ecologically and spiritually. Otherwise, it will not survive. It will not survive in the Third Millennium. We are not talking about the next ten years, but about a whole millennium. The old empires were sending their moronic armies to suppress our people and to retard our quest for light. We are doing exactly the opposite. We are sending our best not to conquer and suppress but to bring more light and more good energy. You have probably noticed how much energy there is in India—radiant bumptious energy of all kinds; in all kinds of places, among all kinds of people, including the poor. I am not talking about the poverty stricken but ordinary Indians who are poor by Western standards.

I was now intrigued and began to be fascinated by Nandi's story. Yet I kept inquiring. Are you implying, I said, that the Indian mission is, colonization in reverse? Instead of going to other lands to exploit and plunder, you are going there to be good Samaritans, to sacrifice yourself for some greater good?

You have got it right, said Nandi.

I interjected: but is it not too much, too naive and perhaps stupid to do that kind of thing in our selfish world? Besides, you seem to be casting yourself in some kind of messianic role. Isn't it old fashion and perhaps again, a bit stupid?

Nandi was patient again as he responded. You are still operating within the same cynical and limited mind-set. This mind-set is one of the problems of the whole Western civilization. From the standpoint of narrow selfishness, any sacrifice is nonsense. But looking deeper into the matter, we are bound to conclude that this narrow selfishness is nonsense. Just look at the entire history of humanity. Look at the whole evolutionary history, in broad outlines, that is. It is the history of cooperation, participation, give and take; and yes, of sacrifice. Prometheus is so much cherished in Western culture because he showed how through the sacrifice of one individual, so many benefits can be brought to others. Without genuine sacrifice, there is no true progress. I will not belabor the story of the sacrifice as exemplified by Jesus. You should know the meaning of this story well. It is a beautiful story which you Western people should remember.

In the Hindu culture, Shiva is the god of creation and destruction. But he is also a guardian, the god of continuous vigilance. He cannot rest even for one second because then, in this very second, terrible things might happen to the people on earth for whom he is protecting. We may say without much exaggeration that in every culture, right sacrifice is appreciated.

Besides, he continued, we are not going to the West to sacrifice ourselves for merely your benefit. Our mission is to renew the world, to re-dress the balance, to straighten injustices. After centuries of being a whipping boy, destiny is calling us to help to create a new civilization, a new world. Thus, we don't go to America to be a exploited and discarded—as so many emigrants have been. The Indic culture is wiser than that. We go because the historic moment is right to implant the decaying culture with new seeds. Just think. How does a superior culture respond to the butchery of a crude materialist culture which thinks that it is the greatest because it has more war toys than anybody else? Obviously, we do not want to be engaged in any military conflict. Besides, this is not our way. Our way is ahimsa, non-violence. Violence never resolves anything. So we need to respond in a subtle way, as is befitting a superior culture. We send our best as a gift to humanity so that they start new enclaves of new light. These enclaves will grow. We have a lot of people to send. Ours is a rich culture. We have bright minds. We have good energy.

3. Outrageous Claims of Nandi

And Nandi continued. Reflect on this. In Western Europe, the most prosperous and so-called successful countries have a negative demographic growth. They are slowly de-populating by their own will. There is no vitality and no life-energy in these people. By the end of the 21st century, there will be only 10 per cent of white people in the world. By the end of the 23rd century, the white race, as such, will more or less disappear. There will be pockets of white people here and there; and maybe some reservations populated with white people. We need to start preparing now—for the end of the 23rd century, and for the Fourth Millennium. We, the Indic people, want this transition to be peaceful, not violent. We want it to be a transition into light, not a bloody upheaval ending in another journey into darkness. This is why we send our best—to prepare the way.

I listened to Nandi with disbelief, fascination and dismay. Could he be right—I asked myself? After a while I recovered my wits and started asking. Are you saying that because of your genes and superior energy you are going to renew the world? What you are saying is outrageous! You don't seem to know what you are saying! Are you serious when you call India a superior culture? Isn't it an expression of megalomania, of outright racism? Do you think that any intelligent person can accept this arrogance, megalomania, crypto-racism?

Hm... responded Nandi. You are using big words which in effect attempt to intimidate me. I have to tell you again that the picture is much larger than you are allowing for. Megalomania, racism, intolerance. Very charged words. Look at the American civilization, nay the American empire. Don't you see how megalomaniac and puffed up they have been. At every junction they have been telling everybody, either implicitly or explicitly, how great and superior they are. Asian people especially have been treated as third rate pulp. The Americans don't even realize how contemptuous and smug their attitudes have been, particularly to the people of color. This is true racism.

And what did this superior American civilization bring to the world, in addition to various gadgets? Violence! Violence on the screen. Violence in the media. Violence in the family. Violence among children —whereby teenagers are killing without reason, as if possessed by a demon of violence. And finally, globalization as a new world order. Globalism is a new form of violence. It is an old fashion imperialism carried out through economic and electronic means.

We, non-violent people of various colors, want to do it differently. Because finally all of us must do it differently. You cry that our quest is a form of racism. But I beseech you to understand that it is not. Racism is this attitude of the mind (and of the heart) which tries to diminish others for your own sake. Racism is full of hatred and venom. We, in turn, bring love and compassion. We are trying to ameliorate the human lot not by diminishing others but by upgrading the entire human race. We do not benefit from the process. We sacrifice ourselves. This is not racism. When Jesus opposed the corrupt ways of the Pharisees and advocated love as superior and the best way for all, this was not racism. Let us remember this example which should be dear to the Western heart.

I found myself short of breath and out of balance. I said, you are using strange analogies. Besides, do you think that America will ever allow what you are postulating to happen—even if it had a remote chance of happening? Don't you see that what you are preaching is going against the grain of history? Don't you see that dominant thinking outlines an altogether different model of the future? Don't you see that your ideas clash with democracy as it is presently envisaged?

And Nandi responded. I am not going against the grain of history. I am merely pointing out the superficiality of history pursued and promoted by the West. Will America "allow" developments which do not favor its present ideology? By bullying and intimidation, America will try to stop these developments. The big club is not the best instrument for creating a new world order. Violence is a poor substitute for wisdom. America is not as strong as it thinks and pretends to be. The inner fabric is weak and fractured. For this reason alone it needs the new Asian immigrants. In its subconscious mind it welcomes them. The U.S.A. should be actually grateful to these new blood cells coming from India. They are very bright and versatile as it has been shown by their excellence at the top American universities and by winning all kinds of trophies in musical compositions. These Indian cells come from a culture which is tolerant. Indian culture has shown that it can accommodate so much and tolerate so much. When the time of transition comes, from the white mind-set to the non-white mind-set, the Indians will not harbor any grudges, they will seek no revenge. They will be ready for a peaceful transition.

And Nandi continued. This question of democracy would worry me if it were true that my proposals and arguments upset or undermine democracy in its true meaning. On the contrary, my schemes favor universal democracy. When new ideas about society and a new world order are proposed and they happen to be at variance with the American dominant ideology, invariably the shouts are heard from the American camp: It is against democracy, it is against our freedom...even if this freedom signifies exploitation of others.

American democracy has worked for America. But even this proposition is open to doubt. The American democratic system has not worked for the whole society, it has not benefited the majority of the people. It really has worked well for the top 10 per cent of American society, the stratum which controls America, its media, its ideology; and of course, its business and its finance sector. Let us face it, the vested interests of 10 per cent of the people of any country which manipulate the rest of the country and which try manipulate the rest of the world cannot be deemed as a paragon of democracy.

Now the population of the U.S.A. consists of 5.5 per cent of the world population. The top 10 per cent of the people who guide, maneuver and "adjust" the course of American democracy translates as only 0.5 per cent of the global population. A rather modest figure—don't you think? Universal democracy is a system which represents the wishes, needs and aspirations of the world population. Would we wish to consider a world model as truly democratic which is governed by and for the benefit of 0.5 per cent of the world population? This is not an expression but a denial of democracy. Yet this is what America tries to do.

I got overwhelmed by this global talk of Nandi. So I tried to bring him down to more tangible questions. You have mentioned that the future belongs to the Asian mind-set, I said. Yet you have studiously avoided mentioning other Asian nations. What about China?

Yes, China is important, said Nandi, very important. However to become a true leader, it will have to overcome its bad karma of the last 50 years. China is a proud, great and spiritually important country. The last 50 years (for all its historical necessity) represent a fall into an abyss. A kind of partial amnesia has occurred. The mind and especially the soul have been blunted and denuded. China will need to recover its soul. Then, together with India it will be a true leader of people. Incidentally, China is not fully aware of how important the Dalai Lama and Tibetan Buddhism could have become for the restoration of the Chinese psyche and soul. Granting a form of autonomy to Tibet would be, at this time, an act of political wisdom. This could signify the beginning of the big wave of spiritual re-awakening for China. Even as it is, China will play an increasingly significant role in the world. By the year 2035, it will be the most significant nation in the world. But we are talking about the 23rd century and beyond. In centuries to come, an altogether different mind-set and values must prevail.

I interjected, you say so Nandi. But why? What is the reason for it all? You spin out your idealistic dreaming and you expect us to believe it. Do you?

Nandi took quite a while before he responded. You people of excessively rational minds, you have lost the capacity for larger comprehension. Your thinking is so narrow. You think that because things have been so yesterday and today, that they will be so tomorrow and 50 years from now, and 500 years from now. It is just foolish to think so. Things were quite different 500 years ago. You forgot this too. This idiotic pragmatic yardstick which we apply to everything—past, present and the future—is lamentable. It is truly a sign of mental deficiency. You see, Western civilization is stuck. The whole Western culture developed in the last millennium is stuck. It has nowhere to go. It has no other visions, perspectives, alternatives. It is stuck in its consumptive quagmire. Its imagination is denuded, its spiritual substance depleted.

But evolution must go on. And it is not going to be only the evolution of electronic chips or potato chips. There are much greater evolutionary forces than those which can be accommodated within the present pragmatic schemes. Evolution is at a new turning point. After it has experimented, during the last four centuries, with the mechanistic instrumentation of the cosmos and of human life, it is now searching for new ways. It wants to go forward and upward. Evolution is not a trivial thing whose purpose is to evolve more efficient gadgets. Evolution is this tremendous magnificent force which helps to unfold what is hidden in our evolutionary potential, which helps to bring to fruition our evolution, our destiny. It is this evolution, the Mighty Maker of New Forms of Life, the subtle sculptor chiseling within us new sensitivities and new powers of becoming, which is now directing the flow of Asian energy to quietly replace the Western decaying world.

A bit shaken and dejected, I said to Nandi, "I hope you are not right." For if you are, this spells a lot of trouble for the world, especially for the Western world and America in particular; a lot of trauma, pain, fracturing of existing structures.

I thought you were going to say, he responded, "I hope you are right Nandi." For if I am not, the Western world is in really deep trouble. You are completely stuck. In agony. You are already in pain and sufficiently traumatized. You are a culture without visions and perspectives. A civilization unworthy to continue, let alone to lead others.

I interrupted. What you are saying is completely crazy. The West is still very powerful and it has the best minds.

It would seem so on the surface, he responded. But it is not so. The West is not powerful. Look at these disempowered people all around. Look at the economic chaos created by the West. Furthermore, the West does not have the best minds. If it did, it would not have found itself in a sea of intractable problems. Yes, your minds are efficient, purposeful, manipulative. But these are the blind minds. They do not see any larger picture. They are spiritually dead.

I protested. Still, what you are saying is crazy or at least unacceptable from the Western point of view.

This may be so, he agreed. I have come here to deliver the West from its curse, not to listen to your sobbing arguments that you are still so great.

There is so much arrogance in your attitude, I retorted.

Listen, it is not so, he said. I have come here to redress the balance. I don't talk to people who cannot understand. I just do my thing. Which means to bring a thorough renewal to the human race. If you have any complaints, talk to my master, Shiva.

- Shiva? Where is he?
- He is in your heart. He is in the cosmic mind.
- Here we go again. The cosmic mind and the truth of the heart. This is what we call irrational.
- Look, what have you accomplished with your rationality? Hell on Earth. Without the cosmic mind and the truth of the heart, you cannot go anywhere; not in the evolutionary sense. This I know. This my master has taught me well.

And he disappeared, refusing to talk any further. I shouted at him while he was disappearing: "Wait, wait ...! How do we make a new departure to light and grace?"

He whispered from a distance hardly audibly: "The human condition is capable of extraordinary new departures if you listen to your inner wisdom."

12

St. Francis : A Saint for All Traditions

1. The Appeal of St. Francis

Christinity has been in crisis for a number of centuries—at least since Luther. Its acute crisis started in the industrial age, and has accelerated in the technological age. Faced with the cornucopia of the technological abundance which promises salvation through consumption, the Christian churches have shrunk in their reach and responsibility. They have been unable to meet the challenge of growing materialism which emerged in the wake of the triumphant technological world view—which itself declared the world to be a machine manipulated by technological devices to man's advantage.

On another level, the churches have been unable to meet the moral challenges of cynicism, nihilism, and the value vacuum, which have crept in as the companions of material affluence. The overall malaise of the Christian churches has been deepened by the ecological crisis. The simple truth is that Christian teaching is ecologically insensitive. Moreover, some have found the Bible to be a blueprint for ecological destruction.

Within the body of Christian teaching, the Franciscan perspective has been profoundly neglected. St. Francis has always been a source of sustaining power within Christianity, a good shepherd who makes us aware of the power of simplicity. I will attempt to show here that the Franciscan teaching has survived much better than the teaching of orthodox Christianity simply because St. Francis' vision is deeper and more universal than the one officially followed by the church. A return to the Franciscan vision may be a salvation for the Christian churches.

Let me first briefly outline Francis' life and thought. He was born in Assisi in 1182, died in 1226. Thus he lived for only forty-four years. As a young man Francis was ambitious. He dreamed of fame and honor but without any definite idea how fame was to come to him. He enlisted as a voluntary soldier for the war that was being fought at the time between the Papal armies and the German armies, on the island of Sicily in the years 1200—1202. While on the way to the battlefield, he heard strange voices during his sleep, calling him to serve the Lord. He heard the same voice the next day, this time being only half-asleep. The voice urged him to return "to the land of his birth." And so he did. This was the end of his military career, and the beginning of his spiritual quest.

After months of lonely struggles with his soul, while continually praying and often weeping at the Etruscan tombs outside the town of Assisi, he spent a day at St. Peter's church in Rome as a beggar in beggar's clothes with his hand outstretched for alms. Through this experience he found a kinship with the poor. He embraced Lady Poverty.

Now, on the slope of the hill outside the city of Assisi, there stood the little church of San Damiano. Francis took a liking to it. The church was in a sorry state of disrepair. One day while praying there, he heard a voice, "Francis, repair my church." He returned to his father's house, packed a big load of finest cloth, loaded it on the finest horse his father possessed, and went to the market. He sold the cloth and the horse, and brought a considerable amount of money to the priest of San Damiano.

The poor vicar was too frightened to accept the money after he heard the whole story. So Francis left an urn with the money on a window sill. Upon returning to Assisi after his journey, Francis' father Pietro Bernardone learned about his son's "theft." He got furious. He decided to try Francis before the magistrate of Assisi. Francis refused the summons, declaring that being a man dedicated to religion, he was not subject to the civic authorities but only to the bishop.

Thus, Bishop Guido was to preside over the trial of Francis in the cathedral of Assisi. On the day of the trial, Francis duly appeared. When remonstrated by the bishop to return the money to his father, Francis said: "My lord, I will gladly give back to him not only his money, but all my clothes I have had of him." Then he took off all the clothes he wore. Stark naked, he put his clothes in front of the bishop.

This act required more than courage. This was an extraordinary act of confronting wealth and authority with ones naked body in the middle of a cathedral. This was an act declaring: Here I am at God's tribunal, and may frail human justice tremble in the face of deeds done on behalf of the needy and the oppressed—even if they violate the existing legal codes. The rest of Francis' life was a continuation of the dramatic encounter at Assisi cathedral. The essence of the Franciscan legacy can be expressed simply:

- Confront injustice and human misery directly. He who does not speak on the behalf of the oppressed, contributes to the crime.
- Redistribution of wealth is our responsibility. The unjustified accumulation of wealth by some is the root cause of miseries of others.
- We stand before God's tribunal, which ultimately means the tribunal of our conscience. To this tribunal of our conscience we are ultimately responsible, particularly as the existing laws so often protect and favor the rich at the expense of the poor.
- Have the courage of being naked. Ultimately you are naked. No garment should muffle the voice of your conscience.
- Have the courage of simplicity. For this simplicity can release from within you great spiritual powers which are numbed by your slavery to mindless overconsumption.

There is no question that Francis was in advance of his age, as he anticipated all that is liberal and sympathetic in modern times: the love of nature, the love of animals, the sense of social compassion, the sense of the spiritual dangers of affluence. Of various aspects of his important legacy, the most important for us is the Franciscan ecological or ecological-spiritual legacy. The worship of nature was for Francis a part of the overall ecological spirituality. We thus hear these incantations expressed in "The Canticle of Brother Sun":

Be praised, my Lord, through Sister Water,
who is very useful and humble and precious and pure.
Be praised, my Lord, through Sister Moon and the stars,
in the heavens you formed them clear and precious and beautiful.
Be praised, my Lord, through Brother Wind
and through Air and Cloud and fair and all Weather,
by which you nourish all that you have made.
Be praised, my Lord, through Brother Fire,
by whom you light up the night;
he is beautiful and merry and vigorous and strong.
Be praised, my Lord, with all your creatures,
especially Sir Brother Sun,
who is day and by him you shed light upon us.
He is beautiful and radiant with great splendor,
of you, Most High, he bears the likeness.

Because of his extraordinary sense of empathy with all creation, because of his gaiety, romantic imagination and universal camaraderie, not only Christians but people of all religions who are acquainted with his teachings are drawn to Francis.

St. Francis' discourses were not numerous, not elaborate, let alone learned. He did not produce anything comparable to the *Summa Theologica* of Thomas Aquinas. He did not produce any systematic theology. His was the vision of the heart, speaking directly to the heart of others.

Francis was not the first man to make voluntary poverty an enormous shining virtue. The Buddha embraced the same ideal 1,800 years before Francis. He too renounced all the riches of earthly splendor; abandoned his palace, his wife, his son, and in beggar's clothes went to seek salvation and redemption. In our century, Mahatma Gandhi, inspired by Hindu ideals, followed a path of simplicity very similar to that of Francis. Those saints of other religions do not diminish Francis. On the contrary, in their company Francis shines as a universal being, as a cosmic being. For the ideals he proclaimed ring true in all major spiritual traditions of humanity. Francis is the saint for all religions. Among Christian saints, Francis is the most popular and most liked.

2. The Road Not Taken

It was a misfortune for Western culture and Western Christianity that it chose the path of Thomas Aquinas and not the path of St. Francis. From the beginning, St. Francis was an extraordinary challenge to the Roman Church, and an extraordinary inspiration to simple Christians. He was on the verge of being excommunicated more than once. He was canonized very soon after his death—in order to avoid a split within the Church. To co-opt him as a saint was a way of blunting the poignancy of his message—that the life of a Christian should be one following Christ's simplicity.

For a couple of centuries after his death, the Franciscan way was alive and vibrant, if only among ordinary people. Then came Martin Luther with his challenge. And then came the Council of Trent of 1545-1563, which tried to find a radical and satisfactory response to Luther. Since the Trent Council, Thomist Christianity has prevailed, and the Franciscan vision has been pushed aside. Why? The reason is not a direct one.

It was not the case that the Bishops of Trent loved Aquinas more than St. Francis. The great problem of the time was how to contain Luther. There were many tricky and muddled theological problems, and Aquinas was so clear in spelling out the Christian doctrines. His vision of Christianity won.

The power to define is the power to control. Thomist Christianity is based on the power of the word, which is the power of the mind. Franciscan Christianity, on the other hand, is based on the power of love, which is the power of the heart. Within the Christian tradition, the mind has prevailed over the heart. And Christianity has become brainy, abstract, wordy—and void of heart. This is our dilemma nowadays, of the whole Western civilization: we are clever and brainy. But our hearts have atrophied.

The mystical trends within Christianity were flourishing until the time of St. Thomas Aquinas. However, as time passed, the rational attitude began to prevail. Aristotle replaced Plato as the foundation of Christianity. Thomist theology is Aristotelian through and through.

Thus Christianity repeats the road of ancient Greek philosophy. We need to remember that earlier Greek philosophies, including that of Socrates and Plato, revelled in holism and bathed in the all-pervading sense of mystery surrounding us. Before Aristotle's time, the logos of Pythagoras and Plato was all encompassing, was in fact a total divine matrix for deciphering the meaning of the cosmic laws. We should be aware that for the Phythagoreans mathematics was suffused in divinity.

With Aristotle we begin the quest for analytical clarity. For the sake of this clarity, things are cut up and parcelled off. Rational justification and analytical definitions are arrived at at the expense of depth, mystery and wholeness.

In the early Middle Ages, mystical interpretations of Christianity abound. The twelfth and thirteenth century mystics have left quite an inspiring and important legacy. Many of these mystics were excommunicated and officially condemned by the proclamations of the Vatican.

St. Francis was one of the mystics. He recognized that the power of the heart is greater than the power of the mind, that the power of things unseen is greater than that of things seen, that the power of simplicity, of frugality, of giving, is more significant than the capacity for acquiring and luxuriating in earthly splendor.

Franciscan powers are exactly those preached by Jesus Christ. Thus Francis will always remain relevant, appealing, and inspiring to those who take the teaching of Jesus seriously. Francis will continually remain a challenge, if not a thorn, to the institution of the Church, particularly when this institution insists on the primacy of the doctrine over the understanding of the heart.

The attitude towards mysticism in the Western world is thoroughly ambiguous. We are uneasy with mystics. They are just not "rational" enough. Our whole culture has been sanitized by rationality. Anything holistic, deep, mysterious, let alone mystical, is often condemned as irrational. We need to remind ourselves of what Albert Einstein says about the mysterious: "The most beautiful thing we can experience is the mysterious."

We have found of late that rationality is a poor substitute for spirituality. So the great question that confronts us is: was the Western mind so made that it had to develop its discursive logos with its distinctive, hard-cutting rationality? Or is this rationality the result of following Aristotle and not Plato? And later that we followed Thomas Aquinas and not St. Francis? I believe that the latter is the case. Whom we follow has enormous consequences for our lives.

Had we followed the Franciscan way, the devastations of nature would not have occurred, and the devastations of our individual lives would not have happened—the two are aspects of the same phenomenon. The Franciscan teaching that all beings in creation are our brothers and sisters is a very powerful and inspiring guide of how to treat nature.

This is what the Native American Indian cultures have believed and followed to the benefit of ecological systems for millennia, until they were ravaged by European settlers. It may be said that all creatures are sacred and are our brothers and sisters in creation. The Franciscan way would have precluded the destruction of nature from the outset. For nature is not a thing "out there" given to us for our use, but a part of our outer self. The Franciscan way would have brought with it a different form of perception, a different form of thinking (which I call reverential thinking) and consequently different paradigms of what is good and effective action.

In 1979, Pope John Paul II proclaimed St. Francis as the Patron Saint of Ecologists. Which was very nice. But more a gesture than the beginning of a substantive change in the policy and teaching of the Church. As I have already mentioned, Francis was canonized very soon after his death. One suspects a similar thing happened when Francis was proclaimed the patron saint of ecologists. The Vatican seems to be saying: "You have now got St. Francis as your patron. You should regard this as an indication.that the Church cares for ecology." However, in order to make Francis a part of the living Christian liturgy, and a part of the actual lives of actual Christians, much more is needed than making St. Francis a patron saint of ecologists.

For the main problem still remains. This is the problem of elevating the human person above all other creatures, and giving the human the dominion over every living thing that creepeth on this Earth. If we are to acquire ecological consciousness we need to alter fundamentally the nature of this teaching. We need much more than the conviction of the sacredness of the human person. Unless this sacredness is extended to other creatures, the gulf will always remain between us and the rest of creation.

There is no easy way to translate the ethics based on the Ten Commandments into meaningful ecological action as long as the human is on the pedestal. In these reinterpretations St. Francis should be our guide. For he represents a new promise for Christianity. It was not only possible for him but indeed inevitable to celebrate the sacredness of the human and the sacredness of all other beings.

From his visions and views concerning the oneness and sacredness of all creation we can derive new, ecologically sound Christian ethics. A new encyclical should be introduced by the Pope proclaiming that all creatures are sacred. We should all work towards this end— by making the Church aware that unless all nature and its creatures are declared sacred, we do not have a solid ethical basis for a radical healing of the planet. Nor is there a basis for eliminating environmental pollution—which is now a more serious threat to the future of human kind than the possibility of a nuclear holocaust.

If we lose the environment, we lose God.

13

The World as a Sanctuary

1. Each Epoch has its Unique Problems

Christianity emerged in order to solve some important problems which the crumbling Roman Empire could not solve. The disintegration of social and individual life in fourth and fifth century Rome was at least partly caused by the fact that the centre did not hold. There was no centre any more; no matrix to support the spiritual life and sustain deeper human aspirations and visions. Christianity created a new centre, and with it a new spiritual matrix. Out of this centre and this matrix grew a new civilization, a new social order, and a new conception of humankind. For a millennium the Christian paradigm held well. From the sixteenth century on it has been holding less well—new problems emerged to which Christianity could not provide an adequate response. As a result new philosophies and ideologies were created to solve specific problems of their epochs.

Marxism emerged in the nineteenth century to solve some important problems. In the epoch of growing prosperity, of enlightened reason and progress triumphant, it was an insult to human dignity and human reason itself that so many people would live in the squalor produced by the satanic mills of the industrial revolution—which exploited them ruthlessly and shamelessly. Social justice was an imperative following from the premises of enlightened reason. At least Marx thought so, and he set himself to rectify the undesirable social conditions which, in his opinion, were responsible for the injustice, squalor, and misery.

The pursuit of the idea of social justice, about which Marxism has been so adamant and passionate, brought about redressing the social balance very considerably, in some countries with paradoxical consequences. In the U.S. we witness a pathological inversion. The working class has become one of the most conservative and selfish, quite oblivious of the idea of social justice. The paradox is that although Marxism (as a global ideology of social justice) has helped the American working class most, this class is the least aware of it and the least receptive to it. There are of course some other "mechanisms" which are responsible for this state of affairs—such as the program of "buying out" the working class, which in the U.S. has been quite successful.

As history unfolds, new problems emerge. In the second part of the twentieth century problems emerged to which neither Christianity nor Marxism offer an adequate response. As the power of technology has grown, so has our domination of nature, to the point that the whole process has backfired on us. Our dominion has become our colony, which we have plundered and polluted beyond belief.

In both Christianity and Marxism, nature is considered a dominion—given to us for our use. The language may be different in each case, but the basic premise is the same. Nature and environment are for us: it is a dominion given by God (Christianity); it is a natural resource which we can and should use for the amelioration of humankind (Marxism).

Christianity and Marxism are identical in elevating the human species above all other species and in disregarding the subtle mesh of unity and solidarity that prevails among all creatures. For this reason both Christianity and Marxism have been taken by surprise by the magnitude of the ecological crisis. Neither of them has found an adequate response, on a deep conceptual and moral level.

Incidentally, Buddhism and Taoism (and Hinduism to a large degree) are much less in a bind with regard to environmental problems. The essential unity with all living beings is an underlying assumption of these doctrines. It follows from them that only a stupid person departs from the Tao (the right path), and in the process causes the destruction of other forms of life and finally our own. Only an unseeing, unenlightened, and partly blind person will cause harm to others without realizing that this harm will come back through the law of *karma* (Buddhism, Hinduism, Jainism). Thus in the very structure of perception of oriental cultures, in their foundations, lie deep and far-reaching responses to the problems of ecological crisis.

In Western culture we have departed from this unitary scheme of things altogether. We have lost the sense of unity. The return to original God-the-Father may be a path of individual redemption but it is not a path of ecological restoration. The return to a pristine version of Communism (which some identify with the early primitive Christianity) may be a path to social justice and a new social equilibrium but not a path to an ecological restoration.

During the last decade many Christian thinkers and theologians have become acutely aware of the missing ecological dimension of the Bible and of the Christian teaching at large. Thus some new interpretations of the Bible were offered, according to which the word *dominion* must be handled carefully—it is not the realm of exploitation but one of stewardship; we are responsible for the well-being of other creatures and not for their extinction. One of the most remarkable efforts in this direction was the creation of the Eleventh Commandment Fellowship, which publishes its own journal and offers an ecological interpretation of Christianity. The eleventh commandment reads as follows:

The Earth is the Lord's and the fullness thereof:

Thou shall not despoil the Earth, nor destroy life thereon.

The founders of the group (which was chiefly inspired by Father Vincent Rossi, the director general of the Holy Order of *Mans*) are not satisfied with spelling out the commandment. They want to make it a part of our daily life. Thus they inspire and admonish us:

Make the Eleventh Commandment the foundation of your personal ethic of the environment.

Learn all you can about the ecological crisis so that you will be able to make informed choices.

Become familiar with the many ecologically appropriate techniques, practices and devices that are being developed. Find ways to use them in your own life.

Yet this is still an isolated voice, almost a voice crying in the wilderness.

The new ecological Weltanschauung has been emerging: a conception of the universe that is open and in part mysterious. New wholistic forms of understanding have been slowly spreading. A new conception of the Earth as alive (Gaia) has met with much sympathy. The rethinking of our entire Western heritage along ecological lines has been under way.

Within the newly-emerging ecological perspective the world is to be conceived as a SANCTUARY. Knowledge is to be conceived as an intermediary between us and the creative forces of evolution; not as a set of ruthless tools for atomizing nature and the cosmos, but as ever more subtle devices for helping us to maintain our spiritual and physical equilibrium.

2. Objective Thinking and Ecological Thinking

Let us be clearly aware that our fundamental problem is not so much polluting factories and poisoned environments, but polluted thinking. Simply put, these factories are an extension of our thinking. We have developed an uncaring mind, really a polluting mind, and the result is careless thinking. Careless thinking creates polluting technologies and poisoned environments. We have to look at the whole process and not only a part of it. To think of how to diminish pollution while continuing to design polluting technologies is not a solution, but augments our problem. We have to see that the links of the causal chain are intimately connected and support each other:

World view influences thinking and vice versa; thinking influences technology and vice versa; technology influences products and vice versa; products influence environment and vice versa.

Because of our excessive specialization and atomization, we have often considered the links of the chain as separate. When we have connected them, our attention was limited to the last three links of the chain, quite forgetting that they were the result of the first two links.

The scientific-technological worldview conceives the universe as a clock-like mechanism. This we know. But we are less aware that the scientific worldview, and its ways of reading the universe, produces its own specific thinking which we call scientific and objective thinking. This form of thinking is good for solving differential equations and for manipulating the world as if it were a machine. This form of thinking does not know the meaning of love, compassion, and caring. In short, objective thinking is harsh and uncaring. Our ecological habitats, the health of our environments, the warmth and harmony of human relationships require a different form of thinking: caring, compassionate, loving.

Humanizing our harsh objective thinking is not enough, is simply not sufficient, and never will be sufficient while objective thinking is the established, sanctified form of social praxis and of general education.

Let us say it quite clearly: as long as we adhere to the scientific worldview and hold it as sacrosanct, as long as we consider objective thinking as the paradigm of all thinking and the most valid form of thinking, we shall of necessity create polluting minds which will go on creating destructive technologies which, in their turn, will devastate our environments.

We need to change the mode of our thinking. We need to develop systematically, and on the level of the whole culture, a new kind of thinking which I call *ecological thinking* which will be the foundation of the healing mind. Already many years ago Albert Einstein prophetically said: "We shall require substantially new manner of thinking if mankind is to survive." We have been slow in recognizing the necessity of this kind of thinking.

Changing the mode of our thinking and the entire cast of our mind is a condition *sine qua non* for stopping ecological devastations and social deterioration. The ecological degradation in the long run leads to the social deterioration and impairment of general health at large.

The healing of our environment requires the healing form of thinking and the healing form of mind. What are the main characteristics of this ecological thinking?

1. It is *wholistic* thinking, which is supremely aware that the whole is more than the sum of its parts; that the nature of the whole so often determines the characteristics of the parts;

that there are subtle interconnections between parts which so often evade the grasp of our analytical tools.

2. It is *reverential* thinking, which makes us aware that things are not only what they appear to be in their physical existence but that they have inherent worth and beauty which goes beyond the physical. Treating all forms of life with respect and reverence, as unique creations of the intelligent cosmos, is a precondition of the ecological reconstruction. Reverential thinking has been practiced in many cultures under a variety of names. Therefore it is not something alien to us but, on the contrary, an essential dimension of our being which brings wholeness to our own life and assures us of harmony with the rest of creation. This form of thinking is particularly prevalent in Buddhist cultures. "There is a Buddha in a blade of grass." This is a figurative way of saying: behold every form of life as sacred. The harmonious meshing with the rest of creation cannot be achieved by employing the mode of thinking that systematically cuts, dissects, analyzes in a cold detached manner, but by an empathetic identification with others; and this is what reverence is about.

3. It is *participatory* thinking. Objective thinking atomizes and disengages us from the larger context of our inquiry and indeed from the larger context of the universe. Participatory thinking, on the contrary, engages us, makes us belong. The framework of participation is joyous because it is united by the bond of solidarity. Participation is the song of creation. Participation is the song of our individual experience. Participation is the glue of social solidarity. To be alive is to sail on the wings of participation. To be morose is to have one's wings of participation clipped.

Thus participatory thinking is crucial to the ecological reconstruction and to social cohesion. In the long run we shall develop a whole new branch of enquiry which will be called the methodology of participation which will supplant, and often replace, the methodology of objectivity. The methodology based on objectivity is actually a young upstart while the methodology of participation is the oldest that has ever been practiced—it is the methodology of life alive. When life discovered the meaning of participation, it discovered the most important modus of its growth. (For further discussion see my *Participatory Mind*, Penguine, 1994).

Ecological thinking is still in infancy, as far as our technological society is concerned; it has been practiced in older cultures. We are our own shepherds. We are responsible for the destiny of the whole planet, of the whole universe. This responsibility clearly spells out care, respect, nurturing of all there is. Ecological thinking is an inherent part of this process of nurturing.

3. "Ecological Person" Versus "Faustian Person"

Careless technology and uncaring/objective thinking create loveless human beings. During the last two centuries we have inadvertently hatched and cultivated "Faustian person" who only lives once, and therefore lives dangerously and at whosoever's expense, even if it means at the expense of future generations. Our Faustian person is a product of the scientific worldview which encourages us to be skeptical and cynical towards everything that smacks of higher values. So Faustian person is cynical, but ultimately lonely and alienated and frustrated; and finally angry inside. This frustration and anger pushes him to try anything (you only live once). So he tries hard drugs and gambles his destiny in the process. You only live once. When there are no higher gods and no higher values, human beings drift. And then they indulge in drugs—for kicks, as a recreation, a way of killing the meaningless reality.

The meaninglessness of present society is the combined result of "objective/scientific" worldview, of the value vacuum or the nihilism of values, and of the Faustian view of man.

Fortunately, this Faustian view is gradually replaced by a new conception, which I call "ecological person," who does not shy away from spirituality for he/she knows that without it his/her life is incomplete, and who sees the universe as meaningful and beautiful—a wonder of creation that produces other wondrous creations.

The ecological person is highly sensitive to the web of ecological and social relationships, and is persuaded that the richness of life consists of entering the various webs of life and participating in them fully and compassionately. Participating always implies responsibility. By assuming responsibility, the ecological person is empowered and becomes the master of his/her destiny.

The ecological person does not reject or ignore rationality, but is not intimidated by experts and specialists, as he looks at the universe through unifying glasses. With compassion and reverence, he/she weaves the self into significant webs of life. Such persons are not alone for they know that the universe is our home. They live in the participatory universe, which responds to the co-creative participatory mind.

This conception signals the return to great spiritual traditions of the past but cannot identify completely with any of these traditions, for this new kind of human being lives in a different world and has a different psyche.

The ecological person is aware of the value of Christianity, Buddhism, and Hinduism, of Marxism and technological progress, but realizes that in the third Millennium we live in a world fundamentally different from other epochs. No other epoch knew the meaning of exploding galaxies and black holes, of sub-atomic particles, of strange weird things such as quarks, of the energy contained in matter, and of the exploding nature in the equation $E = mc^2$. We have exploded it all and we have to put it all together. The task is enormous but so is our imagination and will to do so.

We cannot return to the pious submissiveness of early or even mature Christianity. Nor can we return to the Faustian dream of Marx, who conceived of humans as the conquerers of history and the conquerors of other species. We are not conquerors but an immensely curious species which was given an immensely important mandate. The mystery of our existence and the mystery of the universe should not mystify or bewilder us but inspire to weave ever deeper designs on the crest of mystery. "Life is a faint tracing on the surface of mystery," Annie Dillard wrote.

The ecological person in the participatory universe signifies the miracle of life acknowledged and cherished in the manifoldness of our being. As we unfold and transcend, we employ our rationality to elucidate our spirituality, and we use our spirituality to deepen our rationality. The new perspective offered to us by the ecological worldview may be the twilight of the mechanistic millennium, but it is also the dawn of the age of becoming, in which our destiny will be realized by assuming the responsibility verging on the cosmic, because we are cosmic.

14
Ecological Dharma

Philosophy, as envisioned by Socrates and Plato, was a quest for a meaningful, worthwhile life. Although this quest has been gradually eliminated from the concerns of Western philosophy, it has never been abandoned within the Indian tradition, which has often pursued philosophy as a path to *moksha* (liberation) or as a guide to human destiny. This view of philosophy has been the strength of the Indian tradition and is quite close to the meaning of the term *dharma*.

Dharma has many shades of meaning, but it is essentially a guide on the path of right duty. Dharma spells out our obligation to become liberated. Response to it, as the voice of our inner conscience, requires deep philosophical sensitivity. We also need new insights to see new realms of our *dharma*—our responsibilities in the world. Those who are most sensitive and seeing now perceive that the most important aspect of our present *dharma* is saving the earth.

1. Ecology of Mind

The idea of ecology has been around for a quarter of a century. We have become used to it. We consider its ramifications good, namely, to have clean air, clean water, clean soil. But ecology is much deeper and more far-reaching than cleaning up polluted physical environments. While cleaning the environment is important, it is only a small part of the task. For what are ultimately responsible for the polluted planet are not dirty technologies, but polluted minds—careless, unseeing, alienated. Contaminated minds produce, almost of necessity, contaminated environments.

The present condition of humanity is forlorn, as we dwell in polluted physical, mental, and spiritual environments. Our minds so often resemble a garbage container rather than a beautiful, shining instrument of God. We need to purify ourselves in many ways. Traditional *poojas*, or propitiation ceremonies, are insufficient.

The ecology of mind is still in its infancy. Let us be aware that we need to purify our minds, not through some old-fashioned rituals, but through something more drastic but also more lasting. We need to change the whole structure of our consciousness, which is programmed to manipulation, mechanistic thinking, and an instrumental treatment of people and nature. In effect, we need to create the reverential mind, something I have discussed at length in my book *Living Philosophy* (Penguin, 1992).

The contaminated, mechanistic mind has weakened and sometimes contaminated the sources of our spiritual life. This mind has separated us from the sacred. It has weakened our spiritual life both on the individual level and on the level of whole cultures. By allowing contamination of our minds, we dim our intelligence and blunt our sensitivities, thus making our lives less radiant and more obtuse. Ultimately we are diminished as persons. This consequence is of great importance but usually unappreciated.

We seldom realize that the contaminated physical environment is a shadow of the contaminated mental and spiritual environments. A true ecology heals all three environments simultaneously—physical, mental, and spiritual. Thus our *dharma* must be extended and deepened to include new realms.

Our most important task is both to clean the earth and to cleanse ourselves from mental pollution. Our minds are as polluted as our air, our rivers, and our soil. Preserving the wholeness of the earth and the integrity of our souls is a twofold aspect of our present *dharma*.

2. Green Dharma

Dharma therefore acquires a distinctly green or ecological dimension. Whatever may divide us—our cultures, our tongues, our religions, our economic systems—one thing nevertheless unites us. It is our ecology—our care of the earth, our care of future generations, and our care for the welfare of all sentient beings.

It is not sufficient nowadays to care for yourself and your personal spiritual well-being or even that of your religious community. You must extend this care to the entire earth, for it is your dwelling, your temple, your *sangha*, your vessel in which spiritual attainments can be perfected on your way to Bodhisattvahood and Buddhahood.

If we lose the environment, if we destroy the earth, we lose the way to God or *Nirvana*. We destroy the ground for all possibilities of becoming spiritual and, ultimately, enlightened beings. Previous Buddhas, including Gautama, were less aware of the frailty of the planet earth as the ground for cultivating our humanity and our spirituality. But if this ground is denied, our spiritual journey comes to an end.

Hence the importance of ecological *dharma*, not only for the preservation of the earth, but for the preservation of the conditions that enable us to become fully human, thus enabling us to follow the path of the Buddha or the path of Shiva or the path of Krishna. Seen in this light, ecological *dharma* has an importance second to none. If you are a spiritual person, you must care about ecology, for the earth is your spiritual cradle. **In our times, the ecological and the spiritual become one.** To revere the Buddha or Krishna is to work for the salvation and healing of the planet.

True prayer and true meditation in our time become ecological prayer, which helps to heal all other beings, including the forests, soil, and rivers. This new form of redemption—ecological redemption—is truly universal in nature. It is based on compassion for all beings, all of whom are threatened by our excessive technological activity. To see what is most important for the welfare of all sentient beings (and semisentient beings such as the soil and forests), to see what is most important for our inner peace and our ascent toward Buddhahood, we need a new perspective, the ecological perspective, and a new form of *dharma*, ecological *dharma*.

3. The Dharma of Ecological Philosophy

Much of the present teaching of both Hinduism and Buddhism is steeped in the past, and much of it is a repetition of old dogmas. Non-attachment is by and large a noble and liberating principle. But we need to reexamine its meaning in view of the importance of ecological *dharma*. We must beware of being too detached from the earth. On the contrary, we need to "cling to the earth," though that phrase may alarm some orthodox Hindus or Buddhists. To care for the earth by working for its healing and salvation means to be attached to the earth, though we may say that it is not a selfish attachment. Ecological *dharma* calls for a new reflection on, and indeed a significant revision of, ancient spiritual traditions, including Hinduism, Buddhism, and Christianity.

Ecological *dharma* informs us that the road leading to right livelihood is ecological reconstruction: working close to nature, bringing back labour-intensive occupations, and, in general, working for an ecological catharsis. Right livelihood is essential to our spiritual well-being. Unless we find the road leading us to right livelihood—not only for a select few but for countless millions—we cannot claim that our spiritual message is relevant to our times. Wrong livelihood is destroying people's souls and is undermining the sustainability of the planet.

What is the specific *dharma* of ecological philosophy? It is to reassure us that philosophy is not dead but that, in fact, it has a most important role to play in our time, when wisdom has been replaced by information. Another aspect of the dharma of eco-philosophy is moral guidance. Modernism and postmodernism have disintegrated in the quicksand of nihilism and moral confusion. Traditional philosophy has not been able to help us in combatting this moral decay. Ecological philosophy proposes new imperatives for right moral action and for the moral regeneration of the individual. Moral regeneration is a most important part of our spiritual regeneration.

Yet another, perhaps the most important, aspect of the *dharma* of eco-philosophy is understanding that the ecology of mind, the ecology of the spirit, and the ecology of the physical environment are aspects of one another. The pollution of physical environment inevitably leads to the pollution of the mind and the spirit. And at the same time, the degradation of physical environment is a consequence of polluted minds and sullied souls.

Ecological philosophy is itself a form of *dharma*. Once you understand things with all their interconnections, you must act to bring them back to a right alignment. To understand aright is to act aright. The *dharma* of ecological philosophy tells us that we must put our own house in order.

The *dharma* of ecological philosophy also instructs us that all of us must be teachers. We must spread the light, in spite of all obstacles and the crippling influence of darkness. Right education is the foundation of right awareness, which in turn is the foundation of all right thinking and right action. Right education is the implementation of the right values. An ancient Chinese expression says, if you are preparing for one year, plant rice; if you are preparing for twenty-five years, plant trees; if you are preparing for a hundred years, plant right education.

The *dharma* of ecological philosophy, in a nutshell, is singing the right song with the unfolding universe, which is beautiful but fraught with dangers and pitfalls. May we have enough courage to bear the light that is required of us to make the universe luminous and kind.

Our times call for new resources of imagination, for new resources of inner power to meet the unprecedented peril to the life of the planet and to our own spiritual lives. The two are aspects of each other. A new ecological *dharma* is called for. This *dharma* requires that we be passionately attached to the earth, which of course does not mean a childish clinging to material possessions and their consumption.

The practice of universal compassion in our times requires work of ecological reconstruction and healing unprecedented in history. As the ecological crisis has brought about a sea of suffering, ecological cleansing is the vehicle for the cessation of suffering. Ecology is the noble truth of our time. Eco-philosophy is the *dharma* of our time.

4. Ecology as a Religious Responsibility

On September 26, 1986, thousands of people from all over the world came to Assisi and filled the Basilica of St. Francis and the surrounding area. This was not the periodic annual pilgrimage on St. Francis' birthday. The occasion was much more auspicious. Five major religions—Buddhism, Christinnity. Hinduism, Judaism and Islam—came together in a spirit of unprecedented harmony, to pledge their allegiance to the Earth. During the Assisi Congress it was declared, and since reiterated, that the well-being of the Earth, and its preservation for the sake of future generations, is a spiritual responsibility for all religions.

Religious people disagree on many points. But on this issue they all seem to be in emphatic agreement: that the healing and the preservation of the Earth is our common responsibility, not only for our economic benefit (so that the Earth continues to feed us), but out of our understanding of the holiness of the planet and all its creatures.

To worship God truly in our times is to save the planet. If we lose the environment, we lose God. Healing both the planet and ourselves has today become spiritual work of the first magnitude. Whatever our race and religion, ecology connects us all together. Thus ecology is the religious project of our times. The idea of redemption acquires a new meaning: it means redeeming the world by healing the Earth, since healing the Earth is the spiritual work of our time. This means that to understand religious devotion is to recognize that all religions are forms of worshipping the beauty and integrity of the planet.

This approach could be a point of departure and renewal for many spiritual traditions. It could be the basis for our unity. And what could be more worthy of our collective purpose than working together to save our Earth and implicitly ourselves? Without the vibrant Earth we shall cease to exist.

Spirituality is also, and has always been, the realization of our inner potential, the actualization of the God within us. We need to treat each other according to what we can potentially become: divine lights uplifting ourselves and helping others to heal, to integrate, to become more reverential. But working on ourselves to release and articulate our inner divinity, and working in the outside world to heal the Earth are complementary aspects of ecological spirituality. Instead of the quietistic forms of spirituality which are favoured by many religions, this involves a participatory form of spirituality, a spirituality which resolves itself in the acts of healing in everyday life.

Part of this new spirituality, which I call ecological spirituality, is a new kind of prayer, which I call ecological prayer. Praying to Absolute Deities endowed with divine attributes is well and good. But to save the integrity and beauty of creation, we need to be engaged in ecological prayer. Ecological prayer is acting out the ecological dimension of our existence, and bringing all beings into the campus of our well-wishing. It is bringing a meditative attitude to our daily activities which helps to heal on all levels of being, and is thus a form of ethics in action, based on solidarity and on compassion, and leading to a larger harmony in the long run.

It should be clear that ecological spirituality has a distinctively practical dimension, continually asking us the following questions: How do you work on yourself so that you heal within? So that you heal your mind? So that you become a source of health and support for others? How do you help to heal the diseased educational system, the malfunctioning and carcinogenic social and political structures? How do you help to heal the Earth in your immediate vicinity? How can your lifestyle help to maintain the equilibrium in distant parts of the world by not contributing to frivolous over-consumption?

All these questions are both practical and spiritual at the same time. They require a new kind of awareness, a new kind of commitment, a new kind of yoga. What I am describing is a common religious project for our times. Let us unite together in the common service to Mother Earth, in one stupendous ecological prayer. Then the gods will help us. We need to help the gods so that they can help us. We need to engage in Ecological Dharma, so that the Buddhas bless us in this new holy act. We need to help God—of the Hebrews, Christians, and Muslims—so that God helps us to make God's Earth green and blessed again.

5. A New Response is Required to the Principle of Non-Attachment

As we examine the causes of the ecological crisis, we realize that we are truly in an unprecedented and precarious situation.

Not only have we upset the natural balance of the Earth so that renewal has become difficult. We have also caused immense suffering to the Earth, to all its creatures, and to human beings. This is a new form of suffering, of a kind and on a scale unknown in earlier times.

We have invented so many chemicals which are added to the products we use daily: the food we eat, the fabrics we wear, the paints we use in our houses. So many of these chemicals have a poisonous residue. We are being slowly poisoned in a subtle but unprecedented way. Our health is being undermined, our well-being diminished, our worries and anxieties increased. The diseases of civilization are afflicting more and more people even (and especially!) in prosperous countries.

The lifestyle which accompanies the ecological crisis is one of continuous tension, which comes about as a result of the omnipresence of stress. Stress is one of the new forms of suffering and a killer in our times. Systematic poisoning of various kinds (of food, of the air, of the water we drink) and systematic stress which seems to be people's daily companion, cause a deep sea of suffering unknown in previous history. We must be able to address ourselves to this suffering in a relevant way, by engaging in relevent prayer. Then the Gods will help us. We need to help the Gods so that they can help us.

As compassionate beings who wish, and have the duty, to help other sentient beings, we cannot be oblivious towards those new forms of suffering. Ecological prayer is a new form of prayer, and it outlines a new form of dharma, the dharma of healing— and caring for the Earth.

During a dialogue with Tibetan Buddhists at Dharamsala in April 1991, I chose as my main subject Ecological Dharma. I proposed that *dharma* in our times acquires a distinctly green shade, an ecological dimension. It is not sufficient nowadays to take care of our spiritual well-being, to care about our religious community. We must extend this care to the entire Earth. We cannot be too detached from the Earth, because then we can lose the Earth all together. We need to cling to the Earth. Now the idea of clinging to the Earth and of questioning the principle of non-attachment alarmed many of the learned monks present at the symposium. The opposition to this idea became so heated that I was bound to say: "You seem to be very attached to your principle of non-attachment." The monks got my point immediately.

Needless to say, we have to tread very carefully when we propose "clinging to the Earth" and when we propose a re-examination of the principle of non-attachment. Yet the main point I wish to make is this: We need to cling to the Earth much more passionately than we cling to traditional scriptures. This point applies to all religions. Clinging to the scriptures while the Earth is in distress may not be the appropriate way of participating in divinity.

How should we view the principle of non-attachment in our times? It can be viewed either as a renunciation of the world, or as deeper participation in the world. The Buddha himself chose the latter course. He decided to stay, to help others in relieving their suffering and in aiding their quest for enlightenment. Other great lights such as Zoroaster, Mahavira or Jesus chose a similar course. There have been some great lights who so completely renounced the world that we never heard from them again. We salute their single-mindedness. But we also observe that, by choosing an austere course, which could be interpreted as a special form of non-attachment, they apparently did not help other human beings.

To whom do we owe the greatest allegiance—to our own divinity, or to the divinity of the world as expressed through other beings? This is an eternal question which split Buddhism into the Hinayana and the Mahayana schools. Ideally we would wish to say that we owe our allegiance to both, particularly as our own divinity is a part of the divinity of the world. Yet in practical life, we have to make choices, and so the path of inner liberation is often pursued at the expense of helping the world, or vice-versa.

When our house in completely in order, we have no fear of attachment, and we are not threatened when the principle of non-attachment is questioned. The *dharma* of the bodhisattva redeems the world or at least relieves the suffering of others. This *Dharma* is not afraid of being in the world, with the world, as it absorbs the suffering of the world: the bodhisattva walks on water while not being drawn into it.

6. The Dharma of Wholeness

In recent years, our understanding of the world has changed. In many ways, this understanding has been impoverished, and in many ways, it has been deepened. As astrophysics and the new physics reveal to us the depth of the universe, as we grapple with the idea of the beginning of time, as we begin to appreciate the wonderful alchemy of the universe in the making, we cannot but gasp in wonder. The stories of contemporary science reveal to us new dimensions of the sacredness of the universe. We see that the whole process of the unfolding of the universe has been so exquisite, the forces that have balanced it so delicate, the transfiguration of matter into spirit so relentless and yet so subtle, that we have every reason to feel that we are in one enormous sacred temple. Astrophysicists tell us that the universe is home for human beings. We can go a step further and maintain that the universe is a sanctuary and that we are its keepers, custodians, trustees.

Thus, participating in this universe is participating in its divinity. When the world is considered a sordid place, then withdrawal from it, or non-attachment, is commendable. But when the whole world is viewed as divine, participation in it is holy and commendable. This is the new *dharma* of wholeness : the participation in the whole divinity of the universe. The Bodhisattva in our times is a custodian in the sanctuary which is the universe.

7. The Unavoidability of Suffering

Whenever possible, suffering should be diminished. Spurious, crushing suffering should be eliminated. Yet not all suffering can be eliminated, nor should it be. Yes, we aim at the reduction of suffering, and we even talk about the total elimination of suffering as if this were desirable. But it is not. Can we imagine the world totally void of suffering? What kind of place would that be? A kind of plastic, one-dimensional universe. Can we imagine human beings growing into maturity and depth without any suffering? What kind of beings would those be, ones who never suffered?

Suffering is the source of deeper understanding and compassion, the spring out of which grows wisdom and ultimately enlightenment. So suffer we must. Can we imagine the Buddha himself announcing the Four Noble Truths and the Eightfold Path without previous suffering? What was necessary for the Buddha in order to acquire wisdom, compassion and enlightenment, is necessary for us too. No one can suffer for us to make us wise and enlightened. The enlightened ones, the avatars, show the way. But they cannot be our saviors, for in releasing us from our responsibility, they would bar our path to true wisdom and enlightenment.

Would there be enlightenment if there were no obstacles? The idea of suffering, as a prerequisite of wisdom and enlightenment, leads us to the simple realization that wisdom and enlightenment are human attributes. And so the human species strives for these amidst obstacles and suffering.

8. The New Eightfold Path

In order to understand the nature of suffering in our times, we need to understand how we have increased and multiplied suffering through the onslaught of technology, through poisoning the water, the air, our food, our minds. This suffering is reverberating throughout the whole planet and the lives of its creatures. In those parts of the world where we created affluence through technology and material progress, we also brought about new forms of suffering—the diseases of civilization. The shorthand term for these new forms of suffering is the ecological blight.

It thus follows that ecological cleansing will lead to the cessation of suffering. Ecology is the noble truth of our times, as we attempt to eliminate an enormous sea of suffering caused by people's unwisdom and concomitant greed, quest for power, and loss of hope.

We ourselves are often the murderer's apprentices, as we contribute through our work, research or teaching to the ecological destruction of the planet. So we need to reflect very carefully on the Eightfold Path in order to give it a distinctly green shade, at least as far as the first five principles are concerned.

Our belief systems, and thus our thought structures, have been profoundly influenced by Western rationality, and Western conceptions of the world as a machine to be controlled and manipulated through our knowledge. This belief system has become our second nature. It is reflected in our language and in our action.

This whole thought structure (or the mechanistic world-view) has been destructive to the environment and to our psyche. This we know. By living inside the machine we have created, our beliefs (assumptions), our thought, our speech, our conduct (action) and ultimately our livelihood have all been affected. The way to escape the machine is not to go backwards, to pre-scientific cultures. We have to leap forward, transcend it. I have tried to do so through an eco-philosophy which spells out a distinctive ecological cosmology (right beliefs, right thought, right speech) and a distinctive ecological ethics (right conduct, right livelihood). According to eco-cosmology, the world is not a machine but a sanctuary. This immediately redefines a multitude of things. The human person is no longer seen as a machinist, who manipulates or is manipulated, but as a custodian and guardian of the planet, and everything in the universe. From this conception of the cosmos (and of the human being within it) follows an ethics of reverence, responsibility, frugality, and justice. We need a positive ecological path, which will merge with the traditional Eightfold Path and transform it in the process.

Technological progress has forced us out of our natural niches. We are lost in concrete jungles. We find it more and more difficult to pursue right livelihood. Thus, one of the great problems of our time is to reverse the trend which forces people to do meaningless jobs which by and large are destructive to the environment. Right livelihood is not just an economic problem. Wrong livelihood is destroying people's souls and is undermining the sustainability of the planet. The Buddha was absolutely correct in seeing right livelihood as a spiritual proposition essential to our rightful destiny.

The Ecological Dharma informs us that ecological reconstruction, working close to nature, bringing back labour-intensive occupations, and working in general for ecological catharsis, is the road which leads us to the fold of right livelihood. Thus, the Ecological Dharma appears to be an essential vehicle for bringing us back to right livelihood which is so essential to our spiritual well-being. Unless we find the road reconnecting us with right livelihood—not only for a select few but for countless millions—we cannot claim that our spiritual message is relevant to the present time.

Summary

Our times call for new resources of imagination and inner power to respond to the unprecedented peril to the life of the planet and to our own spiritual lives. These two are aspects of one another. Clearly, a new Ecological Dharma is called for. This *dharma* requires of us to be passionately attached to the Earth, which of course does not mean the childish clinging to material possessions or to consumption. The practice of universal compassion in our times requires a work of ecological reconstruction and ecological healing unprecedented in history. As the ecological crisis has brought about an enormous sea of new suffering, ecological cleansing becomes the vehicle of the cessation of this suffering. Ecology is the nobel truth of our times.

In responding to the present crisis we need to be strengthened by the flame of enduring spiritual traditions, for we remember that thousands of candles can be lighted from a single candle, without the life of the candle being shortened. Yet, we also remember that even the Buddhas can only point the way. The rest of the journey we have to travel ourselves, in a new terrain unknown to previous epochs with pitfalls and traps that often boggle the imagination. We need to have strength and vision, for our journey may be decisive to future generations.

15
Reverence for Life

1. Setting the Stage

The human quest is one and the same through millennia: how to secure meaning, well being, a sense of harmony. On the lower level of human existence: how to secure food, shelter, enough amenities for satisfying social existence. This quest however is expressed differently in different epochs of history. At one time, when the environment was harsh and human tools limited, when human knowledge was in its infancy, and ignorance was in abundance, at such a time the forces of nature were seen as threatening, menacing and often malevolent. To protect himself from these potentially malevolent forces, man created deities and other religious symbols.

As the human story unfolds, man symbolizes more and more realms of his existence. Religions, as distinctive bodies of beliefs, become articulated. The original spirituality, which was diffused throughout all of nature, is now focused. A process of transcendence occurs whereby divinity is vested in a personal God—residing over and above the human realm. This is the story of the Judeo-Christian tradition of the West. God becomes transcendent, no longer present in all the forces of nature around us.

With regard to God so conceived, the first moral commandments are formulated—the laws binding the human to the sacred; and also regulating the relationships among human beings. In the Judeo-Christian tradition, the first moral decalogue, the Ten Commandments, are mainly harsh prohibitions—"thou shalt not." They bind man to the transcendent God who is responsible for man's vicissitudes and his ultimate destiny. Jehova's is a harsh universe, and man lives in constant fear of the wrath of the almighty God.

In the universe so conceived values are predominantly personal. They regulate the relationship: God-man, and man-man (human-human). The importance of nature as a value in itself does not enter the picture because (i) nature is regarded as a threat to be contained; and (ii) because in the monotheistic Judeo-Christian tradition (which is the basis of my analysis here) all power and value is vested in a personal but invisible God, so that the visible cosmos is left disempowered.

Our cosmologies give us not only a picture of the physical universe, but also a set of values which is usually latent in a given cosmology. The Judeo-Christian cosmology-cum-theology, by giving man the dominion over everything that creepeths over the surface of the earth, has articulated for us the Hebrew conception of God and of man as a special creature of God. It has also spelled out highly anthropocentric values. We are still steeped in this anthropocentrism.

Lynn White has suggested that the Bible is a blueprint for the environmental destruction. It would be more accurate to maintain that the Bible spells out the limitations of the early monotheistic cosmology. Given the circumstances, perhaps the early prophets could not do any better. Now, with a hindsight we know better as we are fully aware that these excessively anthropocentric values are part of our present predicament.

The aim of this chapter is not to provide a historical analysis of the Judeo-Christian tradition of values. Rather our aim is to propose a new set of values appropriate for our times and our problems. Before we propose a set of ecological values, let us very briefly look at the various traditions of values which have guided and inspired Western man. The three towering myths which summarize the various value traditions of the West are:

Prometheus

Jesus

Faustus

The heritage of these myths is stored in the psyche of Western people. The Promethean heritage persuasively suggests that life relentlessly unfolds but not without pain. Progress is accompanied by sacrifice. The universe is beautiful but frail. If we forget about its frailty and charge like a bull in a china shop, Hubris follows. To perceive the subtle limits, constraints and frailty of the universe requires wisdom. We have lost wisdom in the West. Hence we have unwittingly invited the Hubris which is our accompanying shadow in the present Western civilization.

The heritage of Prometheus is noble and inspiring. We must reclaim it and incorporate it into our moral structure. The Promethean heritage is part of our overall moral heritage.

As for the heritage of the other myth, that of Jesus, we must be aware of its positive aspect. (The negative aspect is the fundamentalist preaching: "Jesus died for your sins and you must suffer.") It is love triumphant, love that conquers all, love that transforms, love as a positive modality of human experience that must be emphasized. Let us notice that love is almost a spurious category within the universe ruled by the values of efficiency, of control, of objectivity. This is one of the reasons why love is so difficult in our times.

The Faustian heritage is most recent. Yet it is most vocal and most aggressive. The heritage of scientific-technological values can be subsumed under one powerful myth: you only live once; therefore you live dangerously, at whatsoever expense, even if it means at the expense of ecological habitats, of other species, and of future generations.

The recklessness of thinking of the proponents of progress in the West, their sense of conquest, their desire for power and domination, their lack of the sense of harmony are all related to the overall Faustian drive which we have developed along side the notion of Progress. The devastation of natural environments, the brutal elimination of other species and cultures, the ruination of individual existential lives, the disappearance of social cohesion are the acts that cannot be rationally justified. Yet we perpetuate this irrationality daily. Why? Because of the omni-presence of the Faustian fixation: you only live once, therefore you live dangerously; you have a ball on earth, even if you leave behind nuclear deserts.

Now, in questioning the Faustian heritage we are by no means decrying all progress. Prometheus was a harbinger of progress. And what a wonderful harbinger he was! But his was a different kind of progress from our material progress.

Some philosophers and thinkers already in the 19th century became alarmed by the collapse of religious and spiritual values—being crushed by the forces of the chariot of progress. Among the most foresightful were Goethe, William Blake and Nietzsche. They saw what was coming; and warned us. But we did not heed their warning.

Neitzsche's announcement of the death of God was but a dramatic expression of the whole process of the destruction of traditional values and of the instrumentalization of all values. The climate was created in which it became very difficult for a 'rational man' to justify the intrinsic values, especially religious values. From the middle of the 19th century we witness the rise of a new kind of values. First came utilitarianism; then relativism and nihilism. Then in the 20th century, all kinds of instrumentalism come upon the stage leading to cost/benefit analysis. Traditional values have been replaced by monetary values. All these 'new' values in a subtle way support the Faustian mythos: you only live once. There are no deeper intrinsic values. You are allowed to do what strikes your fancy. All is relative—nothing of inherent worth.

We have all become confused, including philosophers, because we have attempted to subject values, particularly ethical values, to the dictates of scientific reason. This reason does not care about intrinsic values; neither does it care for the heritage of values preceding the scientific mind. Therefore this reason attempts to reduce all values to instrumental values. For this reason does not know any better—it is all a matter of efficiency, control and manipulation.

The coercion of the scientific reason takes a variety of forms—from crude, when the zealous scientists tell us that there is nothing in the universe but the cosmic dust: no place for values, for meaning and love, as they do not have the physical dimensions; to more subtle and indirect, when professional philosophers create new theories seemingly to express moral philosophy in a new way but ultimately to submit moral philosophy to the tyranny of scientific reason.

This is what has happened with so called moral philosophy in the 20th century. What we witness is not really a moral philosophy but a high power analytical and linguistic game. Philosophers attempt to dissect the structure of moral propositions in the hope that this dissection will help us to become more enlightened morally. The whole frame of reference is controlled by scientific reason, and the results are expected to fit the structure of this reason. The whole mode of analysis of 20th century moral philosophers is a tribute paid to scientific reason. What we thus obtain is not moral enlightenment but intellectual reasoning about the structure of moral propositions.

In brief, though subconsciously, philosophers nevertheless want to make values comply with the structure of scientific reason. They impose the structure of scientific reason on moral discourse. The result is a set of stultifying abstraction. No wonder that the people cannot recognize in the discourses of philosophers anything that has to do with moral and ethical dilemmas as they experience them.

2. On the Importance of Foundations and of Intrinsic Values

What kind of values I uphold? What kind of universe I live in? What kind of destiny I pursue? These are the questions which are of importance to all of us. These are the questions which are at the heart of our existential malaise—whether we are intellectuals or ordinary workers. Because we have not resolved these questions in any way, we cannot find the key to harmony, we cannot resolve the problem of the meaningfulness of our individual lives; and yet another level—we cannot find satisfactory solution to large scale environmental problems. They are all connected. When the overall harmony, cohesion and meaning evade us, we are at a loss how to deal with particular problems.

In brief, I will try to argue that the resolution to our environmental and ecological dilemmas lies in the matrix of our values. Unless we are able to see in depth what values we behold and how they control our behaviour; unless we are able to establish a new sound, sane and sustainable value-basis. All the dazzling expertise (based on the limited and fragmented vision), all the technological fixes, will be the acts full of sound and fury, signifying nothing.

Ethics is not engineering. It does not ask the question, How to?, but Why? While developing ethics, we do not search for tools for fixing things. We rather search for ultimate foundations which alone can justify our being in this universe. It is very important to bear this in mind in our instrumental age, when we are inclined to reduce everything to a technique. If ethics is a technique, then it is a technique of the soul, following quite a different route from that of present technologies.

We are impatient with general principles. We are impatient with philosophy. We want guides for action now. But that is an attitude of a technician. Ethics, on the other hand, tries to understand a deeper nature of things, and especially why should we behave in this way and not another way? Asking why questions sooner or later leads to foundations, and to foundation-values. Foundation values are a rock on which the whole ethical system rests—whatever its nature. If we do not accept some foundation values, nothing follows. For foundation values give us *raison d'etre* for the whole system, its specific subvalues and its specific modes of action.

I call foundation values the first order values. I call the consequences of foundation values, the second order values. I call specific tactics and strategies for the implementation of the second order values, the third order values. Let us use some examples to illustrate the point.

We should work on legislators to pass appropriate bills to save environments. Our political action (to persuade the legislators) is in the realm of the third order values.

The justification for third order values is in the second order. Why should we work on legislators? Because we value environments. This is in the realm of the second order values. What is the justification of this one? A still deeper value which I call a foundation value. In the systems of eco-ethics which I propose, this foundation value is rooted in the idea of the sanctity of life. The acceptance of the sanctity of life prompts us to protect other forms of life, prompts us to protect threatened habitats, as well as human environments in which life is in peril.

All conservation work, all environmental protection activities, are ultimately based on this deeper conviction of the sanctity of life. Let us be quite clear that if the premise of the sanctity of life is questioned or rejected, the whole design of conservation strategies, and all specific actions for saving environments, hang in the thin air. There is no reason then why we should engage in conservation strategies and environmental and ecological ethics.

Thus the denial of foundation values leads to the annihilation of the values of specific actions. This point has to be stressed over and again. We are so intoxicated with action that we often think that it is the only thing of value. But action has meaning only...if it has meaning. The meaning of action is determined by a deeper principle this action serves.

Foundation values (in any system of ethics) are the terminal points. They provide the justification for the meaning of a given ethics; as well as the justification for the actions performed under the auspices of this ethics. If we deny foundations, nothing follows.

The important ethical systems of our times are those which clearly spelled out their foundation values and built on those values.

Thus for Gandhi, the foundation value was Ahimsa: non-violence.

For Schweitzer, it was reverence for life.

For Aldo Leopold, it was the sacredness of the land.

The ecological ethics, that I have proposed, is based on the idea of the sanctity of life. From this idea, follows the ethical imperative of reverence for life, which is another formulation of the idea of the sanctity of life.

Ultimate ethical principles underlie and justify our rational strategies and practical choices. Such has been the story of great ethical systems of humanity. We shall do well by following the wisdom of past ethical systems without necessarily embracing their specific principles.

In this context we have to see clearly that relativism of values does not represent a value-position but represents an abdication from holding a value position. You cannot build anything on moral relativism. You cannot establish any program of conservation on it, you cannot establish any long range policies for Sustainable Development.

To postulate intrinsic values does not mean to postulate either absolute values or objective values, but values that bind us together, us a species endowed with certain attributes, propensities and common imperatives. Because of analytical difficulties in justifying intrinsic values, the notion has been abandoned by many philosophers, including Arne Naess. This I consider a mistake. We need intrinsic values as the backbone of our conservation strategies, as the ethical basis for right development. I will propose eco-ethics as a set of new intrinsic values. But first let me attempt to clarify the status of intrinsic values. In this endeavor I will build on the proposition that the intellectual insight and the moral insight are two distinctive entities and therefore we must not attempt to subsume the moral insight under the intellectual one because then we wipe out from ethical values what is sui generis in them.

Our intellectual consciousness can declare some things as of intrinsic value only after it is informed by the axiological level, by the values which we cherish in the depths of our hearts and souls. So it is our value consciousness or the axiological consciousness that informs and guides our cognitive consciousness regarding values. This fact is of great importance, for it leads to a new clarification of intrinsic value.

There are no intrinsic values beyond our consciousness as a species and independently of it. Things are not valuable in themselves: independently of our consciousness. It is our consciousness that makes things valuable. This is not an expression of subjectivism. Our intrinsic values are species-specific. In this sense they are intersubjective. Indeed, intrinsic values cannot be subjective because they are trans-personal. But intrinsic values are not objective—unless you are a Platonist.

Thus between the Scylla of subjectivism and Charybdis of objectivism there lies an intersubjective justification of intrinsic values as assessed by our axiological consciousness which is species-specific, therefore trans-subjective. Hence: no attribution of intrinsic value as ontological claims independent of our valuing as a species. Hence: all values properly expressed must result in ethical imperatives and our willingness to act upon these values.

Thus we can uphold intrinsic values and justify them without slipping into Platonism or subjectivism or relativism. But a new justification of intrinsic values requires a new moral insight.

This new moral insight for me, and many others in our times, is the recognition that nature is not an object to be trampled upon and that all other beings were not created for our use, but that nature is alive and we are a part of it; and that all other beings are our brothers in creation. This insight leads (on the ethical level) to the annunciation of the principle of the sanctity of life or reverence for life—from which an ecological ethics is derived.

3. Reverence for Life and Other Ecological Values

Every new ethical insight spells out a new perception, which usually leads to an articulation of a new relationship between man and his cosmos. These new perceptions spell out, or at least indicate, our new responsibilities and new obligations, which sometimes are formulated as commandments. An example of a new ethical insight is Leo Leopold's land ethic.

A land ethic, then reflects the existence of an ecological conscience, and this in turn reflects a conviction of individual responsibility for the health of the land. Health is the capacity for self-renewal. Conservation is our effort to understand and preserve this capacity.

Leopold is one of the champions of the ecological awareness. Leopold's perceptions clearly spell out new values which bind man to the land. The responsibility for the health of the land is one of the essential obligations that we undertake living on the land, with the land, off the land.

For Leopold man's responsibility for the land is an obligation which does not need any further justification: we are it; it is us. It is a good thing in itself to take care of the land. We must do it because it is our responsibility; irrespective of the yields. Eco-values developed in this chapter are an extension and continuation of two insights: of Leopold's land ethic and of Schweitzer's reverence for life.

Among the intrinsic values for out times, the most important is Reverence for Life—born of a vision and conviction of the sanctity of all life. This vision is actually easy to accept; that is before we become influenced and really corrupted by scientific thinking; to be more precise we should say—by mechanistic thinking. This vision is entertained and accepted in the world view of American Indians. This vision is natural to small children in our own civilization. We have to re-learn to appreciate the beauty of this vision.

Yet the scientific/rational mind finds it hard to entertain anything that is sacred. The very term itself *reverence* is difficult to accommodate within the rational frame of discourse. Even such an innocent concept as 'vision' makes some feel uncomfortable. We are told that we do not live in the world of visions but in the world of harsh realities. But we are told wrongly. The mechanistic conception of the universe (and 'harsh' realities following it) is no less a vision than the reverential conception of the universe. Nature can be looked at in so many different ways. We invent our metaphors; and then find in nature what these metaphors assume.

Responsibility is another intrinsic value of ecological ethics. You cannot exercise reverence without responsibility; ultimately responsibility becomes reverence. Responsibility is part of the meaning of reverence. The two co-define each other. There is a whole negative historical connotation attached to the notion of responsibility within the protestant ethics. This negativism is a baggage which we must throw out, so that we can see the concept in its true light: as a radiant principle which enables us to revere the world and appreciate in its trans-physical dimensions. Responsibility is an ethical principle in the sense that if you understand the unity of life, and the fact that you are a part of it; and one with it, then you must take responsibility for life, for all life; there is no other way. Thus the right understanding of the world and in particular understanding of the sanctity of life implies your responsibility for it. It is just that simple. Responsibility is the connecting link between ethics and rationality. Rationality without responsibility is monstrous, as it has been shown by the example of the Nazi Germans. Ethics without responsibility is empty—as it has shown to be the case with formal ethical systems. Responsibility is the spiritual bridge which makes of rationality—human rationality; and of ethics—a nourishing river of the meaning of our lives.

The larger is the scope of responsibility you assume, the larger you become as a human person. If you assume no responsibility, you are hardly a human. Escape from responsibility, which the indulgent society perpetuates, is an escape from your own humanity. If you want to shun all responsibility, there are only two ways—you live as a complete hermit, away from everybody...but this is not possible, for you will be in the company of birds, plants, the mother earth, and the father sun; or more radically—you commit suicide, and this is the last thing which responsible people should do. The truly great lives, like Gandhi's and Mother Teresa's are lives pregnant with immense responsibilities.

Another intrinsic value of ecological ethics is frugality. Frugality must be handled carefully so that it is not confused with abnegation or destitution. Frugality is an altogether positive value, a form of richness, not of poverty. Frugality is a vehicle of responsibility, a mode of being that makes responsibility possible and tangible—in the world in which we recognize natural constrains and symbiotic relationships of the connected system of life. To understand the right of others to live is to limit our unnecessary wants. The motto in one of the Franciscan retreat houses reads: "Anything we have that is more than we need is stolen from the person who has less than he needs." Is this too strongly expressed? People in the third world countries would not think so.

On yet another level—frugality is a precondition of inner beauty. We are frugal not for the sake of others (for this reason too) but for our own sake. Frugality is an optimal mode of living vis-a-vis other beings. A true awareness of frugality and its right enactment is born out of the conviction that things of the greatest value are for free: friendship, love, inner joy, the freedom to develop within. Indeed if you want to buy these things—the more you are prepared to pay the more surely you will destroy their inherent worth.

On a higher level still, frugality is grace without waste. The greatest works of art are frugal in this sense. Grace shines through them; and it is grace without waste. Thus we must cultivate meaningful and elegant frugality. To do so, we will need to develop a new language so that we are not constrained by past connotations which attribute to frugality dreary and tiresome characteristics. Let us therefore be supremely conscious that frugality is not a prohibition, not a negative commandment: be frugal or be doomed; but a positive precept: be frugal and shine with health and grace. You cannot live in grace when you live in poverty. On the other hand, you cannot live in grace when you wallow in spurious luxury. Grace is the divine middle. Already Aristotle was aware of the beauty of frugality when he wrote: the rich is not only the one who owns much but also the one who needs little.

The true image of frugality is Gandhi, whose life was slender in means but incomparably rich in ends; woven into the tapestry of others; confirming the unity of all; and affirming justice for all. An impossible dream? Maybe. But Gandhi has made this dream a reality. Great people are those who make impossible dreams a reality.

Frugality is an aspect of reverence. You cannot be truly reverential toward life unless you are frugal—in this present world of ours in which the balances are so delicate and so easy to strain. The three basic ecological values: reverence, responsibility and frugality are so interwoven with each other, and interconnected that the meaning of each presupposes the existence of the other two. In brief, the precepts: be reverential, be frugal, be responsible are ethical commands following from our deeper insight of the connectedness of life, of the unity of life, and of its essential fragility.

For fear that the importance of frugality may still not be properly appreciated, I would suggest that we now change the slogan of the French Revolution to read:

Humanité, Fraternité, Frugalité

Eco-justice is another value specific to ecological cosmology. Eco-justice means justice for all. Justice is a venerable, ancient concept. We are all familiar with it; particularly as it applies to us. We all demand justice, especially for ourselves. Nearly all past ethical codes accept justice as an integral part of the moral behaviour. Yet in traditional moral codes justice is limited to the human universe. Sometimes it is limited to a particular religion. Then 'infidels' can be mistreated—they are not the children of our God.

Eco-justice as justice for all is simply a consequence of our ecological cosmology; is also a consequence of the idea of responsibility for all; and of the perception of the interconnectedness of all. If the cosmic web embraces us all, if it is woven of the strands of which we are parts, then justice to the cosmic web means justice to all its elements; to all brothers and sisters of creation—as American Indians would say.

It is difficult to render justice to all in this complex and contingent world of ours. This we know. But it is our moral duty to attempt to do so. Moral principles can be annunciated even if it is difficult to live by them.

Now, Conservation is a modus through which we express our responsibility to nature. Conservation is a very special kind of activity. It expresses care, pietism, love, attention; and a lot of hard work to save what we deem worth preservation.

In one sense conservation may be considered an ethical act in itself: an act of caring to the point of fighting for what you consider important to preserve—as I have argued elsewhere. On a deeper level of analysis, conservation is a set of strategies for implementing ecological values in the primary sense. We design various tactics and stratagems to save what is worthy and necessary of protection—be it our individual life, our family life, our social and civic life, or eco-habitats because we value life as such, because we uphold the principle of the sanctity of life. Strategies come after the primary values are established and accepted.

Reverence, responsibility, frugality and eco-justice form the minimal core of intrinsic values for right conservation and Sustainable Development. Ecological values are exactly like other traditional values—they are ideal signposts and imperatives for action. The fact that they may be difficult to implement in practice in no way negates their importance and desirability. Great value-systems of the past were established not because they were easy to practice but because they expressed the imperatives for action whose purpose it was to safeguard life, meaning and human dignity. All genuine values serve life and the quest of human dignity. And so do eco-values.

The ecological values here discussed are only a core. Their application may differ in specific circumstances and they will need a creative extension in various walks of life—just as traditional values did. Let us emphasize, what is here proposed is not a set of specific strategies—how to deal with conservation and development in this or that region, and with regard to this or that problem. What we have proposed is an underlying matrix of values—to guide our thinking, perception, and action in our attempt to establish right relationships with the Earth, with nature, with other cultures so that we secure a meaningful future for ourselves and for the generations to come.

4. Ecological Values and Sustainable Development

How should we see the centrality of reverence for life as the basis for Sustainable Development? To develop or not to develop is not the question. But how to develop is the question. The central question is: what are the aims, goals, purposes and ends of Development?

The ultimate end of all Development is life. Development serves life and positively contributes to life. If life is taken out of the equation, all notions of Development become meaningless. Furthermore, it is not merely life that we value, but quality living—for all creatures. What is at the kernel of Development is not just biological life, but life of meaning, dignity and fulfillment. Unless we respect this conception of life, we need not bother about Development.

Thus, when carefully examined and unpacked, the idea of Development presupposes the life of meaning, dignity, fulfillment, self-actualization. If we look perceptively, we shall see that these concepts of Development which are truly comprehensive assume that Development serves a variety of life, not just economic ends.

We may approach the issue from the other end: if we accept the notion of reverence and of sanctity of life, this enables us to see immediately that Development is not only an economic phenomenon but rather that it is a vehicle of betterment and amelioration of human life on all its levels. Reverence for life does not deny the importance of the economic factor. The satisfaction of basic wants is part of the life of dignity.

At this point we would wish to propose a new concept that of Reverential Development. Reverential Development is not merely a nice adjective which we attach to the traditional (economy-determined) Development, but is of the essence if Development is not to become a bulldozer crushing frail balances of nature and leaving in its wake stupefied consumers. It would thus appear that reverence for life and Development are intricately connected in the framework of thinking and action in which meaning of human life prevails, and in which respect for nature is part of our conscious and compassionate interaction with all there is.

Ecological ethics as based on reverence for life is universal in the sense that in all cultures and major religions there is a latent premise of the worth of life, and indeed of its sanctity. In most traditional religions this sanctity derives from God. What is important for our consideration is not the source of the sanctity of life but its recognition. This recognition alone demonstrates that reverence for life is an implicit premise of most traditional ethical systems. The fact that reverence for life (which we advocate here) coincides with so many religious ethics, based on the sanctity of life, should only reassure us that there is an underlying core of ethical values common to all people and most religions. Ecological ethics represents a new articulation of traditional intrinsic values. It represents the search for meaning, dignity, health and sanity at the time when the Planet is seriously threatened by inappropriate Development.

In proposing a new form of Development—Reverential Development (based on ecological values), we wish simultaneously to bring about: sustainability to the Planet; dignity to various (exploited) people; unity to human kind—fractured by inappropriate Development. In this sense Reverential Development is unitary in the broadest and deepest sense:

(i) it combines the economic with the ethical and the reverential;

(ii) it combines contemporary ethical imperatives with traditional ethical codes;

(iii) it attempts to serve all the people of all cultures;

(iv) the last but not least, it promises to bring about a truce between humankind and nature, including all its beings.

Summary

My main points are as follows:

1. The genetic code makes us into distinctive biological beings. But after the genes have performed their task, we are only half-finished. The other half is still un-made. After we acquire culture and values, only then are we complete as human beings.
2. The values which clarified our status as human beings and which articulated our moral conscience as well as made us sensitive to culture were inspired and guided by religion. Religious values tended to be absolute as they were rooted in the absolute ground of being—God.
3. With the twilight of religion, the religious values have become gradually less and less significant—particularly as the absolute ground for their existence—God has been questioned, challenged and often abolished. "God is dead" (Neitzsche). The triumphant march of the secular world view signified the rise of scientific-technological values, which increasingly tended to be utilitarian, instrumental, relativistic—freeing us from old absolutes but also cutting us from the sources of our spiritual sustenance and deeper meaning.
4. Moral philosophy of the 20th century, stemming from G. E. Moore's *Principia Ethica* (1903), has been more interested in the meaning of moral concepts than in understanding the nature of moral insight—this particular faculty which makes us moral agents. As the result we have accumulated an impressive body of linguistic analyses that have not led to any significant moral enlightenment. On the contrary,

these semantic analyses led to subjectivism and relativism. By mistaking the intellectual insight for the moral insight, we have inadvertently undercut all intersubjective codes of values. Yet in order to be held together as a human family, we must have the glue that ties as together. In brief, we need new values, new normative ethics to live by—not sharp analytical instruments for analyzing past values.

5. Although we have claimed in the West to be liberated and enlightened, we have been trembling in our boots when confronted with the dictates of scientific rationality which has been a censor, a tyrant, and an absolute ruler of what counts as a valid discourse. We have uncritically followed the gospel of instrumental (scientific) rationality which has reinforced the overall drift toward relativism and nihilism of values.

6. Relativism of values or any instrumental approach to values cannot provide a sufficient foundation for any significant program of large scale conservation of nature, which means for any significant program of Sustainable Development. Instrumental approaches to values are based on expedience and short term considerations. Conservation and Sustainable Development are based on the premise that we must preserve the heritage of the Earth and all its species; and also that we must be mindful of future generations.

7. Ecological values are binding us to nature, to the Earth and to each other. They are our new intrinsic values. They are not absolute. But they are not subjective or relativistic. They are species-specific, and thus inter-subjective. They bind us together; and nourish us together—because we are a species of a certain kind connected with life at large in specific ways. All value-systems are ultimately justified by life. Spelling out what is life enhancing in the long run, and what at the same time assures the optimum harmony among the species, is tantamount to spelling out a set of intersubjective values. In this sense, ecological values are intrinsic values for our times. Most important among these values are: Reverence for life, responsibility for all there

is, frugality in our life styles, and justice for all. Martin Luther King has left a beautiful legacy because he told us not what is politic and expedient but what is morally right. To protect life is morally right. To promote Reverential Development is morally right. To foster ecological values is morally right.

8. The very idea of "Development' is not an objective or merely descriptive category. "Development' is a normative term, loaded with values. There is no logical necessity for any development to occur. We cherish meaning, fulfillment, and the idea of living to our full potential. To those end genuine Development (which I call Reverential Development) should be directed.

9. The right concept of Development must be based on wisdom. Otherwise it becomes an exploitive Development which benefits some (in the short run) and ruins most (in the long run). Pursuing wisdom in the long run means enacting right values.

10. Wisdom for our times I call eco-wisdom. Values that express eco-wisdom I call eco-values. Strategies and tactics that truly bring about Sustainable Development that benefits all, or at least most, are based on eco-wisdom, thus eco-values. The pursuit of Reverential Development is therefore identical with the pursuit of eco-values and eco-wisdom.

16

Eco-Mind and Thinking Reverentially

Note: This is one of the interviews (of which I speak in Chapter 9) given some year ago to New Dimensions Radio World Network. The host is Michael Tomes (MT).

We've reached a stage in social evolution when it is imperative that we develop a larger view, to see the whole in order to better understand the parts. Our techno-scientific world-view has achieved much, but its limitations have become all too apparent. The house of cards upon which our energy and economic needs are built is but one result of this lack of vision. Decision-making within institutions has become a completely rational process affected by parochial pressures and the strain of expediency. No longer are human values a consideration, much less a part of the equation. Spirit has been removed. A vital piece of life is missing. Is it any wonder there is confusion, consternation, and chaos? We are in the midst of information abundance, yet there is a dearth of genuine wisdom. Henryk Skolimowski has put forward a new vision, and he calls it Eco-philosophy. It may just provide a positive response to the demands of our time.

MT: *Henryk, what is Eco-philosophy; and how does it differ from what we ordinarily interpret as traditional philosophy?*

HS: Eco-philosophy, as I see it, is a rational reconstruction of the human condition as we approach the twenty-first century. I emphasize the term "rational," for reason at large is not something to scorn. Indeed, I cannot see any reconstruction whatsoever to be accomplished through unreason. However, I do not identify reason and rationality with the precepts of narrow science, or with computer-like thinking. Reason and rationality are a glorious accomplishment of evolution, and for me reason encompasses it all, including all our sensitivities. The generic term for philosophy is *philosophia*, the love of wisdom, and this is what philosophy has been through millennia. It tries to aid us in the quest for meaning, in the quest for an understanding of not only the trivial everyday life, but also of this larger cosmos—its furniture, its intricacies, our connection with it on the physical level and all other levels as well.

Now in the twentieth century, as a result of specialization, all disciplines were forced to specialize. And even philosophy has done it.The idea of scientific philosophy arrived on the stage around 1910 with Bertrand Russell. Then the philosophers from the Vienna Circle in Vienna, in Austria, picked up the idea and pushed it to an extreme. Philosophy became a scrutiny of the structure of language and, in my opinion, was short-changed. Bit by bit, philosophy was made an inquiry into the nature of linguistic propositions. Philosophers became preoccupied, to the point of obsession, with how language works. Distinguished philosophers such as J.L. Austin started writing essays on "Ifs and Cans." If you think how much that is removed from the real quest of philosophy, then you realize that something bizarre has happened.

Nowadays, even analytical philosophers themselves are rather unhappy with the position they have been pushed into. They try to get out of it. Somehow, however, they are stuck. They try to get unstuck in a piecemeal way, while what we need is a total reconstruction, changing the whole mode of thinking, of perceiving and of valuing. It is here that Eco-philosophy comes into focus as a new cosmology, a new way of rethinking it all.

Instead of conceiving the universe as a clocklike mechanism, governed by deterministic laws, in which we are stuck as a little bolt or screw, we can assume that the universe is a sanctuary and we are its custodians—priests if you will. The mechanistic universe was based on the assumptions of the mechanistic nature of the cosmos. Eco- philosophy is based on the view that the nature of the universe is unfolding, evolutionary, and emergent. Because it's emergent, you don't know what will happen next. It is the glory and the beauty of evolution that it is creative, producing new variations—of which the human mind is one. Every new idea is a blossoming of creative evolution. A new philosophy is for me a manifestation of the ability of evolution to create through us. Put otherwise, a new creative conception of the cosmos is a response of evolution—through us!—to get unstuck. For if we are stuck, evolution is stuck. We have got locked in a cul-de-sac and now we are unlocking ourselves by creating new vistas through which we show that we have somewhere to go, and that evolution has somewhere to go.

This is a very short answer to what Eco-philosophy wants to accomplish. It wants to create a new cosmology within which we are at home in this universe and at peace with all creation.

Most of us, when we hear the term "philosophy," have a vision of musty books on library shelves. In our society, philosophy has been relegated mostly to the halls of academia. One doesn't find the philosophical view, or the philosophical approach, very much present in mainstream society or life. We don't often hear our politicians ask, " What are the philosophical implications of this "particular piece of legislation? " That's just not part of the consideration. Why do you think this has happened in our society? Why have we come to this, where philosophy is no longer really present in the everyday, practical side of life?

It is in part the result of the growing specialization in the twentieth century. But it's also the result of a mistaken myth that the glory of the human condition lies in the improvement of our material lot and that, consequently, you have to bank on material progress, on technology and science.

Yet I want to point out to you that those very assumptions of material progress are philosophical assumptions par excellence. We may think that we have thrown philosophy out of the window, that we do not need it. But our pragmatic modes operation, the ways we think what reality is, are all based on some philosophical assumptions. Usually they are rather crude assumptions in which the universe is conceived predominantly as material, and we are conceived as predominantly acquisitive creatures, or comfort creatures. Yet we know that the most glorious moments of our life and in the history of the human species are not the ones in which we live as comfort creatures. So to the degree to which present philosophy has cast us in the image of comfort creatures, it has put a philosophical straitjacket on our being. We are thus victims of a shallow philosophy.

True enough, a good deal of philosophy is contained in those dry books that gather dust on the shelves of our libraries. But in addition to those, there are some very exciting books on philosophy to which we return over and again. If you take the history of your own program, "New Dimensions," what I've been seeing over the years is a development of a new, exciting philosophy. Philosophers do not have the monopoly on creating new philosophy. New philosophy is emerging all the time. For philosophy has always been an in-depth reflection on the human condition. It will be alive as long as the human condition is alive, as long as we persist in being human. Thus I dare say that as long as we search for humanity in ourselves, as long as we search for freedom, we are not going to be confined by shallow philosophy which reduces us to comfort creatures.

In a sense, each of us is a philosopher?

Right. And if you examine in some depth those notions which assert, "We don't need philosophy, we are pragmatic, we are realistic," you find they are based on some philosophical notions. What is it to be "pragmatic"? It means to assume that economic gains are most important in life. Is that true? What is it to be "realistic"? There is a paradox here. What goes under "being realistic" is totally unrealistic nowadays. For we behave in a foolish, destructive, antiproductive way vis-a-vis ourselves, vis-a-vis the environment. And we call it "realistic." When you think about it, it is totally unrealistic.

Thus, we have to evolve a new concept of realism whereby we are less destructive to ourselves, to other beings, to the environment—or expressing it in positive terms—more life-enhancing. And this is another name for Eco-philosophy. It attempts to be life-enhancing. It attempts to show what kind of beliefs and values may help us in seeing ourselves more clearly as human beings, a very special kind of species, who have the responsibility for themselves, but also the responsibility for the planet and, if you will, for the rest of the cosmos.

Henryk, I remember Buckminster Fuller saying that more than seventy percent of the workforce in America is devoted to non-life-support activities, activity in work-a-day America that really isn't oriented toward enhancing life. In a society based essentially on capitalism, with an orientation to the bottom line and profits, how would one integrate Eco-philosophy? I mean particularly society where the bottom line is paramount.

I would look at the situation the other way around. Not how one integrates Eco-philosophy into the existing structure—that concept would be a kiss of death for Eco-philosophy—but rather how one integrates the existing world and its structures into Ecophilosophy.

You may think this to be ambitious, but we have to be ambitious in order to make sense of our life, in order to survive, in order to have a future. We are all searching desperately for a new lease on life, for structures both economic and political as well as human and ecological that are life-supporting—not only to our individual quest for meaning, but also that are life-supporting to the economy at large. What we are seeing is that the capitalistic structures simply do not work even in terms of capitalism itself. These structures desperately need a new lease on life.

I see capitalism as a cycle, a rather extravagant one, of Western civilization. It was one avenue to see how far we can explore the world and what kind of benefit we can accrue to ourselves individually if we say, "Everybody has carte blanche to do as he or she pleases." We have found that in the contingent world we can't do it, because if some pursue their avenue as they please—to the detriment of others—the whole boat begins to tilt sooner or later. And this is what is happening. So I see Eco-philosophy as an attempt to provide a new set of structures whereby existing practices, visions, and ways of interacting with each other can be renewed and translated in life-enhancing forms.

One of the principles of Eco-philosophy is frugality, which must not be mistaken as imposed poverty or abnegation. Frugality, for me, is a positive principle. Frugality is a precondition of inner beauty. You have to pause a little in order to realize that this is how the greatest works of art were created. When the artist imposes on himself severe limitations and out of the chunk of marble creates a marvelous sculpture, this is frugality in the best sense. With limited means creating wonderful ends. This is what frugality is about. This is partly in keeping with Buckminster Fuller's idea of doing more with less. This is what inventiveness and creativeness mean: with limited means creating rich and excellent ends. This is, incidentally, what the Norwegian eco-philosopher Arne Naess advocates: a life which is slender in means and rich in ends.

In the present society, it is just the reverse. We use enormously rich and versatile means, and achieve ends in no proportion to the investment. We have become a people who are developing means for other means which never translate into ends which we can acknowledge as life-enhancing, as adding to our life and as adding to the life of the planet. The other definition of frugality is that frugality is grace without waste. I think we don't have to apologize for using the term "grace," for it is part of the human condition.

On occasion I am asked to give a brief definition of Eco-philosophy. You cannot do it. You need ten to fifteen hours to do justice to the idea which seeks to redefine the lot. Eco-philosophy, like the Buddhist Eightfold Path, suggests that all things are interconnected. Right assumptions about the world lead to right beliefs, lead to right or correct thinking, lead to correct action, lead to right livelihood, and lead to right contemplation. Action is important, but only if it is based on right values and right visions. Otherwise it is blind action. Actually, we so often rush from one form of action to another form of action, thinking that this other form of action is our salvation, while the whole foundation of our action is unsound. Nowadays we have to rethink the whole lot. Another way of looking at the situation in which we are at present is to summarize it in the following way.

Life is short.

Art is long.

Experience difficult.

Truth is enticing to seek.

Difficult to attain.

The delights of being are many.

The delights of becoming are infinite.

And the last phrase is one I want to emphasize. We are the creatures of becoming. This is the nature of evolution. This is the nature of all evolving societies. Unless we continually transcend, we petrify. The problem with our society and with our education is that we have gotten stuck in certain forms of being. And we petrify. Our present social structures and institutions are really interested in self-perpetuation and creating people in their own image. They want supporters which keep the system going. This is one of the reasons why in spite of the fact that we have a huge system of education, it doesn't help us in the quest of enlightenment. Our educational institutions are set to make us obedient ciphers, not to make us free people.

Seemingly another principle in life is resisting change, being comfortable with the status quo. When'you speak of Eco-philosophy, one of the things that seems to be present is constant change. There's always an emergence of new thoughts, new ideas, new ways to think, new ways to do things—that can be very uncomfortable. What about that discomfort and working through it?

Well, it can be very uncomfortable. But living in changing time is always uncomfortable. However, if you live a life that is open and engaging, you always find a response to the unexpected. It is the unexpected, the new, that is the joy and delight of life. In the States, we try to immune ourselves from change because it means insecurity. This is one of our paradoxes: On one hand we say that we are the society that is changing, we are the society on the go; on the other hand, we have tried to create an economic structure of security through which we can be undisturbed. The two do not go together.

We need to go deeper into the nature of the human condition and how we conceive of what it is to be human. If you think that we are unfolding with evolution, that we are creative, you have to embrace change amidst discomfort, for it is a part of the beauty and agony of becoming. And you better persuade yourself that it is good, because it cannot be otherwise. So far as I can see, there is no way to make people comfortable and immune from change and pain unless they are in the grave.

Perhaps we can talk about how we can become more co-creative and overcome the negative view of the world which is so prevalent today. Optimism may be a biological necessity, and it's certainly a principle of Eco-philosophy. Henryk, as you were saying, we are co-creators with evolution and we're the determining factor as to what happens next. Also inherent in your remarks is the idea that somehow we need to celebrate life more than we're doing, that life is rich and full. But so often we're looking at the holes, noticing the gaps, and experiencing problems. When we look around us, we realize that we're in an environment permeated by a constant reinforcement of what's wrong with the world—the negative, the darker view. How does one break through this incredible reinforcement of the negative?

You are quite right when you say that optimism may be a biological necessity. And I would add that hope is not a prerogative of foolish people, but part of the ontological being of man in this world. Once you lose hope, you disintegrate as a human being. Well if so, why are we ridden with the plague of hopelessness, helplessness, and a kind of dreariness? Why do we not celebrate life, when in a sense life fully lived is life celebrated? There are many reasons, I'll just speak of two of them.

One is that the prevailing system of education develops above all the critical faculties, the skeptical faculties, nihilistic faculties. In order to be clever, you always try to puncture everything that is presented to you. You try to cut everything into bits and pieces. This doesn't develop an attitude of wholeness and celebration of life. The educational system says, "If you are clever, try to decompose and destroy everything." But there is a deeper reason still for this attitude of critical scrutiny, of dismembering everything, of showing how you can always cut. This deeper reason is the acceptance of the mechanistic world-view, which assumes that everything is made of discrete atoms which interact in a deterministic way; and which also assumes that the deeper you cut, the further you go. The tunnel/atomistic vision is inherent in our mechanistic world-view.

The other side of the coin is our inability to perceive holistically, in a connected and integrated way. Now, hope requires an affirmation of a meaningful universe which is one coherent whole. The mechanistic universe isolates, separates, detaches everything from everything else. Moreover, it is devoid of human meaning. Hence, we have to transcend mechanistic science to create the universe of hope. If you closely look at the mechanistic scheme, you realize that the celebration of life is not there. "It does not belong to the system," the system does not have the terminology for such things.

The hard-headed scientist may insist that this view of the universe is the right one. I say that his assumptions are myopic and are distorting the real picture of the universe. According to Eco-philosophy, we can choose a celebratory universe in which hope is one of its dimensions. Now which assumptions about the universe are right? There is no logical way of resolving the dilemma. So my response to the question of who is right, the pessimist or the optimist, is not to try to argue out the proposition on logical grounds. Rather, I would propose: Let's see what pessimism is doing to us, on one hand, and let's see what optimism and hope can do for us, on the other hand.

Why should we assume that the universe is dreary? Why not see that it bursts with new forms of life, bursts in joy all the time? We need to embark on the universe that is a place for celebration, and we need to act upon our assumption. Only then we can see the strength and the power of this kind of universe. And to the extent that we are one of its most intricate forms, the universe celebrates itself through us. You cannot disprove logically such an assumption. Let us assume the universe helps us to dwell in it, for we are a part of this universe. There is nothing strange in the assumption that the universe is Home for Man. Intuitively, this view is more convincing than the one which assumes that the universe is a hostile, indifferent, cold place in which we drift like helpless monads.

So what we are doing while developing Eco-philosophy is returning to a connected and hospitable conception of the cosmos, in which we are its right inhabitants and which is home for us. I should mention here that these ideas are developed more fully in my book, *Living Philosophy, Eco-Philosophy as a Living Tree.* (Penguin, 1991).

Many of our institutions, as they have evolved and become a part of our everyday life, have lost the original vision for which they may have been created. They may have been created with a sincere concern for solving a particular human problem, they may have been based on certain values and ethics, but it seems almost one of the principles of institutions that as they get larger and larger the values and ethics and similar concerns are almost pushed out of the everyday decision-making process.

Going back to my earlier question about corporations and living in a corporate society, how do those values and ethics come back into play? From what you were saying, one projection of the future may be that an institution—say, a corporation—might have a resident eco-philosopher to assess how profits and the bottom line may be directly related to that institution's concern with the future overall effect of what it is doing. I'd like to relate that to the importance of institutions once again showing a real concern with human values and with ethics—basically, a return to integrity as an important component in one's everyday functioning.

Well, again, integrity is something peculiarly human. It is not a property of the mechanistic universe. It is not a property of a corporation that makes profit. It is not something that you find in our economic accounting. It is only when you have the peculiar sense that without integrity you are not whole, you are not fully human, that you begin to inject into the system—whatever the system is—a new parameter, a new dimension. And it is at this point that you examine all institutions and realize that, somehow or other, almost each of them alienates itself from the purpose for which it has been originally created. This is part of the dialectics of life.

An institution—or any set of institutions—is created to provide for certain needs, certain requirements, social or individual, and usually it serves those needs for a while. But then once those needs are satisfied, we come to evolve new needs. The institution usually doesn't evolve to cater to these new needs, and it tries to respond in terms of the old needs. After a while, we find the institution quite antithetical to new needs that have evolved in response to life and in response to our own quest for going beyond, for transcendence. To that degree, every institution—whether we take a little civic institution in the city or an institution like the Catholic Church—has a tendency to get stuck and to respond to early needs rather than new evolving needs.

Well, it is the genius of a people or an institution that is able to adjust itself and change with changing needs. Most institutions do not do it. The bigger they are, the more clumsy and the more entrenched they become, and they try to translate our needs into what they can do for themselves. At that point, there is quite a chasm between what an institution is doing and what it ought to be doing if it were doing its right job. And this is what has happened, not only with institutions, but with technology at large.

Technology may be thought of as a form of institution for taking care of our needs. Each and all technologies were conceived for our good, for the betterment of our individual and social life. This is the purpose they served for quite a while. Then they became too big, too independent, too autonomous. And now they are perpetuating themselves and—if we can anthropomorphize a little—have the cheek of claiming us as an appendage to them. At this point it's pathological, it's really bizarre. An instrument has taken over. The sorcerer's apprentice has unlocked the secrets, unleashed the tremendous powers which it is unable to control.

There is something wrong in the process if it leads to consequences that are antithetical to the original purposes. Well, to that degree, we have to really change and scrap lots of institutions, including technology. I'm not saying that technology will have to just be thrown on the rubbish heap of history. But some of its forms that are antithetical to the ends of our life and that are threatening the whole planet, that become a major threat to the whole model of evolution—these have to be revised.

What the humans have done can be changed and undone. To that degree I am a kind of staunch optimist. This is a way of really empowering ourselves, by knowing that it all came as a result of certain visions, certain purposes, certain programs, and that we have to restructure our visions. We can have the courage to say, "We take our destiny into our hands again. We are not so helpless and powerless as we would be made by some institutions."

As to your suggestion that every major corporation might have a resident eco-philosopher to oversee its overall values and its positive contributions to life at large—it's an excellent one! I actually would love to be invited by some corporations as a resident eco-philosopher—and prove to them that it would be a good idea.

Henryk, I would like to relate what you were talking about to a pragmatic, real-life situation. If we look at the institution called health care, and if we look at where hospitals have come to and how we deliver medical services to people, we've reached a point of health care being a privilege and not a right. We're talking about excluding certain people from receiving adequate or the best health care. I think this is an example of an institution that has come to a place where the original vision that it was created for has been lost. Even though there is still a concern to take care of people, we're talking about ways that can only takecare of a certain number of people—those who have the right kind of insurance and the right kind of support in order to take advantage of the services provided. What about that?

Health care is a very good example of institutions that somehow alienated themselves from what they were supposed to serve. Again, you cannot blame the institutions, the hospitals and doctors; there is the whole universe that has gone its own way and become uncaring to our well-being. And this is, again, a matter of in-depth perception, a matter of realizing what health care is about. Is it the maintenance of the machine, that maintains our spare parts? The more sophisticated the machine becomes, the more expensive spare parts become and the more difficult they become to replace. And the more sophisticated the process, the more costly the process, the more difficult it is to provide it to ordinary people.

So the right response is not to try to make the mending process via this mechanistic process less expensive, but to look at the larger picture. What is health care? It is the maintenance of our health. It is our health that is at stake. If you look at the problem of health as not only curing illness, but maintaining our well-being, you change the whole perspective on life, on health. And then you ask yourself what kind of institutions you need to have, what kind of health care you have to have in order to maintain health and keep it in the state of radiance, rather than how to stop this process of prohibitively expensive medical care that is bound to be more and more expensive as the scientific and technological process gets more and more sophisticated. And again, if you are locked in our system, there is no way out. So you have to get out of the system, and go to China.

I went there in 1976. What struck me was that China was a poor country without poor people. In spite of the fact that there were 800 million people there, everybody had basic health care. But it's based on a different principle than ours. And by Zeus, if China can do it, being such a poor country, we should be able to do it. But we'll be able to do it only if we change our perspective. And this perspective is really not the perspective on the medical machinery and how to improve it, but the perspective on life, health, and death. When we talk about institutions and how to cope with them, I think that the answer lies in changing the perspective of the people who run them, changing the entire vision, and saying to yourself: We can do it otherwise.

It occurs to me that the eco-philosophical view would encompass and accept death as being a part of life. One of the problems with modern health care is the constant emphasis on the prolongation of life at all costs. The lives of people who are essentially no longer functioning as living beings are prolonged with technology, thereby creating more occupation of hospital beds, and so on. To some extent, the medical establishment hasn't accepted death as a part of life.

Eco-philosophy tries to do that and tries to suggest that at a certain point the prolongation of certain biological functions is not the prolongation of life. It is just slow death which is already there which we try to prevent, although we know that we can't. And this requires, again, a deeper look into the human condition, rather than new strategy for how to make those people who are already partly departed survive on a kind of vegetative level.

One of the parts of Eco-philosophy is what I call eco-yoga. In addition to rethinking our principles, we have to go in our existential substratum through certain exercises that enable us to perceive the world and people in a new way. One of those principles is what I call reverential thinking. Once you start to think reverentially about other human beings, and about our relationship with ecology and the world, it does something to you. It really changes your perspective.

Part of this value vacuum, part of the problem with ethics, part of the problem with integrity, is that our attitudes and our thinking are so *irreverent*. This objective thinking is a kind of careless thinking. It's nihilist thinking, while life in its *modus operandi* is a very tender phenomenon. When we really take care of life, we take care of life on the basis of a certain reverence for it. I would like to reintroduce reverential thinking as a part of our *modus operandi*, as a part of our daily perception.

So, in addition to the courses I teach at the university, I go to a retreat, you may say, and I run two-week workshops at Arcosanti— which is Paolo Solari's city in the middle of the Arizona desert—in which we try to translate principles of Eco-philosophy into real-life situations. More recently, I have been offering workshops on Eco-philosophy and eco-yoga on the island of Thassos in northern Greece. To enact a new philosophy requires more than just thinking.

Reverential thinking is not thinking about reverence, it is *thinking* reverentially. And there is a difference. In order to think reverentially, you have to, in a sense, rewire your perception, rewire your assumptions. You have to stop thinking always in economic terms: How I can use this piece of land as a resource . . . How I can use this person to my purposes? Thinking reverentially is possible because we know that part of our life is lived reverentially, that is, when we care for those who are dear to us, when we are in love. Indeed, to be in love is to treat the other person reverentially.

So reverence is not an idealistic principle, but one that really is part of our state as human beings. I would wish to emphasize that this principle of reverence for life is something that will help us on our road to the future. Reverence for life is not high idealism but stark realism, if we are to have a humane future.

Henryk, when I first saw the title of your book, The Theater of the Mind, what came to me was the drama that so often is a part of what our mind creates. I thought of how much "theater" we create, which in a sense takes us away from what our real purpose may be. I'd like you to comment on that.

Well, for me life is a drama, the whole evolution is a drama, and indeed the mind is one of the most interesting theaters of all. I chose the title *The Theater of the Mind* quite deliberately in order get away from various scholarly and pedantic titles and the very scholarly, pedantic, and dry treatment of the subject. I think that we have been overwhelmed with the quantity of words, which has the effect of really numbing us. We often assume that the more knowledge we have the more enlightened we become, that the more words we can use the more knowledge we have.

I feel that often the opposite is true. We are inundated by the mountain of information and there is no enlightenment at the end. So I decided to structure the whole book in a different fashion—as a series of illuminations inspired very much by the *Upanishads*. It may be a bit presumptuous to say, but such was my purpose: to write a series of *Upanishads* for our times. *Upanishads* are those immortal stories about life and death, the meaning of the universe and the meaning of our own life. And in those *Upanishads*, the role of the mind is second to none.

In the West, we have made everything pedestrian. Everything is ground to a dry powder of concepts, including the very miracle of mind. I think it is time that we reach for this splendid glorious instrument of evolution, the mind that we have and that is so important for everything else, and give it due respect. But giving it due respect also means celebrating it, realizing that the joy of the universe is the joy of having a joyous mind.

I remember being really excited by a book I read in high school—a book by Will Durant entitled The Pleasures of Philosophy. It excited me because here was an opportunity to explore ideas, to study ideas, to see how people thought and the ways they perceived the world around them. And yet what I saw of philosophy in school courses was often, as you say, pedantic. It was presented as taking dusty ideas out of the past and saying, okay, this is the way they thought and this is what you learn. It was not an evolutionary process. Ideas from the past were being dusted off and looked at in contemporary times, but philosophy wasn't a growing animal. In contrast, when I come in touch with your work, it's clear that you're evolving a philosophy that is both new and at the same time influenced by older and other philosophies. What are these influences? What has most influenced you to move in the direction of this new philosophy?

One doesn't have to be pedantic in order to be profound. And indeed, when I look at the history of philosophy, the great philosophical systems, the great philosophers were those who had the courage to confront problems. When you read their texts, they are exciting although at times difficult. Philosophy for me is exciting because it tries to confront those ultimate questions which are always at the back of our minds.

I was converted to philosophy—or seduced to philosophy—by Plato in my teenage years in Poland. I read voluminously, almost everything. After reading great French writers such as Balzac, Maupassant, and others, I discovered the Greek writers. I read Sophocles, Euripides, and then stumbled upon Plato, whom I first read as a poet. But the reading was so fascinating, and the kind of fiction—science fiction—he unveiled was so spellbinding that I couldn't recover from it. To this day, I don't know whether Plato was one of the greatest fiction writers or one of the greatest philosophers in his attempts to discover what reality is all about.

Of late, I am of the opinion that the greatest philosophical and metaphysical systems are as much created as they are discovered. By this I mean that by imposing a certain architecture on reality, we weave the whole reality around this architecture and then consider this reality as objective. While doing this, we forget that the original blueprint (to which reality conforms) is the human invention. And to that degree, all metaphysics and all reality is human invention!

You gather from those remarks that Plato was one of the greatest and most lasting influences on me. But then one had to move on. While studying in Poland, I got under the spell of analytical philosophy. At that time, Plato was called an old-fashioned metaphysician, a fuddy-duddy. One was encouraged to believe in semantic analysis, in logical calculus, in propositional calculus. The power of logic was supposed to be our salvation. There was a kind of messianic message behind analytical philosophy: If we get our language straight, if we get our mental hygiene right, then we'll be able to solve all problems. This myth prevailed until the 1950s. After that time, the leading minds, that had invented this myth, one after another renounced and recanted it.

However, lesser minds have never been able to do so. We are under the spell of those lesser minds who are perpetuating the myth that analysis is the only philosophy while completely forgetting what analytical philosophy was supposed to be about. It was supposed to be about getting the language clear and precise, so that we could tackle all the problems and solve them satisfactorily.

Present philosophy has become sharpening tools for sharpening tools. Because academic philosophy does not help us in understanding the world and ourselves, we turn away from it. However, we also are aware that because of the unprecedented problems that have emerged in the second half of the twentieth century—such as nuclear waste, the looming ecological catastrophe, and, last but not least, understanding the universe and matter brought about by the new advances of astrophysics and quantum physics—we cannot find solutions to our dilemmas in past philosophies.

Thus, we need to create a philosophy appropriate for our times and our problems. I am neither decrying all philosophy nor advocating a return to the past—be it Plato, the *Upanishads*, or some other mystical tradition. I am in favour of creating a new, comprehensive holistic philosophy suitable for the age of ecology which is dawning on us.

In The Theater of the Mind, *you wrote something that I had experienced in my own life, and that is the incredible similarity in the philosophies espoused by de Chardin and Sri Aurobindo. Though they here in some sense contemporary, they didn't know one another, and you make the connection between them. De Chardin was a Catholic, Sri Aurobindo was an Indian, came out of the Hindu system. How about that connection? what does it mean?*

Teilhard de Chardin was one of the great influences on me in recent times. I have been fascinated by his story of evolution as one of the most thrilling adventures of the human mind.

To try to reconstruct and shed light on such a phenomenon as total evolution is like holding the whole universe, from its inception, in one's palm. I've tried to puzzle out how Teilhard arrived at his system. When I discovered Sri Aurobindo, who arrived at a very similar system, I couldn't believe it. There is, of course, the theory that the *zeitgeist* has worked through both of them. *Zeitgeist* or not, I thought there must have been some influences.

So when I was at Pondicherry in southern India, where Sri Aurobindo Ashram is located, I finally got to some people who knew the entire opus of Aurobindo and also were aware of Bergson. One lady had done a doctorate dissertation at the Sorbonne on Bergson and Aurobindo. I said to myself, "Right, this must be the connection." I asked her point blank, "How much did Aurobindo learn from Bergson?" She said, "The influence is so great that I would not be able to distinguish one from the other."

We know, of course, that Teilhard was very greatly influenced by Bergson as well. So this is the connection. Bergson's influence is really tremendous, though not obvious.

You see, evolution goes on. And so does our evolution about the meaning and the significance of evolution. Darwin published his *Origin of the Species* in 1859. It was exactly the year in which Henri Bergson was born—1859. When Bergson was a mature man, about forty or forty-five, the whole impact of Darwin was already absorbed. So Bergson could really accept the idea but also look at it in a different way. This is what he did. He came up with the idea of *creative evolution.* He conceived of evolution not merely as a process of chance and necessity—as Monod and other Darwinists and neo-Darwinists tried to make us believe—but as something much more subtle, much more miraculous. In his work *Creative Evolution*, he put this point across, and it is from those views that both Aurobindo and Teilhard learned. Now, when we move into the second part of the twentieth century, the impact of Bergson is already more accepted. One of the evolutionary biologists, Theodosius Dobzhansky, said: "As it was important in the nineteenth century to see the connection between the human species and other species—that we are brothers of chimpanzees and other apes and other animals—so it is equally important in the twentieth century to see what distinguishes us from lower forms of life". What I see as happening is that we are articulating the idea of evolution. And it is such an awesome, complex, and beautiful idea that we are far from fully understanding it.

My whole book, *The Theater of the Mind*, is a series of articulations of the idea of evolution. In a sense, it is a celebration of evolution through the dancing mind, through the theater of the mind.

Henryk, what about the idea of the super jump, the quantum jump that can occur from one thing to another? One often thinks of evolution as gradual, taking thousands of years. And yet throughout history we see this indication of the quantum jump. What about that?

Well, in a sense we are all waiting for this quantum leap of evolution that will carry us all to the realm of enlightenment whereby like pure angels we'll be able to solve all our problems. I think that this state may be a bit away from us still. However, I accept the idea that evolution does not progress smoothly from one stage to another. It is not like building a pyramid. Evolution is discontinuous process whereby after a discontinuity occurs there is a leap to a new level, and this you can trace in various ways.

Take the history of science. Until the second half of the twentieth century, the view prevailed that science is like a monolithic pyramid to which scientists, like masons, add one stone each. If you look at the picture of the evolution of science as presented nowadays by such people as Karl Popper and Thomas Kuhn, it is a different picture altogether. It is a dramatic picture, a discontinuous picture, reminding us more of a kind of Shakespearean stage in which main actors— basic theories— like kings in old tragedies are slain and new ones emerge. After a new paradigm emerges, the old paradigm is dethroned like an old dynasty. This is also confirmed by psychologists, according to whom our own individual development does not proceed smoothly from year to year. At certain points, there are periods of tension which is so great that we do not know who we are any more. After the process of inner transformation, as it were, a new person has emerged. For instance, a teenager has become a young adult.

The Polish psychologist, Dombrowski, calls this process of inner transformation through pain "positive disintegration": Disintegration of an older personality occurs and a new personality emerges. The person has been able to reintegrate. Hence positive disintegration. But some do not make it. And hence the tragedy. This kind of process occurs not only once, but probably three or four times. We shed off the old skin in pain in order to acquire a new one. Thus we can see that in actual life evolution proceeds through continuous stages, but also through discontinuous ones.

A similar idea is also expressed, though in different terms, by Ilya Prigogine. He talks about dissipative structures which occur when an organism or environment is under such great stress that it is unable to bear it any more: There occurs a disintegration, after which there is a reintegration on a new level whereby the old tensions and stresses can be accommodated. This is another way of acknowledging that evolution is discontinuous. When unable to bear old stresses, forms of life reintegrate on a new level. I think those are different names for a very similar idea. A leap is made which is accompanied by pains and some trauma.

I am inclined to think that we as a civilization are going through a similar process. Hence so much tension and pain in societies and individuals. There is no way of knowing what will be the result of this leap. The nature of the emergent evolution is such that the new stage, the emerging stage, is unsimilar to the previous one. Let us hope that it will be a truly creative one and that it will enable us to find structures and solutions adequate to our present problems.

You mention that evolutionary change frequently involves pain and trauma. We can apply that to our own individual evolution as well, our own individual living of life and growing and evolving. Sometimes we go through painful times, traumatic times, and yet usually after that period is behind us we can see how it was a growing process. We can see how we went into that stage as one person and, out of the process of the pain and the trauma, we became another person. An evolutionary process took place there at an individual level.

Quite so. But it is much easier to see it after the fact than when we are in the period of transition and pain. Those periods are confusing, because we are in between two stages, in between two paradigms, as it were.

The point is thatt individual evolution happens in the same way as the macro evolution dues. I think that is an interesting point to make, that personal evolution is the same as planetary evolution. And that would make the connection, too, that as we evolve so also will the planet and the cosmos evolve.

It is perhaps a thought to think of, but not to celebrate, that pain may be a precondition of growth. We do not want to acknowledge the idea while we are in the process of pain. But perhaps it is inevitable that real growth is accompanied by pain because it is the pain of transition from one state of being, within which we are comfortable, to another state of being. Becoming is always difficult.

There is a Buddhist prayer that actually asks for suffering because that is the way to growth, that is the way to enlightenment.

That is beautifully put.

Sometimes we need, and it can help us, to see our suffering in a different way and experience it.

Let us reflect deeper on our culture which so often tries to avoid suffering at all costs. The consequence is that avoiding suffering at all costs happens at the great cost of developing a kind of anesthesia, and this itself is a form of suffering. I would rather acknowledge the suffering as an instrument of vital growth than have the numbness that leads to atrophy and another form of suffering. To put it briefly: As long as we live, as long as we grow, as long as we become, we must not avoid suffering because this is how this universe is made. In the universe of angels it may be different, but in the universe of contingent human beings that is just the way it is.

I could be wrong about this, but my sense is that often, when we think of philosophy, we tend to see it as some kind of subject that gets studied. We go to books and study someone's philosophy, what they wrote, what they put out, maybe centuries ago, or more recently. It's a particular philosophy, and we study it. And somehow in that process we lose something of the value of philosophy. I'd like to hear you talk about how you see the relevance of philosophy to the living of our lives, even the relevance of the study of philosophy to how we live our life. Does philosophy have anything to do with what we are doing?

It has a great deal. One way of looking at philosophy is to consider it as the study of ideas of the past. Very respectable, very good for your general knowledge. But there is another way. You then look at philosophy and consider it as a form of life. Philosophy is a form of life itself. What we witness today is a separation of philosophy from life because in our atomized, analytical society everything is separated from everything else. No wonder culture atrophies.

In a society in which everything is separated and analyzed *ad infinitum*, philosophy is on one shell and life is on another shelf—and indeed so often life is on a shelf. When I talk about the relevance of philosophy for life, I think I am not alone. In his book *Small Is Beautiful*, E.F. Schumacher emphasizes very strongly that the most important task for our times is not so much an economic reconstruction, although this is vital and necessary, but what he calls a metaphysical reconstruction or a religious reconstruction—looking deeper into our philosophical and metaphysical foundations and seeing what has gone wrong.

In this sense philosophy is vital, because many of our problems stem from the fact that we started to look at the universe in too limited a way from the seventeenth century on. The metaphor of the universe as a clocklike mechanism has constricted not only the meaning of the universe and the meaning of cosmos for us, but also the meaning of our own life. We have somehow strangled ourselves.

So what I am trying to do in *Eco-philosophy* and other books is to look for alternative philosophical and metaphysical foundations. We have to realize that the mechanistic way is only one way and not the best one. It is pernicious nowadays. Although it has brought great material rewards, it is counterproductive in the long run. We have to create another matrix, another architecture around which we can weave reality and the cosmos. It must be an architecture of the cosmos within which our life can breathe, and thereby our philosophy will be life-enhancing. We need to establish a symbiotic relationship with the cosmos and other forms of life. This cannot be done within the mechanistic universe which splits and disintegrates everything in the mortuary of our analytical thinking.

Life-enhancing philosophy is one that tries to bring to bear such a conception of the universe which is Home for Man. In it, we are part of the flowering of the great blossom of evolution. Within such a conception of the universe, we are not pitted against other forms of life and especially we are not pitted against each other.

On top of the mechanistic conception of the universe, we have grafted Social Darwinism, "*homo hominae lupus est*," man is wolf to a man. And those two conceptions, which are philosophical par excellence, are working towards our own undoing.

What I am saying is the following. Our philosophical roots are not nourishing us any more. They are responsible for our plight. We'll have to change those roots, this whole foundation, so that it becomes again a tree that is nourishing us, that connects us with the universe, with other forms of life, and with our ultimate destiny which some call God. We cannot live in a shattered, meaningless universe. Human beings crave for meaning and this meaning is part of our nature. So rethinking our foundations is not only an intellectual exercise, it is part of the quest for meaning. It is our existential necessity.

To that degree, I not only do not apologize for what I am doing. On the contrary, I think that I am a part of a new wave whereby life takes itself seriously again and wants to assert itself in meaningful forms— simply wants to flourish. *The Theater of the Mind* is homage paid to life, which not only crawls but has the capacity to fly.

Hearing what you are saying, it seems to me that a life-enhancing philosophy would go beyond the notion that there is only rational thinking and would include the intuitive process. Intuition so often gets excluded when philosophy is presented as a rational, linear, logical-mechanistic type of process.

In my conception of the mind in *The Theater of the Mind*, I distinguish three minds. The first I call analytical or discursive mind. The second I call the mind that is made of all the sensitivities that evolution has developed. Intuition, compassion, and aesthetic appreciation are included within the second mind. We can enjoy various aspects of the universe only insofar as we possess appropriate faculties. I call these faculties "appropriate sensitivities." Through them we elicit from the universe what is there. Among those faculties, intuition, insight, emotional responses are very important.

When we look at each other, straight eye to eye, we see much more than the eye. We see the whole soul of the other person. We see in a sense the whole history of the person. We see the whole history of the species. This is not an exaggeration. Because eye-contact is so important, because we have this sensitivity built into our eyes, built into our mind, we can carry on many conversations beyond mere words. We talk eye-to-eye.

In my "Mind 2," love is also included. Love as an evolutionary, and *existential*, phenomenon is both emotional and rational. As long as human beings are alive and are not crippled, love between two human beings is both beautiful and rational. We do not need to apologize for it. We need to celebrate it.

The scope of what I call Mind 2 includes all the sensitivities that evolution has ever evolved, from the first tropisms of an amoeba to the genius of Einstein. Mind 2 is the whole spectrum of these sensitivities. Within this spectrum, human life is lived. We need to evolve a new broadened concept of rationality which accounts for the whole spectrum, for the entire mind. We don't want to throw out rationality and become anti-rational or totally emotional. I insist that both rationality and emotions, insight and abstract reasons are capacities which evolution and human beings have evolved and which we enjoy.

All these sensitivities have to be incorporated into a larger symphony of life, plus those other faculties, sensitivities in *status nascendi*, which have not yet been fully articulated—as, for example, premonitions. As evolution is not completed, new sensitivies are being articulated. The "third eye" is perhaps this sensitivity which enables us to see beyond seeing. So often we do seem to be able to see beyond seeing. What is the phenomenon of extrasensory perception if not the phenomenon of seeing what our eyes cannot see?

There is a way of integrating all those developments—from the development of the first reactions of the amoeba to the development of faculties in mystics and in people with extrasensory perception— that makes sense within the spectrum of the sensitivities of evolution. It is for this whole spectrum that we have to create a new rationality. I think that we can do it. And we can rationally defend it. I myself refuse to be browbeaten by narrow rationalists who try to intimidate us by telling us that the searches beyond the empirical that extend to the mystical are not rational, and therefore are not worthy of human beings.

We need to salute evolution in all its flowering. We need to see its greatness in our capacity for compassion and in our capacity for abstract logic. The riches of evolution are immense. We have every right to participate in them because we are a flowering of evolution. We also have the responsibility to defend this participation as a rational process.

It occurs to me, Henryk, what could one do that is more important than exploring ideas and seeking wisdom? What else do people do?

I am glad that you have said it. We must be aware that exploring ideas and seeking wisdom have a great value. But we must not stop at this stage. We in the West have a great propensity to be little squirrels, to hold on to those great ideas and think that because we have read them all, accumulated them in our abstract coconut, these ideas themselves will make our life better, fuller, and more beautiful.

I think the second stage is to be able to translate those ideas into our lifestyles, and I think that in this process the Eastern philosophies are much better. We in the West are very long on theory and short on practice. In the East, I often feel, it is the other way around. They are very long on practice and often short on theory. In the West, you have the paradox that you cannot act upon the idea unless you understand it. So we create elaborate great theories and we try to convince ourselves that the theory is right. But in the end we do not do anything with it.

Henryk, you just struck a chord. I used to feel that, too, about the Eastern approach. When I first became exposed to Hindu philosophy, the Upanishads and Vedanta, there was an emphasis on getting the experience of becoming one with the universe, as opposed to developing the philosophy behind that experience. Then I came in touch with the Tibetans. And it's really extraordinary. They emphasize the practice, but they have an incredible philosophy behind it. They have what seems to be an endless supply of literature and tradition. It's recorded in writing, and is the bedrock philosophy of their practice.

Yes. I have envied Tibetan monks for their capacity to lead a connected life wherever fate and vicissitudes brought them. They seem to be able not only to survive, but to flourish in such a way that they become exemplars. We look at their lives and wonder how it is possible to have such a connected life in those very distressing and disintegrating times. It may be so because of their integrated philosophy, whereby general Buddhist philosophy is combined with rigorous practices and yogas which make this philosophy one's inner reality. When I was commenting on the paradox of the Western mind, what I meant to suggest is that so often after we have learned the theory we say: "Well, now I know the theory, and the theory should work for me." And we stop at that. This is not really a living philosophy. I think that for the last three centuries we have over-emphasized the abstract quality of knowledge and the importance of ideas in one's mind at the expense of life as a living form. So many great minds, including the Buddha, said that the art of living is second to none. What is important, therefore, is to be able to find the ways whereby good ideas are interiorized, whereby they reach the level of our being, change our consciousness, and we become them.

For this reason, I have developed of late, as a parallel to my Eco-philosophy, what I call eco-yoga. At first when one hears the term, one thinks it's a bit of a joke. But it isn't, because no good ideas, no good principles, no wisdom that one accumulates in the abstract part of our brain is good enough unless it can inform you how to live. Unless it becomes living wisdom, it is not wisdom.

To find a way whereby a good idea is translated into the layers of your being is itself a creative act. For this reason, I have claimed that we have to make a radical transition in our culture from what I call the methodology of objectivity to the methodology of participation. The whole of life is participation, while methodology of objectivity in a sense denies this idea. Within our methodology of objectivity, everything is an object, set apart, put in the laboratory and cut with our analytical scalpels. In contrast, the methodology of participation is based on empathy, on understanding other forms of life in their own terms—on understanding the underlying unity of it all. It is a holistic one. It is one that requires that you take responsibility for all. If you are aware that you are a part of a greater whole, you have to take responsibility for this whole.

My eco-yoga is a part of this methodology of participation. It took us time to develop fully the methodology of objectivity to where it became enshrined in our schools of academia. So it may take us a considerable time for new insights to be transformed into new participatory strategies, whereby our research and our learning will be based on the idea of participation, empathy, compassion, rather than dissecting, objectivizing, and separating.

Sounds to me, Henryk, like a Western philosopher has taken on the nondualistic thinking of the East.

When you look at evolution holistically, you realize that it is one total process. You remember our friend Anaxagoras, who was Socrates' teacher. Anaxagoras claimed that all is mind. Then the history of philosophy developed along different avenues. But now when you look at how important mind is in co-creating with the universe in creating realities, it makes sense to say that at a certain point of analysis, mind becomes indistinguishable from reality itself. This conception I call Mind 3—to return to our earlier discussion—mind as coextensive with reality. The idea of mind, *nous*, in Anaxagoras, is so important that it is conceivable to think about the doctrine which I call "noetic monism," one which asserts that mind is inherently woven in every aspect of reality and every perception of it. Through this conception of mind, we can resolve many of the spurious dichotomies and various dualisms which we inherited from Descartes on. Our various activities—loving, doing logic, creating new worlds—are parts of the same mind. Doing different things, we are all parts of the same mind which functions in different capacities.

You're talking about what might be called universal mind, that we're plugged into.

Universal mind, that's right—of which we are aspects and which we articulate. I think that this idea of nondualism, Advaita in Hindu philosophy, can be now justified in a new rational way. Part of my rethinking concerning the nature and place of mind in the universe goes in this direction.

We have to simultaneously re-define three things: reality, knowledge, and the mind. By trying to understand one part of it, we simultaneously throw light on the other two parts. For each concept defines the other two. The conception of mind informs you what knowledge is and what reality is. Conversely, a given conception of knowledge immediately delineates for you the scope of the mind and of reality. It follows that if we start with a wrong concept of reality—for example, that it is some kind of clocklike mechanism that is detached from us—we immediately receive a distorted conception of knowledge, one that accentuates the accumulation of physical fact; we also receive a very screwed-up conception of mind as a Tabula Rasa, a blank sheet of paper on which experience writes. You can see that if you make one basic step that is wrong, the whole thing falls into pieces. This is what happens with Western culture and Western philosophy. We have to reconstruct it. You and I.

So you and I. And you're suggesting too that we have to take our minds, our little minds, and expand our notion of what our minds may be capable of.

Our little minds which, I put it to you, are not so little if we allow them to be as great as they potentially are.

17

A New Logos for a New Civilisation

1. Transcending Ecology

Ecology has quite rightly been hailed as one of the positive visions of humanity in the second half of the 20th century. It has been a holistic discipline giving us a sense of the holistic nature of the world and of our own lives. It has served as a rallying point for many idealistic and compassionate impulses aiming to help Mother Earth.

On another level ecology has been an island of sanity surrounded by the sea of insanity, an exception to the turbulent angry and aggressive modes of life of the 20th century.

The time has come to look for a new vision. We need to transcend the view of ecology as a separate island of sanity surrounded by a sea of insanity. As we are in the Third Millennium, we need to broaden the whole conception of ecology, we need to change the sea of insanity into a friendly sea. We cannot forever fight as a doomed outpost, righteous as we are, responsible as we consider ourselves to be. We are one with the sea surrounding us. All is one.

Ecology and ecologists have been somewhat stuck during the last 20 years. We have not been winning people's hearts and especially people's consciousness. Often we have been alienating people by our impatience and our inability to convince them. We have been unable to create a more complete picture. We have been successful in developing various techniques for monitoring environmental disasters. We have been less successful in bringing wholeness and peace to people's hearts and minds.

Ecology must be a complete guide to a sane, meaningful and joyous living. It cannot just be an economic guide to sustainable future.

We need to embark on a new voyage, on a new venture. This voyage transcends ecology while incorporating it in our new logos. The logos, which has guided civilization in the second and the first millennium will have to give way to a new logos. We are at a turning point in our evolutionary journey. Evolution wants us to bring, from within ourselves, new resources of imagination, new forms of thinking—to create a new harmony, a new peace, and a new meaning for particular individuals, for the human family, for the whole biotic family. Our aim is not to create a new Pax Romana, a new world order for some privilege human beings, but a Pax Cosmica, a new sense of order which, while releasing from within us new freedom and new imagination, weaves us beautifully into the underlying cosmic tapestry. We are cosmic beings. This is where we belong. This is where we came from. To weave ourselves into the underlying structure of cosmic patterns, to be nourished by cosmic sources of energy is a privilege, prudence and wisdom.

2. A Brief Encounter With Western Logos

Logos is a most fascinating phenomenon of the human mind and probably of the cosmic mind. Let us first ponder for a while about the nature of logos which has shaped our cultures and minds during the past millennia. And then see what kind of shape the new logos wants to acquire.

The history of civilized man is short. The history of philosophy is even shorter. Logos burst on the scene of ancient Greece like a super nova. And then created a wondrous variety of beautiful things. It is still a mystery what logos is and how it operates.

We, in Western World, are the beneficiaries of this Logos. We are greatly indebted to it, for better and worse. I use this phrase "for better and worse" advisedly. We are fully aware what a splendid guide of the mind logos is. We are less aware that it is also a tyrant, tyrannizing us to serve it. That it serves us is a good thing and we are proud of it. That we serve it is a bit puzzling if not disturbing. But we have been slaves of it—particularly this abstract form of Logos we call scientific rationality.

So from the early articulation of Logos around 500 B.C.E. by Anaxagoras, who was a teacher of Socrates, to Socrates and Plato. And what a splendid logos Plato possessed. Then to Aristotle, another stupendous embodiment of Logos. Then to the Stoics and ...all kinds of decadent philosophers—cynics, hedonists, Epicureans. They too used Logos masterly and consummately to justify their existential plight.

By and large historians of philosophy do not realize that hedonism and cynicism were subtle inventions of Logos to give the people, who felt that history had passed by them, a sense of importance, even though that importance is a bit perverse: "look at me, I can deride everything. I can prove that nothing is important and has no special value." A splendid defense of people who themselves feel unimportant. (In our times we see this spectacle over and again.)

In medieval theology Logos flourishes in a new form. Its ornate arabesque patterns, describing the nature of the inscrutable God, are so refined that even theologians themselves were at a loss to comprehend them. Whatever we say about the nature of God is invariably a product of some logos. Designs of God cannot be conceived outside of logos. This point is not fully understood.

Then from the 17th century on Logos is married to Mechanos, a new force, or vision, which wants to reduce everything to some kind of physical relationships. An impossible, if not a ridiculous project. And yet look how splendidly we have re-interpreted the bulk of knowledge of the world into mechanistic and physicalist relationships. What a triumph of Logos! But also what a tragedy of Logos. I hope you are beginning to see what I am trying to say. Our Logos is so powerful that it can prove almost anything. For instance that the whole universe is a clock like mechanism. What a triumph of reason! What a folly of reason!

During the last four centuries our mighty mechanistic logos is doing its mighty work trying to impose itself on all human, social, ecological, spiritual and cosmological relationships. The result is manipulation of nature, destruction of ecological habitats, withering of beauty and spirituality of human life.

Now where were the philosophers in this whole misadventure? Surprisingly they have been helping this conquering logos; often being slaves to it. It is really astonishing how unmindful the philosophers have been while being swept and deluded by the mighty conquering mechanistic logos. There were some exceptions of course: Spinoza, Kant, Goethe, Nietzsche. Their logos was subtle and deep. But the dominant mechanistic logos brushed them aside.

The whole Western European philosophy proved to be dry like a bone, abstract, unable to find alternatives to the civilization that was strangling itself. And so it was with the 19th century German philosophy which celebrated many triumphs—if by these we mean the creation of abstract philosophical systems. The curious thing is that whether we take the system of Hegel or of Marx (diametrically opposed to each other in one sense) they each exemplified the qualities of this abstract disembodied logos, which was so remote from the human universe and from deeper human aspirations. There is no question that the 19th century German philosophical systems were the triumph of a powerful logos. But we cannot be proud of this logos.

As we entered the 20th century we were still in the in the clutches of this abstract logos, especially as far as Husserl's phenomenology is concerned. Martin Heidegger is trying to strike in a new direction, by devising a new program of liberation. He attempted to go to the source, to the very beginning of philosophy. But how well has he succeeded? How important was his revolution in philosophy? Why was he so desperate toward the end of his life, announcing the end of philosophy and proclaiming that only god can save us?

And thus we come to our times, in which we have the whole richness of the great philosophical traditions at our disposal and in which we feel so impoverished philosophically; in which we have a whole mountain of knowledge at our disposal, but in which we feel so confused and disempowered by this knowledge.

We feel that the whole world is out of joint. And we ourselves feel out of joint—in spite of enormous knowledge we possess, and in spite of the powerful logos that seemingly is at our disposal. We have created a new world which has outstripped our understanding. We are bewildered by not being able to understand the world through the knowledge by which we have created it.

3. The Faustian Bargain

When we look back at the last four centuries of the development of Western culture, the question impresses itself on us: were there some other hidden trends and forces which played a significant role in addition to the obvious forces of rationality, science and technology?

One such force, barely noticed, is the myth of Dr. Faustus, or the Faustian myth. It emerged on the European scene in the late medieval times. And it attached itself to Western imagination tenaciously ever since. Goethe has contributed much to its popularity. But Goethe was only a vehicle serving this myth.

Yes, the poetic depth of his vision is compelling. Yet we must not overlook the fact that this vision serves to enshrine a rather repulsive conception of man who rolls over others regardless of the consequences.

You only live once and therefore you live to the brim, even at the expense of others; even at the expense of eternal damnation. Such briefly is the content of the myth. It is really quite extraordinary to notice how many individuals have been possessed by this myth; how many individuals are possessed by this myth as if nothing mattered, only an instant gratification now!

Moreover and this is a point of great gravity: if you look deep enough you can see that the whole Western civilization is possessed by the Faustian myth, is mesmerized by the roles of conquest, conquering, using others to our whims.

If we consider the whole civilization as a collective mind then we see clearly that it has been infiltrated by the Faustian ethos. You only life once and you don't care what happens next. Somehow, somewhere the Faustian bargain has been struck: We have decided to pawn our deeper assets for the sake of cheap gratification now. Just look around with a discerning eye and see. Perhaps you also should look at yourself. How much of Dr. Faustus is in you? How much is he manipulating you from within?

Goethe should not have redeemed and saved Faust in the last scene. It was a bad piece of theology to allow Faust to go to heaven—after his abominable life. It only encourages others to think (if only subconsciously) that whatever bad deeds and even atrocities they commit, they might somehow be redeemed and saved. To have created a pathological destroyer, for this is what Dr. Faustus was, and then sweetly send him to heaven through a sacrifice of an innocent girl, is a major fracture of Western imagination.

There is karma that follows one's life. There are consequences of good deeds and bad deeds. We should not allow ourselves even for a minute to think that whatever atrocities Western civilization has committed to other people and to nature, it will be all forgiven and forgotten. We carry the shadow of our deeds behind us. This shadow is called in the Indian tradition Karma.

I am aware that I am treading on egg shells. I am aware of the almost mystic status of Goethe's thinking and visions in German speaking world. I am aware of the Christian underpinnings of "Goethe's solution" of Faust's problems. I am aware how deep and subtle myths can be when they in dwell in our psyche. Yet there are times that we have to look at them gently, compassionately but unwaveringly.

Let us observe to begin with that myths are extraordinary entities, really powerful fields of energy, which emanate from the nefarious lands of our subconscious. We often think of them as metaphorical stories of ancient times. Which they are. We sometimes think of them as fictitious stories which have nothing to do with reality. Yet myths have a lot to do with reality. They are a crystallized form of human energy encapsulated in symbols and stories. They are a residue, a sedimentation of past experience, of past problems, of past dilemmas, of past dreams and nightmares.

The most extraordinary aspect of the myths is that the dilemmas, ambiguities and agonies they encapsulate, still reverberates in present human psyches. Even when we try to push the energy of these myths down to our subconscious—as irrelevant and antiquated—this energy has a way of popping up in unexpected ways, through subliminal and obscure channels.

Meeting with the myths is like an encounter with ghosts, our own ghosts, the ghosts of human psyche. Usually in our busy conscious life, we are unaware of them, they are forgotten. What remains is only a faint recollection, a faint awareness of ancient ramblings in our own psyche of the energy so peculiar and so startling that we don't even want to know what it is. Only when these myths, the hidden layers of ancient energy, are disturbed by some unforeseen circumstances, they suddenly manifest themselves and take possession of us in unexpected ways as if saying: don't you ever dare to ignore us; you might think that you are a master of your own life, but we are co-masters. Therefore myths must be treated with a great care and with full awareness that they may be indwelling in us, especially the myths specific to our culture.

The myth of Faustus is powerful. And so much so that we really do not want to know how pervasive and deep it is. It pervades all strata of Western society. It indwells in brash successful businessmen and polished and sophisticated brokers on Wall Street; in macho men of Hemingway's elk and in learned intellectuals wanting to out-shine others, while craving public acclaim.

In Germany, the country of Goethe, the Faustian myth may be expected to possess nuances, twists and ramifications of its own. For all his deep sensitivities and appreciation of genuine feminine qualities, Goethe was a male. Whether he was acting out his subconscious or whether the myth as if possessed him, the outcome is alarmingly striking: Gretchen must be sacrificed so that Faust can be saved. I know, the actual plot is more subtle. Gretchen is willing to sacrifice herself so that he overcomes his blindness, can see and then be saved. This act of supreme sacrifice is hailed as a gift of women to save the unseeing men. Sometimes it is treated as a gift of God showing the superiority of women over brutish men. But this is a cover up justifying male ruthlessness.

By sublimating the story, many are taken in, particularly women. They feel great and elated that they are so important by being in a sense, chosen to redeem the world and men. In actual fact, Goethe's rendering of Faust's story represents a continuation of the tale of slavery and butchery of women. True, the story is presented in such a sublime, poetic and enthralling manner that even women feel and are convinced that it must be right. While in the background the devil is sneeringly chuckling how easy it is to ensnare male egos to commit damning deeds and how easy it is to persuade women to serve these damning deeds by sacrificing themselves for damned men.

Let us say it very simply. If human freedom is to prevail, if women are to be part of this freedom, they must not be coerced into submission and made into sacrificial scapegoats. 5000 years of male dominance, of coercion, aggression and manipulation is enough.

It has been through the male conspiracy that the Faustian myth has been perpetuated, the myth which has glorified the selfish, the aggressive, the power-crazy. Goethe was part of this conspiracy, whether he was aware of it or not; probably he was not; he was used by the myth. After Goethe, theologians and philosophers have attempted to justify and sanctify "the Goethe solution"—the sacrifice of Gretchen to save Faust. Women should not condone this "solution". For they are merely sacrificial lambs in the story. Alas, they have allowed themselves to be duped to feel that their sacrifice has been such a noble affair. This may be seen as a cynical outreach of the myth. But not a path to women's freedom and liberation; neither is it the path to men's authentic and genuine freedom. One additional remark. Let us see it with all the clarity we possess that the ethos of conquering, power-crazy technology and the ethos of unmindful, power-drunk Dr. Faustus, are really twin faces of the same destructive, devil inspired energy. Conquering technology loves Dr. Faustus because it is him.

4. The Tribunal of Life

We have been sailing through vast seas of logos and some turbulent waters of the realms of myth. Both Logos and Mythos are part of our heritage. And we need to understand both to transcend our present predicaments.

We have already stated that there are two major obstacles to overcome, two big traditions that work against us. One is objective. The other is subjective. The objective one is rationality, science, and in general the mechanistic world view. The subjective is the Faustian predicament, the relentless drive to dominate and manipulate. Actually, some early roots of this tendency to domination can be found in the Bible when God tells the people "I give you dominion over everything that exists on this earth." This is an invitation to domination which becomes plunder.

We have mentioned the excessively abstract, cerebral nature of Western philosophy over the last centuries. One of the consequences of this form of philosophy is detachment and alienation from life. It is a philosophy which celebrates itself.

We can retort by saying this philosophy is rational at least. How rational is it? How rational is our rationality itself? To our surprise we find that

Rationality cannot assess itself.

It assumes that it is a very good thing. It wants us to believe that it is so. Both philosophy and rationality must stand a test, a tribunal higher than what they say themselves. This tribunal is Life. We furthermore find that

Knowledge cannot assess itself.

It assumes that it is a very good think. It wants us to believe so. We have great difficulties of late to believe that scientific knowledge is so beneficial to human society.

Scientific knowledge, and its very rationality, have been driving us forward and forward relentlessly. We are told that science is objective and so is rationality. Why are we so driven by them? Why is science and rationality so susceptible to manipulation? Why are science and rationality so easily used for the conquest of nature? Is some other force behind the whole process? Is the Faustian quest built into the nature of science? If so, then science may not be such a rational endeavor.

Let us finally notice that

The feedback of life is the criterion of worth and validity of both rationality and philosophy.

This applies to science as well. Science must stand the tribunal higher than itself. This tribunal is Life. Science must be life-enhancing. Knowledge that destroys the world is pathological. We should start looking deeper and think more critically. If we do, then we may come to the conclusion that the whole foundation of Western civilization, based on science, is not really rational.

Furthermore, we need to take seriously the feedback of life. We are very fond of repeating that we should think with consequence. If the consequences of our thinking are undesirable or negative; if the consequences of our actions misfire and lead to negative results, then there is something wrong with the premises. Let us use a well known logical law to express the idea precisely.

$(p \rightarrow q) \rightarrow (-q \rightarrow -p)$

If p, then q; then: if not q, then not p.

This law is known from medieval times as Modus Tolendo Tolens; which in our language means the law of re-transmissibility of falsity. It asserts that if q truly follows from p, or in other words, if p implies q, then if q is shown to be false (or negative), this makes p negated and false.

The power of this law is considerable. Its consequences are actually tremendous, that is, when applied to science and rationality vis a vis life. We are not saying that science is not powerful when applied to certain tasks, particularly to the manipulation of mechanistic aggregates. We are saying however that science and its rationality have consistently failed the Tribunal of Life.

We have now enough feedback from life to confidently assert that life in so many forms have been saying NO to so many intrusions and mishandling it by science. The time has come to think with consequence and understand what is actually happening. The time has come to respect logical laws and especially the law of re-transmissibility of falsity which we have mentioned. And this law, when applied to science and life, shows that life has so often negated the validity of science and its tableau of undoubted truths. Let us remember: the feedback of life is the ultimate criterion of worth and validly of science, rationality and philosophy.

We shall express the main point of our discourse in simpler terms still. If there is a black box (BB), which consistently leads to negative consequences, although it should generate positive consequences, then there is something wrong inside this B.B. The reasoning is simple and it must be respected.

Our Black Box is science, technology and rationality. Our negative consequences is feedback from life; and ecological and social disasters. For how long can science and rationality go on pleading that they are wholly good and that we are to blame when they misfire. For how long can we disregard the evidence of logical laws and our own sense of feedback which informs us that "there is something basically wrong with the Black Box of science and technology?"

In older traditions it was said: "By their fruit you will judge them." T.S. Eliot has expressed it more poignantly:

Of all you have done in the past
You eat the fruit
Either rotten or ripe.

Because science, technology (and their underlying rationality), are bearing rotten fruit, we must disengage ourselves from them and escape from their perilous clutches. This is not a question of cognitive or aesthetic predilection. It is a question of life and death.

This discussion demonstrates again that Western Logos is sick and bearing rotten fruit. Thus it is our imperative to develop a New Logos. Let me emphasize that it is not a question of improving "our science and technology here and there and make them less harmful." It is a question of changing the black box entirely. For it is malfunctioning all the time. We are so slow in understanding this.

We cannot be constantly haunted by the questions: How to live rationally in a world which is insane? How to live beautifully and in grace in the world which is brutal and violent? How to aspire to sanctity in the world which derides everything that is noble and holy?

Our supposedly rational science and technology have made this world brutal, violent and insane. From the depth of our inner sanity, we must refuse to accept this world, and its underlying pseudo-rationality, for it is an angel of necrophilia and of irresponsible Dr. Faustus. Therefore, with the help of a much larger Logos, which we call cosmic logos, we shall re-draw the boundaries of present rationality, we shall redefine the nature of knowledge, we shall develop life-enhancing technology. We shall create a New Logos much more attuned to the beat of Universal Life, much more in harmony with the universal laws of the evolving Cosmos.

5. Life-Enhancing Knowledge of the New Logos

Just thirty years ago there was a generation which was not afraid of asking big questions, not afraid of challenging the status quo, not afraid of proclaiming: "Be realistic. Demand the impossible." Were these people hopeless romantics, utterly devoid of common sense? No, these were normal people. In comparison, we, the people, who tolerate, and in a mute way give consent to the crap, poison and pollution which our civilization has developed as a way of life, are sub-normal people.

Reaching for the stars has been the old longing of humanity. If you don't long, dream and aspire, you are half-dead. What is the use of a comfortable life if your spirit is dead? What is the use of your good income if you don't fulfill your evolutionary destiny? Why is the human mind and human soul so low? Why are we so busy creating plastic gadgets and oppressive environments? These questions need to be taken seriously, otherwise we shall be drifting—to further numbness and perhaps oblivion.

In asking these questions, we are assuming that the Third Millennium cannot be as low and barbarous as the Second Millennium. We are furthermore assuming that the awakening of humanity and a new chapter for all will not happen through the economic expansion and by "bringing prosperity to all." For this has been a false teaching of the economists which has wrought untold damage. We are postulating that a tremendous leap forward will be made through the creation and articulation of the New Logos.

To be normal is to dream, to aspire, to hope. Hope is the spring eternal. It is the spring from which humanity has drunk from time immemorial. So we must go on dreaming and hoping for a new future. Without dreaming and hoping this future will not be created. Like a spider, we shall need to weave out of ourselves new webs and designs. Have you ever watched a spider at work? What an exquisite example of a creator at work!

In addition to dreaming and hoping, we shall be developing new knowledge, new awareness, new relationships through which the New Logos will manifest itself. And this New Logos will be our companion, guide and inspiration. But also a part of our inner selves: as we shall develop this logos, so we shall become in its image, so we shall create the world in its image.

Any form of logos is an extensive edifice which comprises: a view of the world, a view of the human, a view of the divine, as well as tactics for living and the criteria for a fulfilling life; as well as the admission of some invisible forces which guide it all—myths, divine forces, gods.

Let us examine these various aspects of the New Logos, starting from its main pillars, or the underlying assumptions on which everything rests. For the sake of clarity and succinctness, I will first mention the nature of these pillars or assumptions, show their interrelations and interdependence and only later discuss their deepest roots and consequences in some detail.

The three pillars of the New Logos are:

(1) The World is a Sanctuary

(2) The World is Participation.

(3) The World is in the process of self divination.

Let us take an Olympian perspective and see how the three assumptions complement themselves and are necessary for each other. Let us not approach these assumptions through the microscopic scrutiny characteristic of present mechanistic logos; especially let us not submit them to analytical scrutiny from the positions of the present logos—for this would be a futile exercise as we are in a new territory, outlining a new reality.

The three assumptions, explained in the briefest possible way maintain that:

* The cosmos is on a self-actualizing journey;
* this is a journey of becoming—from bottom up, or the roots—onto life, consciousness and divinity;
* through evolution the world becomes a sanctuary;
* participation is also a vehicle of individual transcendence by allowing individual humans to choose these forms of life which lead to grace and divinity—thus to life conceived as a sanctuary.

We shall now elucidate further the meaning of the three pillars, and of the points made above.

All knowledge must be ultimately accountable before the Tribunal of Life. This we claimed in section 4, while discussing the vicissitudes of scientific knowledge and showing that the knowledge of Mechanistic logos is failing life in important respects. How different is the knowledge of the New Logos? Is it truly is truly life-enhancing? We go to our first pillar.

The world is a sanctuary. From this it immediately follows that you are a sanctuary that everybody is a sanctuary. This is an important realization: you can claim your dignity, your sense of worth, your aspiration to deeper and spiritual life because you are a sanctuary. But this realization also entails important responsibility. To dwell in a sanctuary is to behave reverentially, responsibly, ethically. Our ethics no longer has to be imposed on by the almighty church or by the sanctions of society. It simply follows from our understanding of the world as a sanctuary and of ourselves as a sanctuary. What an important liberation!

One of the consequences is that we must not be luke-warm or tentative about our behaviour in real life. You are a sanctuary. You live in a sanctuary. Thus you behave appropriately, that is to say, reverentially. You are a shepherd of being. You take care of nature, of ecological habitats, of other people; yes, of yourself—your body, your health, your destiny. This is your responsibility. You are responsible for the whole heritage of life, and of your own strand woven into the magnificent tapestry of life. You want to be responsible before the Tribunal of Life. You are responsible before this Tribunal, even if you wanted to escape its judgments. So behave accordingly. Show that your truly understand. Show what a beautiful piece of the cosmic design you are, how intelligent you are, how caring you are—by caring of yourself as a sanctuary and by caring of the world as a part of your outer skin. All is connected. All is participatory. All is on the Big Journey of Becoming. The knowledge of this journey is so pregnant, so compelling, so inviting. This is one aspect of the knowledge of the New Logos. Its life-enhancing nature does leave any shadow of doubt.

The New Logos is not afraid of admitting that it cooperates with new emerging myths of humanity. One of them is a myth of Gaia, the Sacred Mother Earth, which is a living being, and which requires love, care and responsibility. Another new myth is simple: the world is a sanctuary. Once we accept this vision so much of darkness and negativity are dispelled almost automatically.

The new logos is not afraid of so called "rational criticism" of the defenders of the present scientific mechanistic mind-set. The defenders of the status quo are likely to say that one does not mix myths with true knowledge. And they will be so wrong. For the present scientific world-view is precisely such an admixture of myth and reason. Let us remind ourselves that the Faustian myth is now inexorably woven into the structure and pursuit of scientific knowledge. But not only this myth. Two further myths woven into the mechanistic mind-set are: the myth of Free Market and the myth of Globalization. There is no rational justification for either of the two myths. They are just assumptions. They have been pushed onto us as revealed truths. These two myths have caused great damages to many societies and cultures.

Yes, we want to be rational. Let us be so. If we have a choice of either selecting life-enhancing myths, such as Gaia and the world is a sanctuary, or life-tormenting myths, such as Free market and Globalization, we should not hesitate which to choose. We should opt for life and not for its destruction. The rationality of the New Logos is lucid and merciless. It unmistakably points out that you cannot rationally behold knowledge, which is destructive of life.

The New Logos is aware that we have many methodological "hang ups"; which is to say, constrains built into our mind which try to regulate which knowledge we should deem as acceptable and which we should reject; or at least consider as suspect. These constrains are a legacy of the scientific mind. This mind not only promotes its specific knowledge. It also imposes on us its methodology. This methodology is its watchdog. On the surface it appears to be benign, as it seemingly only wants us to distinguish what is genuine and what is humbug. But in its actual mode of operation it is a censor and dictator, which tells us what to choose and what is to reject. This methodology, in actual fact, often effectively blocks our search for new perspectives.

Given the power of existing methodology, we might be discouraged by the daunting task of creating the New Logos. Some might say that the task is too big, too unrealistic. Our response would be as follows: what can you lose? Only your chains and delusions that you have lived in the best of all possible worlds. We are staggering under an oppressive burden, which civilization has imposed upon us. The present strains and stresses, manipulation, chaos and nihilism are just too much to bear. And we know this. The whole civilization has put itself on an unrealistic course.

Let us therefore be realistic! Let us release ourselves from the chains and aspire to higher goals of human destiny. Let us reclaim the meaning of life. Let us embrace the mystery—the mystery of human existence and of the world. But can you do this without making yourself an irrational fool? Yes, you can. Listen to Albert Einstein's voice on this matter.

> The most beautiful thing we can experience is the mysterious. It is the source of all true art and science. He to whom this emotion is a stranger, who can no longer pause to wonder and stand wrapped in awe, is as good as dead: his eyes are closed. What is impenetrable to us really exists manifesting itself as the highest wisdom and the most radiant beauty which our dull faculties can comprehend only in their most primitive forms.

6. The Participatory Universe

To understand the meaning of the self-realization of the cosmos, without mystifying it on the one hand or vulgarizing it on the other, means understanding the meaning and role of participation—as an essential part of the creative process. The participatory universe is this kind of entity which participates in its own becoming. This becoming signifies the creation of living molecules out of the cosmic dust; and furthermore, creating Mozarts and Einsteins out of the living molecules. Participation of the cosmos in this process entails also participation in its own growing awareness.

How does the cosmos see? How is it aware of itself? Through its various tentacles and extensions which are its eyes and its radar-like antennae. All the creatures are the sensitive antennae of the living cosmos which is feeling and sensing itself as it develops and unfolds. We can present this process by an image. The universe is a big U. Let us imagine that this U has an eye. When this eye looks at the universe, what does it see? Itself! Almost an astounding realization.

This is a participatory process at its most sublime. In this process the role of the mind is absolutely essential. In this process our role is essential. We are the minds and the eyes of the universe. Through us the cosmos unfolds, meditates, refines itself. At first this idea is starling. Then it becomes so natural. For what else can we be if not an array of energies, sensitivities and comprehending powers of the cosmos?

Participation informs us of not only of the cosmic process of becoming. It also informs and guides your own life and the life of people around you.

What you participate in, that you become

To understand this precept leads to profound consequences. Our life has been cheapened and trivialized. Yes? Yes. Why? Because we have been forced to participate in endless pursuits, which have no meaning and which are trivial, of no consequence to our life. Our life has been denuded of the deeper contexts, made shallow and rushed. Why? Because we have been prevented from participating in deeper contexts. For what purpose? "To make the economy function better." We have accepted this argument. But deeper down we should ask ourselves: why should we participate in the plethora of activities which do not contribute to the meaning of our lives but, on the contrary, which undermine the integrity of our lives? This is not rational. This is not sane. And we know it.

What you participate in, that you become. If you participate everyday in playing bingo, you become a Bingo Zombie, your mind will become as shallow and passive as the bingo game requires. If you spend endless hours watching trivial TV programs, you become a "couch potato" as the American expression aptly describes it.

Thus, choose well the forms of your participation. Choose them very carefully. Through participation we make ourselves who we are. "He who thinks of God becomes God." So speak the Upanishads. Properly understood, this means, if you participate in the context of God, if you identify yourself with the attributes of this context, if you consciously attempt to refine the structure and ethos of your life in the image of these attributes, you are on the path of divinity. This is the meaning of participating in the divine. The Dhammapada has put it in this way: "What we are today comes from our thoughts of yesterday. And our present thoughts are paving the way of what we shall be tomorrow. Life is the creation of our mind."

How have you treated your mind today and yesterday? What kind of thoughts and activities have your participated in to prepare a beautiful life of tomorrow? The karma of mind is even more powerful than the karma of your diet. If you eat bad food, poisonous food, you will poison yourself, or at least you will make yourself sick or emaciated. If you think inferior and trivial ideas, you make your life inferior and trivial. What you participate in, that you become.

Participation is the song of creation. And it is a song of your individual existence. The most significant forms are those in which you extend yourself, in which you stretched, in which you are creative, in which you realize your deepest potential, your destiny. In such forms of participation you are reaching for the stars, you are self-realizing yourself, you are part of the self-realization of the cosmos.

Our deepest participation in this world is co-creation. Yes, we co-create with the universe and all its subtle forces. What a wonderful expression of our dignity! What a beautiful example of living in meaning. We live in the world which is a sanctuary, and we are a sanctuary. As we maintain both sanctuaries with pride, joy and responsibility, we again express our dignity. We must be intelligent in reading aright the meaning of the New Logos in order to see how everything is beautifully connected and really integrates itself on a deeper level.

Among the specific attributes of the human, who integrates himself/herself into New Logos is a new sense of freedom.

We are were born to freedom

This freedom is so intoxicating that it almost paralyzes. To use it well, efficiently and beautifully we have to learn to fly. The past period of crawling or of being chained is over. We cannot be chained to the old deterministic anchors of the mechanistic world view, or to the old commandments of the wrathful angry god. But

We need to fly in control.

This is one of the prerogatives of the New Logos: you need to learn to fly. But you must fly in control. We must not crash like Icarus.

These are some of the aspects of the knowledge of the New Logos. To appreciate these aspects, one has to take the desiderata of the New Logos seriously, one must embody them in one's own life, one must re-create reality in the image of these desiderata. Otherwise, we are left with words, words, words. But we do not want the new desiderata to be just words. Therefore, we must embody them in our own lives—to restore our dignity, our humanity, the very meaning of life. This is what reaching for the stars truly means. Without reaching for the stars, we are doomed to a reduced existence.

Summary

Our story of the New Logos is part of the ancient story of the cosmic logos. We are part of the cosmic logos. We are no accident. The Cosmos is self-realizing itself through us. We are at present at a new turning point of the evolutionary journey of the cosmos and of ourselves. We are an inherent aspect of the journey of the cosmos. This turning point demands and requires of us new resources and courage and new outburst of fresh imagination. It demands of us flying in control—as a part of our new freedom.

We are not claiming some special privileges and powers for ourselves. We only postulate eliciting these powers from within which are there and which are necessary for continuing the evolutionary journey of the cosmos and of ourselves; of ourselves and of the cosmos—as we are inherently intertwined.

Some may be startled that we demand too much for the New Logos. But realizing god through our own journey is not an ordinary venture. We tremble as we think of it. But we go forward elated as there is no greater joy and privilege than to dance with the creative cosmos.

The dawn of the New Reason is coming. It is the dawn of the New Logos for which the New Civilisation is wanting, for which future generations are waiting. We cannot deny the cosmos to sing through us its new song. We are not slaves of the creative cosmos. We are its proud heralds and messengers. We should not curse fate for living in difficult times. We should be grateful for participating in this auspicious journey.

18

Cosmocracy—as the Next Stage in the Development of Democracy

Prologue

Our existing concepts have been in use for centuries and sometimes millennia. Many of them are worn out. We have extended the boundaries of our world and of our mind. In the process we have changed ourselves. We need new concepts to acknowledge the world we have created. Cosmocracy is one of such concepts—one of the new windows through which we can look onto the new worlds.

In one sense, cosmocracy pre-dates the historic political systems, including Democracy. When humans lived in an essential unity with nature and cosmos, they governed themselves according to the principles of cosmocracy—they knew that all powers come from the cosmos and reverentially obeyed the orders of the cosmos. Then they broke away from nature, created more anthropocentric forms, of which Democracy was one; and then they estranged themselves from nature. Cosmocracy, here proposed, closes the cycle and tunes us back to the essential unity of all things.

We need not only new concepts. We need concepts which are life-forms. Cosmocracy, which I am advocating, is not only a proposal for a new form of government but a proposal for re-arranging life in new life-forms—out of which a suitable, life-enhancing, non-exploitive forms of government will naturally follow.

1. On the Origins and Meaning of Democracy

Political systems do not arise out of political expediencies but out of a deeper desire to actualize the hidden potential of man and of the human race. Thus political systems are extensions and embodiments of philosophies, religion, and ideologies. They are not merely political entities to be justified through their own assertions.

To understand a given political system in depth means to unravel its underlying philosophy, its history, its concept of the human. A mere analysis of the meaning of the concepts of a given system, which confines itself to its internal structures, or worse still—merely statistical correlations within the system, is a facile exercise which leads to facile conclusions. True political science is nothing short of political philosophy.

Democracy did not arise merely because people wanted power (Demo-cratia—power of the people). It arose because ancient Greeks wanted to actualize a certain ideal of man. Already in the 6th century B.C., the Greeks were aware of their distinctiveness from their neighbors. They were especially aware that one of their ideals was to seek freedom. They referred to other peoples as barbarians not only because the others could not speak the language of the Hellas, but also because they were not free people.

While searching for the right freedom, the Greeks asked themselves: what is the best form of living together, providing, of course, that man is a social animal? Those who were anti-social, who refused to participate in public affairs, were called by the Greeks 'idiots.' The Greeks found that the best expression for social life was to live in a Polis. How should the Polis be governed—to secure optimal freedom for the individuals? It should be governed democratically: Thus Democracy was born to safeguard freedom.

Freedom for the Greeks was a vehicle for the enlargement of man. It was not a license for "doing as you please", nor was it an indulgence to satisfy one's own whims. True enough, freedom was cherished in its own right— as a dimension of human existence. But it was also valued as a condition enabling individuals to pursue the path of self-realization leading to

Enlightenment, and ultimately to godhead. The highest ideal, as we remember from Socrates and Plato, was the quest for self-enlightenment, as a part of spiritual realization. Thus freedom in this context serves spiritual ends—of man's self-realization and ultimate fulfillment.

Let us emphasize our point. Democracy, which is a vehicle of freedom and a pre-condition of it, serves not only social ends but also spiritual ends. It is a social structure which enables the individual to pursue a life of social richness and spiritual fulfillment.

Thus in the original Greek context, both freedom and Democracy, served spiritual ends. These ends were determined by the conception of man—as envisaged by Greek philosophers and poets. Democracy was not the football of crass politics and of lobbying groups (as we think of it today), was not the pursuit of power by some people, but was rather a pursuit of Enlightenment —in a common social structure. Our more recent conceptions of Democracy, as a vehicle of power-seeking of rival groups, or as a vehicle for amassing individual power through legal means, is a far cry from the original conception of Democracy.

Equally far removed from its original design is the idea of Democracy as freedom from constraints, especially from the constraints of the oppressive structures of the church. Democracy was not meant to be a secular structure. The Greeks did not see Democracy as opposed to religion; rather as a vehicle of the realization of a certain religious ideal. Only with the advent of the 18th century French Enlightenment is Democracy juxtaposed against religion. It is then wedded to secularism.

Now, let us see the picture of Democracy as it has evolved in modern times. Within the confines of the French Enlightenment—inspired and guided by the ideals of Reason and material progress—Democracy and secularism are seen as co-defining each other. But that was not the way the Greeks saw Democracy. In their context, Democracy combined with reason was not animical to the spiritual quest but indeed a condition and dimension of it. This point needs to be especially emphasized, namely that Democracy is not a servant of secularism and part of its definition, but on the contrary, that it may serve spiritual ends and can be conceived as an aspect of the spiritual conception of man. The redefinition of Democracy along spiritual lines may be one of the most important tasks of our times.

The conclusion which clearly follows from our arguments is that it may have been a mistake leading to a corruption of Democracy when we have subsumed it under secularism, and moreover tied the meaning of Democracy with the progress of science and technology.

It is now acknowledged that wherever we look, we see Democracy in tatters. The various political systems which have assumed the name "Democracy" are pale shadows of the original intent. The fundamental reason is that Democracy, or various attempts aimed at Democracy, have been placed in the wrong context, the context which invariably distorts the meaning of Democracy and perverts its potentials and aspirations. And what do I mean by this wrong context? The combined matrix of materialism, secularism and the conception of power as domination.

As we said at the beginning, every political system arises out of larger ideals concerning human destiny and what life is about. In the context of the post-Renaissance utopias (Thomas Moore, Francis Bacon, Campanella and all), which have promised salvation on earth through material progress and the subjugation of nature, Democracy has become a hostage to the Faustian quest—of grasping for power, of control and domination, of manipulation of some groups by other groups through legal and 'democratic' means.

In the present world, I would see Finland, Sweden and Norway as somewhat approaching Democracy. Some people label these countries as Socialist. If these countries are Socialist, then one is bound to conclude that their form of Socialism is part of the definition of Democracy. Indeed, let us have the courage of our thinking, let us notice that the original conception of Democracy, in ancient times, entailed a form of Socialism. If you were only for yourself, unconcerned with public good, unwilling to work pro bono publico, you were called an 'idiot'. Thus a form of solidarity, a form of compassion, of working for public good was universally expected and strongly endorsed. This I call 'minimal socialism'. I submit that this minimal socialism is an inherent aspect of Democracy and its defining characteristic. Put otherwise, cooperative behaviour is a pre-condition of both freedom and survival.

It follows from our argument that the United States cannot be called a Democracy because it is too selfish a form of society, too deficient in public good. The pursuit of power and selfishness is not the pursuit of Democracy. It is rather the pursuit of power and selfishness. For this reason one would be inclined to call America Cratio-cracy—power to the powerful.

Now there is another term, which seems even more appropriate for the description of the overall socio-political system in the U.S. The United States is a society, which is youth-oriented. The adulation of youth is so intense and so uncritical in it, and so little attention is paid to wisdom of the elders, that the whole society could be called Infanto-cracy.

The Social Contract by Jean-Jacques Rousseau asserts that if there were a nation of gods, Democracy would be a suitable form of government for them. For ordinary human beings it is too perfect a form of government. If Rousseau's assertion is taken as a gospel, then it provides a ready justification for our apparent failure to implement Democracy in actual social realities: Democracy is too perfect a form of government for human beings.

However, upon a deeper analysis, we shall find that Rousseau's assertion does not really make sense. For let us reason: if there were a nation of gods, they would not need to govern themselves democratically. They would govern themselves theocratically, by electing the god, which would be most omniscient. Indeed, they would not even need to elect such a god. They would automatically assume their responsibilities. They would not need any form of government.

Rousseau's argument is deficient in yet another way. By its very meaning, Democracy is not for gods but for people. The Greeks did not think they were inventing a political system for gods. Gods do not need our help to devise a political system for them. The Greeks were inventing Democracy for themselves. And they tried to live it.

It may be argued that with the exception of the Golden period of Athens, in the 5th century B.C., Democracy never existed elsewhere. Even if such were the case, this would not yet prove that Democracy is impossible, but only that it is very hard to implement.

All cardinal virtues are difficult to attain. Yet we strive for them. These ideals are compelling not because they are easy to reach but because they present something highly desirable. And so it is with Democracy. The very meaning of the term 'democracy' has a magic spell over us. Why? Not because of the abuses of Democracy of which we are plainly aware. But because of our longing for a 'perfect' system.

Democracy is in a sense a religious ideal. Perhaps the connotation which the ancient Greeks attached to the term still lingers on. We long for a political system which would be a vehicle for freedom and at the same time an instrument of self-perfectibility.

2. The True Sources of Power

Every political system is an embodiment of a specific concept of power. Theocracies are an embodiment of spiritual power. The Athenian Democracy was an embodiment of the power of freedom and the power of self-realization. The Industrial Democracies have become embodiments of physical power. So often it is power in order to control and manipulate. Now the reduction of the meaning of power to its physical aspect is a corruption of power. The consequences of this corrupted concept of power for Democracy are enormous and unfortunate.

The root cause of the corruption of power, within our political system and within the variety of forms of social life is, in my opinion, the progressive secularization of the Western world and the Western mind. Secularization is the determining matrix which begets materialism, and, accompanying it, the process of universal reification (or objectification or 'thingification') of the natural world and the human world. The result is a radical impoverishment of the cosmos. Both the human and the physical worlds are impoverished as we try to screen out the elements which do not fit into the quantitative-physical matrix. In the political and social spheres this signifies the impoverishment of Democracy as well as the human relationships which we try to 'objectify', to reify, to quantify.

All of this has been the result of a philosophical mistake. This mistake was committed at the beginning of the 17th century, at the time when we started viewing the world through the spectacles of a mechanistic metaphor. This philosophical mistake is mainly responsible for the rise and increasing domination of the Faustian concept of man—a reckless creature, who lives only once, who has lost all his great inspiring ideals and who therefore seeks the meaning of life in living dangerously—often at the expense of other beings. This philosophical mistake is largely responsible for the malfunction of Democracy.

The Greeks were independent and often arrogant but their arrogance was tempered with the awareness of hubris. We are the children of the reckless Dr. Faustus. And we have forgotten about hubris, and nemesis following it.

In brief, the philosophical mistake we made in the 17th century, assuming the universe is nothing but a clock-like mechanism, has borne countless negative consequences. Among them is the adulation of physical power and our submission to its imperative. Here is a graphic summary of the forces that have shaped the industrial democracies, and our individual lives.

SECULARISM

↓

THE IDEAL OF MATERIAL PROGRESS

↓

SCIENCE AND TECHNOLOGY AS TOOLS OF DOMINATION

↓

THE MYTH OF PHYSICAL POWER

I will now outline an evolutionary approach to power, which enables us to understand present pathologies of power as well as those other conceptions of power which, in the long run, are more important than physical power.

Power is an universal attribute of life. The source of all power is evolution. Entropy is the inexorable march of the universe toward chaos and disorder. Life is this unique organization of matter, which is capable of combating entropy. The capacity of life to combat entropy is often called syntropy. Syntropy manifests itself not only in biological organisms but also in social and political institutions.

The ultimate purpose of all structures endowed with power (including political structures) is to combat entropy and enhance life. The institutions and people who contribute to syntropy represent a legitimate use of power. Let us emphasize the point: the purpose of power is the propagation of syntropy through the transfer of will, which is life-enhancing. This is accomplished in the social universe through the creation of institutions which promote life in the long run and for the largest number of people.

We are aware that all systems are subject to entropy. Left to themselves, they have a tendency to degenerate. The degeneration or pathology of power reveals itself very clearly when, instead of being the instruments of syntropy, social and political institutions become the instruments of entropy. From an evolutionary point of view, such a state of affairs represents a degenerative shift. That this has happened to many present-day social and political institutions, is obvious to everybody. The enormously negative consequences of the concept of power as brute force are too conspicuous to be ignored.

Power without authority is illusory. This is why Jesus prevailed over the Caesar. This is why Gandhi prevailed over the British. Gandhi's example is luminous in its clarity. A little frail man against the might of the British Empire! I proposed earlier that power is an universal attribute of life. Gandhi's moral authority is an enigma from a rational point of view. Why would this little man command such an enormous respect? Why would any man command any respect? The answer does not lie in a rational analysis but in the understanding of those deeper faculties which underlie moral authority.

There are three levels of power. The first level is power as physical control. The second level is power as authority. The third level is the power as moral authority. What is the source of moral authority? It is the power, which resides in holy men, shamans, healers. These persons possess extraordinary faculties. These faculties become the basis of their authority. We should see it very clearly: moral authority or authority as such, is not given to us, Deus ex Machina. Rather it is a crystallization of some inner powers which those who ascend to authority possess.

In traditional cultures, the chief was vested with political power because he possessed those extraordinary faculties which made him a medicine man or a man of vision. We can approach the relationship among the three realms of power from the other end. Because a given person possessed extraordinary inner faculties, he had authority. Because he had authority, he was vested with power.

We have now distinguished three conceptions or three realities of power:

1. Power conceived as domination through brute physical force, characteristic of most political institutions of our times.
2. Power conceived as authority which is a transfer of will. The person of moral authority compels others to act as the result of some moral imperative.
3. Power conceived as the possession of extraordinary inner faculties, whereby things are accomplished as though by magic, which only means that those who do not possess extraordinary faculties are at the mercy of those who do possess them.

In present Western culture, dominated by the mechanistic paradigm, power as authority is belittled, and power as the possession of extraordinary faculties almost completely ignored, much to our peril. Gandhi's political power was no doubt the result of his moral authority. His moral authority, in turn, seems to have been the result of his special faculties which made him a holy man (the term 'holy fool' would be equally appropriate), whereby people were inspired and renewed by his mere presence.

Let us draw some conclusions. Power is not an isolated concept. Its meaning is determined by the entire social, cultural and civilizational context. Since medieval times we have profoundly changed the context of Western society. Correspondingly we changed the concept of power.

The triumph of the West is the triumph of the Western context, and this means the triumph of Western secular ideology, with its concept of material progress and its concept of power. The three concepts: secularism, material progress, and physical power co-define each other. We should be aware that the triumph of the Western context includes both industrial capitalism and industrial socialism. The communist countries (while they still existed) accepted secular ideology, material progress, and power as domination in almost the same degree as we did in Western Democracies.

We are now ready to broaden our discourse still further. All power resides in the cosmos. We are repositories of this power, including political systems, which are built of the elements of power which the cosmos provides.

Since the time the Bible was written; since the time the Greeks conceived of the Polis; since the time Thomas Moore and Francis Bacon wrote their secular utopias; since the time Newton conceived his mechanics as the ultimate model for the explanation of the universe, since all these times, our knowledge of the universe has immensely broadened and our perception of our place in this universe has considerably changed; particularly during the last 100 years. All these changes challenge our imagination to conceive new political systems. We can no longer accept the biblical conception of man. Nor can we accept the role of the conquistadore, in the service of whom all nature and all cosmos revolve. Nor can we accept the conception of democracy as serving a select few.

3. Eco-cracy or Eco-democracy

We are beginning to accept the idea of designing with nature rather than against nature. The acceptance of this idea leads to reverence for natural systems. Now the idea of reverence for natural systems, translated into the language of political science means Eco-Cracy. Ecocracy means recognizing the power of nature and of life itself, means observing the limits of nature, designing with nature, not against it, creating ecologically sustainable systems, reverence for the planet—not its continuous plundering.

Genuine students of Democracy, in our times, must realize that we are in the 21st century. Thus our understanding of political realities cannot be confined to the internal and often superficial analysis of the relationships within present governmental structures, nor even the analysis of the relationships between technology and society, for there is often a conflict between technology and nature.

Let me put it succinctly. Technocracy and Ecocracy aim at fundamentally different goals. Technocracy aims at efficiency, control, manipulation and (so often) 'profit now'. Ecocracy aims at sustainable systems which can support and bring well being to human species and other species in the millennia to come.

The Industrial Democracy, in truth, is no longer Democracy. At best it is the pursuit of Democracy within one nation, and often at the expense of other nations—if only indirectly, via complicated socio-economic mechanisms and determinants. This form of Democracy does not deserve the name of Democracy, as it does not lead to increased freedom, but to new forms of slavery among nations.

A true understanding of Democracy in our times, when by Democracy we genuinely mean an instrument of justice, freedom and social amelioration of people, not only in some pockets of the globe, but the world over, is one which inevitably ties Democracy with Ecocracy and which insists that true Democracy is an Ecocracy. Now if a new term is to be coined, we should introduce the idea of Eco-democracy—not as a fancy term signifying the peppering of Industrial Democracy with some ecological jargon, but as a term signifying a new structure with profound social and political consequences.

In this interconnected and co-dependent world of ours, the notion of Democracy must take on a new meaning. Democracy can no longer be limited to the city-state (the polis); it can no longer be limited to one nation. Democracy must be so conceived that its execution in one nation does not harm (if only indirectly) other nations and does not harm Nature itself.

Let us put it in positive terms: Democracy in our times must be conceived as such a form of government that benefits all nations in the long run, and which at the same time, respects and enhances natural systems. This inter-nation and inter-species Democracy, I call Ecocracy or Eco-democracy. When we think how global and interconnected our problems are nowadays, this notion of Eco-democracy impresses itself on us as almost obvious. Moreover, a system which I describe as Ecodemocracy, or a very similar one, is a necessity for our survival.

Ecodemocracy does not provide a set of ready blueprints concerning how to set up genuinely democratic forms of government within societies and among nations. Rather it re-conceives the meaning of power. From a new understanding of power comes a New Enlightenment concerning the way we conceive "power structures"—whose purpose is not to oppress and manipulate, but to enhance life in the long run.

The purpose of all structures created either by evolution or by human industry is the enhancement of life. A truly enlightened philosophy is one which illumines the unfoldment of life, which is in sympathy with life growing and transcending itself, which helps the human mind to see the greatness of life, and which helps the human species to design with life, with nature, with the underlying structures and the laws of the cosmos. This philosophy I call ECO-PHILOSOPHY. I have formulated some rudiments of such a philosophy in my books: Eco-philosophy, Designing New Tactics for Living (1981), Living Philosophy—Eco-Philosophy as a Tree of Life, (1992), The Participatory Mind (1994); and in other books.

Ecodemocracy, along with Eco-philosophy, unapologetically maintains that if ecological habits are ruined, if the ecological ship goes down, our dexterous manipulations within the existing power structures will be seen as the proverbial shuffling of deck-chairs on the Titanic.

Human systems must be in congruence with natural systems. Human welfare should be furthered alongside of the welfare of other species. Such is the meaning of universal Democracy. Such is the meaning of Ecodemocracy.

Ecodemocracy includes among persons not only human beings but also other living beings. To extend the notion of Person in such a way is not a violation of the existing usage. In many past and present systems of beliefs, all living beings have been accorded the status of persons and have been cherished as endowed with a divine spirit. The Native Americans have no problems in referring to foxes as brothers and ravens as cousins. Nor did St. Francis have any problem with recognizing birds and other animals as his brothers and sisters. These belief-systems, which recognize the bond of solidarity between all beings, are ipso facto expressions of the universal Democracy or Ecodemocracy, which I am advocating.

4. From Ecodemocracy to Cosmocracy

After we have explained the notion of Ecodemocracy or Ecocracy, the road to Cosmocracy is now open. Cosmocracy emerges as we generalize the idea of Ecodemocracy. Cosmocracy is a generalized idea of Democracy in yet another way. Universal Democracy, when it is extended to all beings, becomes Cosmocracy. Cosmocracy simply signifies the recognition that all powers come from the cosmos. Celebrating the cosmos as the power-giver leads to a political system which is rooted not in a one-sided notion of physical power, nor in the idea of Democracy for a select few (as the Greeks conceived of it), but in those tremendous forces which brought life and human societies to existence. Our global ecumenical thinking must inform us that we are all connected within the stupendous tapestry of the evolving cosmos. This recognition must inform us that seeking justice, freedom and good life cannot be confined to a few select societies. Cosmocracy is Democracy for the entire cosmos.

Some semantic purists might argue that "Democracy for the entire cosmos" is a meaningless phrase. Let us see whether they are right. The expression simply conveys the idea that all forms of being are entitled to their existence. It furthermore conveys the idea that all beings are entitled to their respective forms of self-actualization. This last point is important and needs to be commented upon further.

All life, including human life, is a process of self-actualization. If we cannot understand that, then we cannot comprehend the meaning of our own lives. Let us make another important point. The right to self-actualization is a continuation of the right to existence. Every being has the right to exist. And by the same token, every being has the right to self-actualization. The right to self-actualization is thus one of the main principles of universal Democracy. Eco-justice becomes at this point cosmic justice, becomes the celebration of life unfolding. And that is what Cosmocracy is all about. The idea of self-actualization emerges as one of major importance for both Ecodemocracy and Cosmocracy.

Cosmocracy as proclaiming universal justice for all beings, and the right to self-actualization of all beings, is perhaps a novum against the present political scene. But the tenets of Cosmocracy are not new vis-á-vis the major spiritual traditions of the past. When the Buddhists talk about compassion as a vehicle for helping others in their self-actualization, indirectly they attempt to bring about cosmic justice. We may go a step further. When we contemplate Buddhism, Christianity and other major religions in some depth, we can see them as vehicles for self-actualization of individuals.

Self-actualization and self-fulfillment are thus important gospels of major religions. The ideal of cosmic justice is in accord with the main tune of world religions. However (and here is the rub), in most major religions (with the notable exception of Buddhism), self-actualization is limited to humans. Within the framework of Cosmocracy, self-actualization embraces all beings. To claim the right to self-actualization for all beings is not only reasonable but necessary once we understand the intricate, interconnected and exquisitely woven embroidery of the cosmic evolution of which we are an intrinsic and celebratory part. Cosmocracy signifies not only the proclamation of cosmic justice, but a celebration of the cosmos.

Cosmocracy is here presented as a political structure which attempts to make sense of self-actualization on the cosmic scale, and also on the scale of social arrangements within human groups and nations. Cosmocracy is a restatement of the Kantian moral imperative: "Act as if the maxim of your action were to become through your will a universal law of nature." We generalize

Kant's principle and assert: act in such a way as if the maxim of your action were to become a yardstick of cosmic justice. Such a principle would not be a bad foundation for a political system of the future—whether we call it 'cosmocracy' or by some other name.

Indeed we need something as universal and as far reaching as cosmocracy to bring the human family together. Furthermore, we need a comprehensive framework of cosmocracy to be able to talk intelligibly about the phenomena which are connected but which appear disparate because of our present limited frameworks. The meaning of justice; the meaning of Democracy itself; the meaning of rights of unprivileged cultures; the rights of defenseless animals, and the right of down-trodden nature are inherent parts of our present problem-ridden planet. Cosmocracy enables us to talk about these phenomena in one coherent frame of reference.

5. Participatory Politics in the Participatory Universe

The idea of Cosmocracy as a possible blueprint for future political systems receives powerful support from recent explorations in physics, and from the picture of the universe which presents sub-atomic and quantum physics, unveils to us. The broadening and deepening of our view of the universe is one of the most exciting aspects of our times. For the first time since the Renaissance, we have arrived at perspectives, visions and concepts which enable the physicist, the social scientist, the humanist and the religious thinker to feel that they belong to the same unified cosmos; unified not through a unified physical theory but in a deeper, more embracing sense.

The insights of this new wholistic universe have not sufficiently penetrated political science, which desperately tries to make itself in the image of the old Newtonian science—by insisting on atomizing and quantifying phenomena and putting them in the physical(ist) framework, while physics, at the cutting edge, has far transcended the rigid, atomistic precepts of Newtonian mechanics; and now tends to treat the whole universe wholistically and through concepts which certainly are trans-physical—if the physical is defined as the tiny material corpuscles which Newton postulated. We are at the dawn of a new picture of the universe. Political scientists should become aware of it.

The astrophysicist John Archibald Wheeler may have been the first to announce, in an articulate way (in the early 1970s), the idea of the Participatory Universe. He wrote, "The universe does not exist 'out there' independent of us. We are inescapably involved in bringing about that which appears to be happening. We are participators. In some strange sense this is a Participatory Universe."

In the early 1980s, drawing from the insights of Wheeler, on the one hand ("In some strange sense this is a participatory universe"), and building on the insights of Teilhard de Chardin ("We are evolution conscious of itself"), I have developed the theory of the Participatory Mind. This theory, on the one hand, attempts to vindicate the claims of the New Physics about the participatory nature of the universe; and, on the other hand, attempts to fill the missing dimension in Teilhard's opus—which wonderfully describes the unfoldment of evolution but misses the role of the mind in the whole process. Consciousness is one of the key terms in Teilhard's story. But strangely, it is consciousness as if there were no minds. The theory of the Participatory mind provides an epistemological foundation to Teilhard's cosmology.

The participatory theory of mind maintains that our world is the creation of our mind. But not in a solipsistic manner a la Berkeley (esse-percipi), but in a participatory manner: we have become aware that we can elicit from reality only that much as our mind is capable of conceiving. This is precisely the sense in which we say that we dwell in a participatory universe.

We elicit what is potentially 'out there' in continuous acts of participation. Participation is of the essence not only in our cognitive acts but also in our social activities and political endeavors. Tell me what you participate in and I will tell you who you are; and what the meaning of your life is.

We become that in which we participate. As we participate so we become. If we participate all the time in trivial matters, we become trivial persons. These ideas are anticipated by the ancient teachings of the Hindu philosophy and of Buddhism. Thus we read in the Upanishads: "In truth who knows God becomes God." (Mundaka Upanishad). The matter is even more strikingly expressed in Dhammapada, one of the chief texts of Buddhism: "What we are today comes from our thoughts of yesterday, and our present thoughts build our life of tomorrow. Life is the creation of our mind."

Already at the beginning of the 19th century William Blake was aware of this strange process of interaction between reality and our inner knowing faculties. He wrote:

But to the eye of the man of imagination
Nature is Imagination itself.
AS MAN IS , SO HE SEES.

The ancient Greeks anticipated it all. Thus Parmenides has said: "No mind, no world." This powerful insight is very contemporary. When spelled out, it unveils the structure of the universe which is quite different from the one we are used to.

We now have the background for connecting our earlier discussion of Cosmocracy with the more far-reaching ideas of the New Physics, particularly these concerning the Participatory Universe.

All political systems are about participation. All Democracies are about participation. But the nature of this participation—its depth and ramifications—are different in different epochs. The Athenians of the 5th century B.C. enjoyed a great Democracy. Their participation in the affairs of the state, and of the cosmos at large was deep, multifarious and intense. They thought themselves large people, and indeed cosmic people, and participated in the cosmos accordingly. To this very day the word 'cosmos' is used in everyday Greek language to designate that in which we partake and of which we are a part.

In the industrial world, we have reduced the meaning of Democracy to a much narrower scope precisely because we have diminished our forms of participation in it. We are consumers, not participators. It can be granted that consumption is a form of participation. And here is the rub: it is such a lowly and diminished form of participation that it cannot lead to genuine fulfillment. Self realization through consumption is a parody of older spiritual quests.

Industrial Democracies favor expertise and specialization. This is another reason why they discourage our participation as complete and whole beings. They prevent us from becoming self-reliant, independent, complete. In a subtle but pervading way they inhibit us as spiritual beings. Industrial Democracies are controlled by the ideology of secularism. In the secular world there is no place for God and for higher ideals, including self-actualization in the spiritual sense. This is one of the reason why present Democracies are a poor vehicle for self-actualization.

One of the central points, which I wish to make is as follows: The plight of Democracy and the demise of the quality of life of Western people is the result of the shrinking scope of our participation in the wake of which comes the impoverishment of our relationships with the cosmos—all of which are the consequences of our cripplingly narrow world view.

Summary

Democracy is never a thing in itself but always a set of structures and institutions, which reflect the world view of a people. Therefore, our attempts to salvage Democracy or to build new sustainable models of Democracy cannot be successful if we are to remain in the old crippling paradigm. The resurrection of Democracy must go hand in hand with an erection of a new world view.

A truly participatory Democracy is not a superficial game of playing with your personal computer—and punching choices, which others have programmed for you. A genuinely participatory Democracy signifies a genuine participation—in the vast riches of the cosmos. Participatory Democracy in the Participatory Universe, as unveiled by the New Physics, signifies Cosmocracy. Cosmocracy is Democracy for the entire cosmos.

Cosmocracy can be illuminated from two different perspectives: that of the Participatory Universe ("We are inescapably bringing about that which appears to be happening"); and that of the ecological paradigm: our understanding of sustainable social systems invariably leads us to Ecocracy and, upon deeper analysis, to Cosmocracy.

Thus the concept of 'Cosmocracy' is not a fancy linguistic gimmick. It is born out of our deeper awareness of how things are connected in this extraordinarily complex and interdependent universe in which our thinking and our minds are not static photographic plates but real movers of history as well as shapers of the nature of reality.

If the concept of Cosmocracy appears too grandiose and too much to swallow, the question is: what else is there to get us out of the present rut? Democracy is a beautiful concept with a glorious past. But it was invented twenty-five centuries ago! Even the best concepts wear out. "All things wear out," as Heraclitus insisted. We need new visions and new concepts for the new world we have created. Our modes of knowledge, our categories and concepts are old and stale. We need new windows on the universe we have erected. Cosmocracy is one of these windows. It is a worthy successor of Democracy. It is a daughter of Democracy which has outgrown its parent.

19

The Meaning of Politics in a Spiritual Perspective

The art of good government is possible
when people become aware
of the spiritual principles
underlying all life.

Political institutions are a shadow of our souls. Put otherwise, political institutions express and embody the wisdom of the people of the time. If there is no such wisdom among the people, these institutions express their unwisdom. The state of our wisdom and the state of our soul are closely related.

Our institutions do not work because our souls do not work. Our spiritual blight affects our individual lives and our institutions alike. Let us state it clearly. We cannot have good political institutions if our visions are cripplingly narrow and our wisdom lamentably limited. Thus, the road to good political and social institutions is by deepening our wisdom and by broadening our visions: which is to say by enlarging our souls. This is the only way. And there is no other way.

Our technology is stupendous. Our technical instruments often dazzle in their capacity to perform. However, our political institutions cannot be conceived of as merely technical instruments. Perfect technical instruments are often perfectly insensitive to the human needs and desiderata. Wise politics needs much more than good technical tools. It needs empathy and deep understanding of our inner longings.

What is then the right recipe for building a political system or for reconstructing a political system? Do not concentrate on merely reforming the institutions, especially by trying to make them into "perfect" technical instruments. Acquire wisdom. Mend and enlarge your visions. Go deeper into yourself. Then your institutions will work. And only then.

Yet, here is the rub. It is one of the most difficult things for any people, to admit that their institutions do not work because of the smallness of their souls. For the institutions are most of the time conceived as being "out there", as instruments regardless of who we are. Yet, we must remember: these institutions are a shadow of who we are.

We blame our institutions for our plight, for our dissatisfaction, for our unhappiness. Why? Because it is very hard for us to admit that we have the institutions we deserve, that we are responsible for these institutions, that they reflect our inner selves, that is to say, our inner worth. I am aware that the kind of statements I make are not welcome. Often they are ignored as annoying. Why? Because they pose too much challenge to ourselves. Yet, if these statements reveal the truth, then the conclusion is: don't blame institutions for what they are. Blame yourself for what you are. And don't hide. Hiding accomplishes nothing. Are you prepared to change yourself? No. So, don't expect the institutions to change. The institutions only reflect who you are, including your indolence, your lack of responsibility, your waiting for "Godot".

Don't expect politicians and even political scientists to help you, for they are completely conditioned by the past and possessed by the collective unwisdom of our time. They cultivate your smallness. They think that by putting you into the cast of your smallness, you are comfortable there. Deep down you are not. Let us call the poet Goethe as our witness. He said:

To treat man as he is
Is to debase him.
To treat man as he ought to be
Is to engrace him.

Politicians and social scientists want to treat us as we are, constantly reducing us in our stature and possibilities. We know that we are pretty low in our lowest aspects. But this is not the ground for celebrating our humanity. We celebrate our humanity by aspiring to what is best in us, by attempting to become what we can potentially become, what we ought to be in the best sense of the term. Only then we enshrine our deepest humanity, give a testimony to who we truly are

Social scientists are obsessed nowadays with measuring. But what do they measure? To measure empirically our unwisdom, as expressed through our consumptive attitudes, is not a scientific confirmation of who we are. It is rather a sad capitulation of the scientific mind to the lower realm of human possibilities.

When they work to our advantage, political institutions must lead the people, must be like great religious symbols to which we aspire. And while aspiring to them, we change ourselves in the process. It is thus clear that political institutions must not follow the people, especially, if by following the people, we mean reducing the people to their lower selves. For it does not help much if we create political institutions in the image of reduced people.

To break this vicious cycle we need to ascend to a higher perspective, to a spiritual perspective from which we can see things more clearly and with a greater depth and understanding. Thus, we need to see that satisfaction and happiness also mean the inner peace and the nourishment of the soul. Some are allergic to the term "soul". Let us not be led astray by words. We are simply saying that inside of us there is this human core which is trans-physical and trans-biological. It has its needs and demands, the satisfaction of it is as indispensable to the meaning of our life as the oxygen is to our lungs. We know this truth well.

Now, this human core, which has traditionally been called soul, is something without which our uniquely human life withers. Social and political institutions must safeguard all aspects of our being. If social and political institutions neglect our inner lives, or are in collision with our inner selves, then we whither. Such institutions are not worthy of our support and allegiance.

I need not belabour the fact of the plight of present political and social institutions (particularly in the developed world) in providing the shelter for our spiritual life. To respond that these institutions are secular in character and that we live in a secular society is to miss my argument. It is so, for two reasons. One is that our spiritual or inner life must not be confined to the religious life and religious institutions. The separation of the state from the church, of our civic institutions from our religious institutions does not mean neglecting and eliminating our inner lives, our spiritual quests, our inner core. Spirituality and religion must not be confused with each other or conflated with one another. To gaze at the stars and to see in them an immense temple does not require priests, church, or religion.

The second reason is even more important. The so-called secular society, delivered on the wheels of material progress, may not be much of a society, if by "society" we mean such an arrangement of human life through which this life is enhanced and not dwarfed. If by the secular society we mean one in which "*homo homini lupus es*" (man is wolf to a man); in which we witness the growing violence on the streets, and in the family, in which we witness the growing injustice as the poor become poorer and more dispossessed, then we might want to take a deep breath, pause for a while and ask: might it all not be a manifestation of the sickness of our soul? If our reason continuously deceives us and leads us astray, then we need to go deeper—to the structure of our wisdom and the state of our soul. For not infrequently our deeper maladies have their source there.

We are so used to the idea that politics is the arena for the selfish, greedy, and rapacious, that we tend to forget and disregard the examples that prove just the opposite. These examples which show that politics is for the noble, self-less, high minded, and idealistic are numerous. There is much we can learn from these examples, if we choose to. More important still, they show that the politics as the exercise of the power of the soul is possible and that when it is practised thus, it brings about remarkable and positive results.

In ancient times in China there lived a sage Kung-Fu-Tse, whose name has been simplified in the West as Confucius (551-479 B.C.). He was renowned for his sagacity, wisdom, impartiality, justice, and the capacity to see through the distant consequences of human actions. In due time he was invited by the king of Lu province to govern the kingdom. And he ruled for twelve years with the blessing of the king and the growing happiness of the people, showing what wisdom can do when consistently applied in social-political affairs. Confucius' rule was so successful, while the prosperity and peace of the people in the kingdom was growing, that the neighbouring kingdoms were astounded and became envious. This was a clear demonstration that politics could be a noble and beautiful art benefiting all.

Then one of the neighbouring kings somehow bribed the king of Lu, whom Confucius worked for, and suggested that Confucius should be sent for a holiday for one year. So he went for a holiday. He was not assassinated nor did he die in ignominy. But he never returned to rule again, though he wanted to.

For Confucius the ideal consists of the harmony between the superior individual and a well ordered society, which is based on the mutual moral obligations of the five basic human relationships between: ruler and minister, father and son, elder brother and younger brother, husband and wife and one friend to another. Government is to be conducted through the ruler's moral example. The difference between the mature man, whom Confucius calls a superior man and an immature man, whom he calls an inferior man, is that for the former the rule is moral principle.

One of the conclusions is that we need to mature spiritually to produce such people as Confucius and then we need to allow them to show us what the art of government is about. For what is going on with present governments is not so much that they are led by unwise and often selfish people (which is undoubtedly true) but that the people who elected them are unwise not to know and not to demand any better.

Confucious' teaching has survived over two millennia and is still inspiring people. It does not really matter that Confucius was Chinese and his teaching may be more resonant with the Chinese psyche than the Western one. What matters is that he is a shining example of a philosopher who built his philosophy on spiritual principles and yet was capable of applying this philosophy to practical and political affairs with such a success that he can truly be called a philosopher king.

We should not conclude too rashly that the political influence of Confucius ceased with his death. It still continues. Nowadays some Asian nations, after tiring of American domination and Western decadence, which is imposed on them as modernity, return to the Confucian teaching in order to combat what they consider as an ideological imperialism. In places like Singapore, but not only, the respect for the traditional Confucian values is said to be the backbone of the social cohesion as contrasted with Western alienation and disintegration. Thus, the political legacy of Confucius lives on and is seen as remarkably sustainable. Why? Because it is based on something deeper than the expedient values of political manipulation.

Ashoka was an Indian king who ruled in the third century B.C. (269-232). He was a man endowed with an extraordinary strength and physical and spiritual powers. Through his military genius and extraordinary physical prowess, he conquered all the neighbouring kingdoms and truly unified India at the time. And then one day, after a huge battle, seeing the rivers of blood running in front of him he woke and decided that this was not the way. He became a follower of the Buddhist creed of compassion and non-violence. He did not relinquish his kingdom. He did not run to a cave in the mountains to repent. Instead he ruled as a spiritual monarch. And remarkable indeed was his rule and his achievement.

First he built 84000 stupas (Buddhist monument/chapels) in all the villages and towns of India. Each of them was a visible commandment that compassion, social justice, and non-violence were to be the foundation of society. Then he carved in rock his famous edicts proclaiming that social and political life was to based on the spiritual foundations of justice and compassion. Only in the nineteenth century did we start to rediscover the famous Ashoka edicts. So far, we have found over forty of them. How many are still buried in the jungles or under the mounds of earth we do not know. But what we did discover is impressive enough! The rocks carved by Ashoka's messengers are as far apart as Pakistan and Burma, some two and one half thousand kilometres. Communication and transport were not easy at the time; they are still not easy on the Indian subcontinent. Yet, with remarkable will and persistence, Ashoka wielded his vast empire into a political organism based on Buddhist philosophy.

He did not create a religious state run by the monks, although he sometimes considered himself a Buddhist monk. He was a truly enlightened monarch. He ruled single handedly through his various emissaries who ran from one end of his empire to another carrying his messages and overseeing that justice and non-violence were observed. Though Buddhist to the core, the language of his messages, and of his edicts, were often not explicitly Buddhist. The country was still dominated by the Hindu Brahmins—particularly in remote villages and these were not to be antagonized. Yet, Ashoka did more in spreading Buddhism throughout the Indian sub-continent than all the Buddhist monks taken together.

The remarkable thing is that Ashoka's purpose was not to be a religious missionary. His purpose was to establish good government based on the principles of justice and non-violence. As it happened, he succeeded in both: in establishing good government and in spreading a deep spiritual awareness among his people, an awareness which was based on Buddhist principles.

Ashoka's case (and also the one of Confucius) is more telling and more paradigmatic than we are usually aware. It is simply not the case that these were two wise men who stumbled on good principles which helped them to rule. The spiritual principles and good government are part and parcel of each other. As the spiritual awareness spread and became accepted by the populace, good government became possible and indeed inevitable. Here is an important conclusion: the art of government for the people and with the people is possible when people become aware of deeper spiritual principles underlying all life and the forms of sustaining government.

Index

W